Acclaim for *Roadblocks to Equality* by Jeffery Klaehn — 2

"In *Roadblocks to Equality* Jeffery Klaehn has assembled some of the most cogent writers on issues of justice, gender and media in a collection of essays that helps us connect the struggles of everyday life with those of global proportions. Exploring themes of desire, sexuality and commodification across boarders, boundaries and human bodies, these essays unmask the powerful forces that shapes our lives and map the pathways for new directions."
—Robin Andersen, Director of Peace and Justice Studies at Fordham University and author of *A Century of Media, A Century of War*, and *Consumer Culture and TV Programming*

"*Roadblocks to Equality* is a first-rate book: comprehensive, thoroughly researched, and grounded in several disciplines. This compilation reports a multidimensional examination of western women's perspectives of, and interventions in, the labor force, as content, producers and consumers of cultural industries, in human rights, and politics. The chapters go beyond the scope of one country as they relate to realities in Canada, the United States, and Great Britain."
—Dr. Leen d'Haenens, Department of Communication, Catholic University of Leuven (Belgium)/Radboud University Nijmegen, The Netherlands

"*Roadblocks to Equality* engages timely critical issues of concern to women across a variety of social, cultural and political boundaries. The collection provides important scholarly interventions addressing the challenges that arise from women's contemporary struggles in relation to globalization, human rights and political economy and perhaps more importantly, considers the possibilities of resistance and hope for transformative futures."
—Jasmin Zine, Dept. of Sociology, Wilfrid Laurier University

"It is heartening to see women—and men—boldly address persistent gender inequities in contemporary lives, refashioned by complex political, economic, and cultural economies emerging in the twenty-first century. With perceptual acuity and feminist insight, the essays in *Roadblocks to Equality* implicitly recognize the battles won and possibilities the future holds."
—Jyotika Virdi, Communication Studies, University of Windsor

ROADBLOCKS to EQUALITY
Women Challenging Boundaries

ROADBLOCKS to EQUALITY
Women Challenging Boundaries

Jeffery Klaehn, editor

Montreal/New York/London

Black Rose Books No. MM363

National Library of Canada Cataloguing in Publication Data

Roadblocks to equality : women challenging boundaries / Jeffery Klaehn, editor

ISBN 978-1-55164-317-5 (bound) ISBN 978-1-55164-316-8 (pbk.)

1. Women--Social conditions. 2. Equality. 3. Women--Economic conditions. 4. Women's rights. I Klaehn, Jeffery

HQ1121.R59 2008   305.4   C2008-902981-X

BLACK
ROSE
BOOKS

C.P. 1258	2250 Military Road	99 Wallis Road
Succ. Place du Parc	Tonawanda, NY	London, E9 5LN
Montréal, H2X 4A7	14150	England
Canada	USA	UK

To order books:

In Canada: (phone) 1-800-565-9523 (fax) 1-800-221-9985
email: utpbooks@utpress.utoronto.ca

In the United States: (phone) 1-800-283-3572 (fax) 1-800-351-5073

In the UK & Europe: (phone) 44 (0)20 8986-4854 (fax) 44 (0)20 8533-5821
email: order@centralbooks.com

Our Web Site address: http://www.blackrosebooks.net

Printed in Canada

Table of Contents

Dedication

This book is dedicated to my beloved godmother, Shirley Marie Russo (nee Harnack), who unexpectedly passed away while the book was being completed. She was loved by my entire family, and by everyone she ever knew, and is missed terribly. When I was younger, she was the person who always encouraged me to read, to dream, and to imagine. As I was growing up, whenever I needed to know something for school, no matter how obscure this may have been, I knew that I could always call Aunt Shirley and she would have the answers for me. Throughout my entire life, at every single family get-together that we ever had, I would no sooner walk into the room and she would be calling my name (she always called me 'J.J.') and a moment later she would have me in her arms, be giving me a big kiss on the cheek and that hug of hers that always made me feel so special and happy to be there in that moment. Every memory I have of her is so good. She was so loved—the most intelligent, most beautiful and most wonderful person I could have ever wished to have been part of my life, and I am so thankful to have known her and to have had her as such a significant, influential and positive force in my life for so many years. She continues to inspire, will always be loved, and will be remembered, always.

—*Jeffery Klaehn, October 8, 2008*

Acknowledgments

First and foremost, thanks to my parents. My mom, especially, Sharyn Klaehn, I'd like to thank so much for all the love that she has given to me throughout my life, and for the support she gave me while I was putting together this book. Mom, this book is for you.

That's my mom on the cover of the book, incidentally.

Thanks mom!

I would also like to acknowledge with much love my late Aunt Minnie, who was an influential part of my life as I was growing up. My grandmother, Mable Harnack, by her example, personifies what it means to be a strong and independent woman for me and I want her to know that I've so much respect and love for her.

James Winter, thank you for being so great, and for all the support.

Thank you to each of the contributors to this book. It has been my absolute pleasure working with you. I am happy to have made some wonderful new friendships in the process.

Thank you also to Neetin Kalsi for her timely assistance as the book reached the end station, and thanks also to Anna Wilk for her support and encouragement.

Preface

Roadblocks to Equality is a unique edited collection which brings together a range of original scholarship devoted to central topics and issues of importance to women and women's lives within contemporary society, including globalization and the sex industry, political economy, women in higher education, and violence against women.

The book is divided into four main sections: Women and Political Economy; Women and the Culture Industry; Women, Violence and Human Rights; and Politics, Knowledge and Age.

Women and Political Economy features essays on the separation of the public economy and privatized care work, the political economy of women's everyday lives; the importance of universal, affordable childcare in light of women's often low-wage, service-sector employment is also explored here.

Women and the Culture Industry includes chapters that reflect upon how women are represented in advertising, and considers how women have responded to those perceptions and representations to advocate change. This section also features chapters devoted to women and global communications and the issue of pornography and the question of men's responsibility.

Women, Violence and Human Rights features chapters on globalization and the sex industry, the state of women's rights and human rights internationally, the Montreal Massacre, and women's experiences of separation/divorce sexual assault in rural Ohio.

Politics, Knowledge and Age leads off with a chapter that explores ways in which aging is a gendered experience and examines why aging and women's activism matter. Women in higher education and girlhood studies are also considered within chapters featured in this section of the book.

My original vision was to create a book that would take up a range of issues, moving across various boundaries or borders, and one that would have international dimensions.

The book includes contributions from scholars in Canada, the United States and the United Kingdom. This was by design, as with the other edited books I have done in the past, I strove to have contributors onboard from around the world. My original title for the project was *Women Across Borders*—I very much like the metaphor of moving across and through borders of various kinds—although the new title (suggested by the publisher) is one that I also embrace: it carries different connotations, but conveys the central essence of the essays within the book concerned to explore inequalities and boundaries of various kinds that women encounter within the contemporary social world.

—*Jeffery Klaehn, Kitchener, Ontario*

Notes on the Contributors

Patrizia Albanese is Associate Professor of sociology at Ryerson University, and author of *Mothers of the Nation: Women, Families and Nationalism in Twentieth Century Europe* (University of Toronto Press, 2006) and co-editor (with Tepperman and Curtis) of *Sociology: A Canadian Perspective, 2nd ed.* She is currently doing (SSHRC-funded) research on Quebec's $7/day child care program and is working on a project on household work and lifelong learning (with Dr. Margrit Eichler, OISE/UT). She has published chapters in edited collections on motherhood and nationalism, Canadian families, and childcare in Canada. She is currently working on a book on childhood in Canada (expected 2009, Oxford University Press), and is co-director of the Centre for Children, Youth and Families at Ryerson University.

Susan Bryant is Adjunct Faculty in the Department of Communication Studies at the University of Windsor, where she has been teaching since 1999. She holds a Ph.D. in Communication from Simon Fraser University and a Master's in Environmental Studies from York University. Her research interests focus on gender and labour, gender and technology, critical theories of technology, and culture and the natural environment.

Walter S. DeKeseredy is professor of criminology, justice, and policy studies at the University of Ontario Institute of Technology (UOIT), Oshawa, Ontario, Canada. He has written 12 scholarly books and more than 60 scientific journal articles on a variety of topics, including woman abuse in intimate relationships and crime in public housing. He also jointly received (with Martin D. Schwartz) the 2004 Distinguished Scholar Award from the American Society of Criminology's (ASC's) Division on Women and Crime, and in 1995, he received the Critical Criminologist of the Year Award from the ASC's Division on Critical Criminology. In 2007, he won the UOIT Research Excellence Award for his many contributions to a social scientific understanding of woman abuse and other social problems.

Natalie Dias is a fourth year undergraduate student majoring in Honors Sociology and Global Studies at Wilfrid Laurier University, in Waterloo, Canada. Her research interests include gender, advertising, popular culture, social theory, and social inequality.

Peter Eglin is Professor of Sociology at Wilfrid Laurier University in Waterloo where he has taught since 1976. He is author of *Talk and Taxonomy: A Methodological Comparison of Ethnosemantics and Ethnomethodology ...* (1980). With Stephen Hester he is co-author of *The Montreal Massacre: A Story of Membership Categorization Analysis* (Wilfrid Laurier University Press, 2003), *A Sociology of Crime* (Routledge, 1992), and co-editor of *Culture in Action: Studies in Membership Categorization Analysis* (University Press of America, 1997). As a student of ethnomethodology and conversation analysis he investigates the use of categories for describing persons in practical reasoning in talk and texts in various settings, most recently gender categories and the category "feminist." He is currently beginning a study of university-specific work as an interactional accomplishment. He is also exercised by the question of intellectual responsibility in a number of human rights issues, notably state terrorism in El Salvador in Jeffery Klaehn's *Filtering the News* (2005), near-genocide in East Timor in Jeffery Klaehn's *Bound By Power* (2005), and Israeli crimes in Palestine.

Danielle Fagen is a prevention/intervention professional at a private non-profit organization that works with individuals and families affected by drug and alcohol issues in Athens, Ohio. She has published an article related to her M.A. thesis in *Feminist Criminology*, which the official journal of the American Society of Criminology's Division on Women and Crime and she is an adjunct instructor at Ohio University.

Kathleen Gotts is a graduate of Carleton University's School of Journalism and Communication. Her thesis was a woman-centered, qualitative communication study of the campaign strategies and discourse used to advocate the legalization of midwifery in the province of Ontario, Canada, from 1979 to 1989. Besides her research in women's political activism and communication, another of her key interests is how risk is communicated in public health messaging.

Sylvia Hale is Professor and Chair of the Department of Sociology at St. Thomas University. Her major publications include the widely influential *Controversies in Sociology* textbook (Copp Clark, 1995) as well as The Elusive Promise: The Struggle of Women Development Workers in Rural North India (McGill University, 1987). She is also an award-winning educator. Her research interests include the family, development, and political-economy.

Mandy Hall is currently a Ph.D. student at the University of Hawaii-Manoa. She has published refereed articles in *Feminist Criminology* and *Critical Criminology*, which is the official journal of the American Society of Criminology's Division on Critical Criminology. Her areas of concentration are critical criminology, violence against women, juvenile delinquency, and drugs and crime.

Robert Jensen is a journalism professor at the University of Texas at Austin and board member of the Third Coast Activist Resource Center http://thirdcoastactivist .org. His latest book is *Getting Off: Pornography and the End of Masculinity* (South End Press, 2007). http://www.southendpress.org/2007/items/87767. Jensen is also the author of *The Heart of Whiteness: Race, Racism, and White Privilege* and *Citizens of the Empire: The Struggle to Claim Our Humanity* (both from City Lights Books); and *Writing Dissent: Taking Radical Ideas from the Margins to the Mainstream* (Peter Lang). He can be reached at rjensen@uts.cc.utexas.edu and his articles can be found online at http://uts.cc.utexas.edu/~rjensen/index.html.

Neetin Kalsi is completing her MA in Sociology at Wilfrid Laurier University. Her research interests include race and ethnicity, knowledge, cultural practices, and social inequalities.

Jeffery Klaehn is widely published as a cultural commentator and critic. His scholarly writings have been published in national and international peer-reviewed journals, including the *European Journal of Communication, International Communication Gazette* and *Journalism Studies,* and are required reading for many media-related courses at the MA and PhD levels throughout North America and the United Kingdom. He is the editor of and main contributor to *Filtering the News: Essays on Herman and Chomsky's Propaganda Model* (2005), *Bound by Power: Intended Consequences* (2006) and *Inside the World of Comic Books* (2006). His research interests include popular culture, media, discourse, politics, universities, education, and human rights.

Michèle Martin is a professor in the School of Journalism and Communication at Carleton University. She has a Ph.D. in sociology from the University of Toronto, an M.A. from the Université de Montréal and a B.A. from the UQAM, both in communication. Her research is in the historical sociology of technological development, political economy of communication and socio-cultural analysis of the media. Her particular area of interest is the political economic development of forms of communication and their impact on society.

Martin's books include *Images at War: 19th Century Illustrated Periodicals and the Development of National Identities* (University of Toronto Press, 2006), *Victor Barbeau, pionnier de la critique culturelle journalistique* (Presse de l'université Laval, 1997), and *Hello Central? Gender, Culture and Resistance in the Formation of Telephone Systems* (McGill-Queen's University Press, 1991). Her articles appear in such journals as *Réseaux, Histoire sociale/Social History, Labour/Le travail* and *Journal of Communication Inquiry*. She also presented many papers in various international conferences. Michèle Martin has been visiting professor in different universities: the Goldsmith College, Oxford University; the London School of Economics and Political Sciences; the Institut Français de Presse, Uninversité Paris II; the University of Bucarest, Romania. She teaches the political economic development of communication technologies, socio-historical study of the media, politics of visual representation, feminism and communication theories.

Claudia Mitchell is a James McGill Professor in the Faculty of Education, McGill University, and an Honorary Professor in the Faculty of Education, University of KwaZulu-Natal. Her research focuses on visual and other participatory methodologies particularly in addressing gender and HIV and AIDS, teacher identity and gender, and the culture of girlhood within broader studies of children and popular culture and media studies. She is a co-founder of the Centre for Visual Methodologies for Social Change at UKZN which focuses on visual methods and media education. She is the co-author/co-editor of eight books including several books on girlhood, *Seven Going on Seventeen: Tween Studies in the Culture of Girlhood* (with J. Reid-Walsh) , *Girlhood: Redefining the Limits* (with Y. Jiwani and C. Steenbergen) and *Combating gender violence in and around schools* (with F. Leach).

Michael Parenti is a political scientist, historian and media critic. His books include *The Culture Struggle* (Seven Stories, 2006), *Superpatriotism* (City Lights), *The Assassination of Julius Caesar* (New Press), and *Contrary Notions: The Michael Parenti Reader* (City Lights). For more information visit: www.michaelparenti.org.

Richard Poulin is Professor of Sociology at the University of Ottawa and is an expert in globalization, sex trafficking and the sex industries. He has been researching and writing about pornography and prostitution for more than twenty years and has published a range of books, book chapters and journal articles in all of these areas.

Jocey Quinn is a Professor of Education at the Institute for Policy Studies in Education (IPSE) London Metropolitan University. Her work takes a cultural approach to Higher Education and Lifelong Learning and she is particularly interested in the relationships between knowledge transformation and social justice. She has published widely and has conducted national and international research in this field. This includes research on the impact of the mass participation of women in Higher Education and on working class 'drop out' from HE. She is currently writing two books *Culture and Education* (Routledge) and *Learning Communities and Imagined Social Capital: Learning to Belong* (Continuum).

Jacqueline Reid-Walsh is a specialist in historical and contemporary children's literature, culture and media and fascinated by girls culture. In these areas she has published on topics ranging from early moveable books and Jane Austen's' juvenilia to Nancy Drew mysteries and girls websites. She is co-author of *Researching Children's PopularCulture* (Routledge: 2002), co-editor of *Seven Going on Seventeen* (Peter Lang, 2005), and currently co-editing an encyclopedia of girls popular culture (with Claudia Mitchell). She teaches at Université Laval and Bishop's University.

Carole Roy is an Assistant Professor in the Department of Adult Education at St. Francis Xavier University, Nova Scotia. Her book, *The Raging Grannies: Wild Hats, Cheeky Songs, and Witty Actions for a Better World* (2004), was published by Black Rose Books and selected for the 2005 Amelia Bloomer Award by the Feminist Task Force of the American Library Association. She is interested in women and activism, creativity and social change, and is currently a recipient of a research grant from the Social Sciences and Humanities Research Council of Canada (SSHRC) to look at film festivals as tools of adult education and community building.

Martin D. Schwartz is professor of sociology at Ohio University. A former visiting fellow at the National Institute of Justice, he has written or edited (often with Walter DeKeseredy) 11 books, more than 60 refereed journal articles, and another 50 book chapters, government reports, and essays. Active in the battered women shelter movement since the 1970s, he has received the Lifetime Achievement Award of the American Society of Criminology's (ASC's) Division on Critical Criminology, and the Distinguished Scholar Award (with DeKeseredy) from the ASC's Division on Women and Crime. He has been co-editor, deputy editor, or a member of the editorial board of 12 journals and has won a variety of teaching and service awards, including the Ohio University title of Presidential Research Scholar.

Nancy Snow is Associate Professor of Public Diplomacy in the S.I. Newhouse School of Public Communications at Syracuse University and Senior Research Fellow in the Center on Public Diplomacy, University of Southern California. Her most recent book is the *Routledge Handbook of Public Diplomacy* with Philip M. Taylor. A Fulbright scholar to the Federal Republic of Germany, Snow served as a United States Information Agency (USIA) and U.S. Department of State (DOS) official in public diplomacy and international exchange. Dr. Snow is the author of numerous book chapters, articles and books, including *The Arrogance of American Power: What U.S. Leaders Are Doing Wrong and Why It's Our Duty to Dissent*; *Information War*; *Propaganda, Inc.: Selling America's Culture to the World*; and *War, Media and Propaganda: A Global Perspective* (with Yahya Kamalipour). Her books have been translated into five languages. Her opinion writings have been published in the *Los Angeles Times*, *Newsday*, *Adbusters* magazine, and the *Washington Post*, among others. She is a *magna cum laude* Ph.D. graduate in international relations from American University's School of International Service in Washington, D.C., and a *summa cum laude* political science graduate from Clemson University in South Carolina. Snow is a lifetime member of the Fulbright Association. She edits a website devoted to American persuasion, influence and propaganda at www.NancySnow.com.

Tanya Terzis is currently completing her MA in Sociology at Wilfrid Laurier University. Her research interests include poverty, social inequality and human rights.

Anna Miroslawa Wilk holds an BA from York University and an MA in Sociology from Wilfrid Laurier University. She has a wide range of research interests, including family, social policy, gender, education, human rights, and media.

WOMEN AND POLITICAL ECONOMY

The chapters in this section explore women's experiences in the workplace and their push toward wage equity, support for working mothers, and the importance of universal, affordable childcare. To my mind, poverty is a defining characteristic of women's political-economy—while progress has been made, perhaps it is time to redefine the boundaries of debate. Perhaps it is time to do more than is currently being done to actually address the problems here in real, concrete ways. —*Jeffery Klaehn, editor*

In volunteering at a local soup kitchen and getting to know many people I can now call my friends, I have come to appreciate and realize the harsh realities of what impoverished women living in the same community as myself go through, as well as the limited choices they have in their lives. Their choices are those of diapers for their children or tampons for themselves, of eating this month or paying rent, and of shampoo or soap. Women's poverty, even in a country that appears as equitable and affluent as Canada is often said to be, is an unfortunate but undeniable reality. And this poverty seems to permeate the city in which I live, but do you know what? The vast majority of people turn a blind eye to the living conditions of their fellow community members. And in my view, this is where the problem lies.

In looking at why and how women are experiencing various inequalities today, I feel it is important to first consider the ways that power operates in the social world. And where do we generally get most of our ideas about how the world works? The media is owned and operated by those in power. Why do stereotypes exist and what stereotypes do you normally associate with poverty? An image of a 'lazy man' with his hands outstretched, 'begging' for a 'hand out?' What stereotypes do you connect with women and poverty? The picture of a woman living in hostels with her children, unable to make ends meet with the high cost of day care and the low minimum wage from the full- or part-time job she is likely to have? Or, how about this—an image of a woman who is living in poverty after she has left an abusive relationship?

My view is that the corporate-owned media have a vested interest in obscuring the issue of poverty. It is easier this way, to justify social policies that maintain the status quo. So it is that some are systematically disadvantaged, but you'd never really get this from reading the chain-media newspapers or from watching the nightly news. You wouldn't hear much about the roadblocks to equality. And this is important, the implications widespread.

Women are mothers, daughters, sisters, aunts and grandmothers—how they are represented in the media impacts various political processes, and these in turn influence where economic resources and attentions are directed, and the structural conditions that impact women's lived experiences.

Tanya Terzis, MA student, Sociology, Wilfrid Laurier University, Age: 23

Chapter One

Enforcing Boundaries: Managing the Separation of Public Economy and Privatized Care Work

Sylvia Hale

HISTORICALLY, the rise of industrialization is credited with bringing about the separation of production from consumption. In pre-industrialized agricultural economies the extended family household was the centre of both productive labour and the maintenance and care of family members. People produced what they needed and consumed what they produced. Households that engaged additional apprentices, labourers, or servants, routinely serviced them as they did extended family members, providing their food, housing and clothing, along with the education of young apprentices. The prevailing analysis holds that this integrated organization of labouring and caring work changed fundamentally with industrialization. As manufacturing became centralized in factories in Montreal, Bradbury argues,[1] workers increasing went 'out to work' for wages, while caring work was done at home. Artisans found it less onerous to pay a living allowance to apprentices and have them return home at night than to house and care for them. This separation in location of activities is seen as bringing about a gendered specialization of labour. Typically, it was men who did waged work outside the home while women necessarily remained in the home to care for children and other family members.

Industrialization is further associated with a conceptual shift in the definition of 'economy' to separate commodity production for profit from subsistence consumption in families.[2] What goes on inside families is conceptualized as a separate sphere of activity from the economy. The two spheres are seen as linked through the breadwinners' wages, a proportion of which is given to household dependents in the form of a housekeeping allowance. In commonsense discourse this gendered separation of spheres of work is naturalized, with women seen as naturally homemaker-mothers and men as naturally breadwinner-workers. A combination of economic and biological determinism is held to explain the separation of spheres, with minimal choice or human agency involved.

The first section of this paper critically examines historical evidence for these claims. What is in question is not the descriptive generalization that the separation of male paid employment from unpaid female homemaking actually happened, but why it did. What were some of the active practices that produced and enforced this separation of spheres historically. The second section of the paper will explore how similar practices are being sustained or undermined in contemporary society.

Policing Families: Producing the Homemaker/Breadwinner Model

Donzelot's seminal analysis of 200 years of State policies towards families in industrializing France during the eighteenth and nineteenth centuries, in *The Policing of Families*[3] challenges the view that the nuclear family form or a breadwinner/homemaker model emerged naturally from the conditions of industrialization. He argues instead that this form emerged over a long period of time, as the result of a regime of state-managed reproduction of social order, operating through emerging professions that were the precursors of contemporary psychology, psychoanalysis, education, social work, criminology, juvenile courts and probation.

The prospect of factory wages encouraged masses of young men to flood into the growing cities from the rural areas to escape military service and the impoverished drudgery of farm labour. In the cities they filled the rooming houses, brothels and taverns that expanded to accommodate them. Rural women soon followed, seeking work as factory hands, house servants, and in the sex trade. Few of these people had either the inclination or the resources to form family units or to raise children. Infants born in these chaotic conditions were abandoned in very large numbers into orphanages or 'foundling hospitals.' Among the more well-to-do classes, women were raised for lives of idleness and decoration as the status symbols for the newly rich bourgeois class. They routinely farmed out their infants to wetnurses and their older children to the care of house servants. Girls who lacked sufficient dowry for a good marriage were often sent to convents. There they would be educated and used as workers in convent-workhouses that might eventually provide them with a dowry. Men commonly refused to marry unless a woman brought sufficient dowry with her to raise his status and to compensate him for the upkeep of her and her children. The French army explicitly forbad men to marry or to legitimate their children unless they got a dowry.

Nowhere in this picture is there an image of the nuclear family with male breadwinner and female homemaker and caregiver that is taken for granted in later accounts. Donzelot's central question is how did the institution of 'family' in this model nuclear form come about? He looks at the active practices of the State and the professions or 'disciplines' employed by the State that combined to bring about this re-formation of 'the social.'

A primary incentive for State intervention was the high death rate among children left in orphanages or left to the vagaries of wetnurses and house servants, and the poor physical and mental quality of those that survived. Donzelot estimates that as high as 90 percent of children left in orphanages died, as did two-thirds of infants left with rural wetnurses. Survival rates were better for the children of elite families that could afford the exclusive service of a supervised wetnurse. But rich families could not buy the good-will of house-servants, who routinely took out their spite on children in their charge. Together these practices threatened both the state's ability to raise armies and maintain dominance in the colonies, and the interests of the bourgeoisie in a stable labour force. The better-off classes generally felt under increasing threat from diseases and crime emanating from the slums. They shared interests in getting men out of the brothels, children out of the orphanages, servants out of elite households, and women out of the convent-workhouses that threatened the profits of other businesses.

The solution was found in raising the status of motherhood. Physicians and psychoanalysts collaborated with elite women to raise their status from decorative status symbol to authority figure in the home, responsible for education, hygiene, and management of the domestic economy. Middle class women were in turn employed by the State to train lower-class women in domesticity. Incentives were offered in the form of child allowances to encourage and enable women to keep their infants, and social housing to encourage men to get out of the brothels and rooming houses. The incentives came with threats of intense surveillance. Women had to manage their children and maintain their houses at a level that would keep their men out of brothels and at home. If they failed, family allowances and social housing would be withdrawn. If children misbehaved, juvenile courts placed their mothers under tight surveillance. Women were pressured to save and manage on the meagre wages that their men brought home. Families that sought State assistance forfeited their privacy to State investigators who incessantly intruded into their lives. Employers as well as the State had an interest in pushing women out of factories. Employers feared that if women earned enough money to support a home, then men would be inclined to live off them rather than do the low-waged, heavy labouring jobs that employers wanted men for.

In summary, what Donzelot describes is the emergence of a regime for managing social life that enforced strongly gendered boundaries. Women were made responsible for the care of children, the maintenance of health and hygiene in homes, and the disciplining of male workers, in return for heightened status as homemaker-mothers and child allowances. Men were pressured into taking money home rather than to the brothels, in return for the privatized homemaking services that women provided. The nuclear family model was further enforced by segregated labour markets in which employers were willing to hire women only at such low wages that women could not support themselves without a male wage. Essentially similar practices of State child allowances, heightened surveillance of low-income families, and state-supported professions extolling and enforcing ideologies of motherhood and homemaking were adopted across Europe and Canada. Discriminatory labour markets were pervasive.

Industrialization in Canada: Enforcing the Homemaker Boundary

The commonsense view that historically most women 'chose' to stay home rather than seek paid labour is challenged by Bradbury's account of industrialization in working-class Montreal. She gives insight into details of the economic and broader social practices that combined to push women out of the paid economy. Records show that a high proportion of women actually were in the paid labour force at least for periods of their lives, if only through taking in piece-work sewing from factories. Bradbury notes that 64 percent of females were recorded as paid workers by 1891, 98 percent of them in dressmaking and millinery trades. What they encountered, however, was pervasive discrimination in the labour market. Women employed full-time in factories typically earned wages of $3-4 per week compared to $7-8 for men. In effect, the factory wages paid to women were so low that there was no point in going out to work. They could earn more money at home by taking in boarders, doing laundry, peddling lunches to factory workers, taking in piece-work, and scrounging the streets for food for a household pig or chickens. One boarder typically paid more per week than a woman could earn in a factory. Most working-class women and girls earned such low wages that they could barely even cover their own food and clothing, let alone run independent households.

The further irony was that among the poorest of poor families, where even marginal extra income earned by women might have made a difference, women's full-time unpaid work in the home appears to have been essential for the survival of other family members. Women were stretched to their physical limits to keep people alive.

They had to care for infants, and meet the bodily needs of children and adults under appalling conditions. Records show entire families living in single back rooms, the poorest in damp basements adjacent to communal pit toilets, where cooking had to be done on open-fire stoves in the room, and where there was nowhere to store food, and no piped water. Illness, disease, malnutrition and death were commonplace. Wage labourers, who were typically away from home some 14 hours a day, 6 days a week, could not shop, cook, feed themselves or clean their clothing. A woman's labour in the home was vital. When a wife died, as frequently happened during childbirth, a husband typically had to find another woman to replace her immediately, or give up children to an orphanage. In effect, the cheap wage-labour economies of factories and dockyards in industrializing Montreal were parasitic on the backs of the unwaged housework of women .

Could this pattern of segregated wage-earning by men and unpaid caregiving by women have been accomplished differently? Was it inevitable that women be forced out of the paid labour force in order to protect children from neglect? A rare case study in which employed women successfully integrated wage-working and care-giving strategies shows that this history of forced segregation was not inevitable. The crucial factor making the difference was higher base wages for women. Joy Parr[4] describes family relations in the small town of Paris, Ontario, in which women were the primary breadwinners. Penmans knit-goods factory, the only major employer in Paris between the 1880s to the 1950s, actively preferred female workers. Females were considered more highly skilled and nimble-fingered at working the knitting machines, and able to turn out a higher quality product than were men. Without alternative employment, the large majority of men left the town to seek work elsewhere. The majority of women in the town were thus both primary breadwinners and primary care-givers.

In this female-centred town, the boundaries of public economy and private care-work were never sharply drawn. Routinely across the town, neighbours marketed all forms of domestic work - child-care, cooking, laundry, and cleaning, allowing flexibility for individual women to alternate between paid work at home and paid work at the factory. There are also stories of women sharing boarding houses with other single women and their children, so that they could pool their childcare and other domestic work. One woman, perhaps one with a new baby, might elect to work at home in exchange for a portion of the wages of other women who worked full ten-hour shifts in the factory. Penmans even arranged that women with newborn infants could take a knitting machine home, so that they could earn some income, although less than in the factory. During the depression years of the 1930s in particular, when paid work was in short supply, women often pooled available wage-work shifts between them.

The central question raised by this case study is why this pattern of integrated labouring and caring work has been so rare historically. In the nearby town of Knetchel, for example, where the primary employer was a furniture factory hiring male labour, Parr records no such pooling or marketing of domestic work. What seems to have made the Penmans knit-goods factory experience so different was that skilled female knitters could earn enough money in their 55-60 hour work weeks that marketing some of their domestic work was a realistic option. Under the conditions described by Bradbury, employed women could not afford to buy any assistance with caregiving work.

In summary, Parr's study shows that women could and did combine wage-earning and caregiving under conditions where they themselves earned and directly controlled sufficient money to make possible the marketing and pooling of caregiving work. Across most of industrializing Europe and Canada, however, such conditions rarely happened. Cheap wage labour economies depended on the hidden, but nonetheless essential caregiving work of women. Employers found it ultimately cheaper and more efficient to drive women out of the paid economy entirely than to pay them more. If women would work without wages to provide for the bodily care and maintenance of male workers, and to reproduce and raise new generations of workers, then employers and the State gained access to a higher quality of more stable male workers. Male workers in turn could be more effectively exploited, or paid less, because so much of their subsistence needs were being met with free labour. The State allied with these business interests by providing subsidized family allowances to unwaged women, under conditions of intense surveillance to ensure that the caregiving work got done. Networks of new professions arose to discipline the emerging social order, enforcing and idealizing the homemaker/ breadwinner nuclear family form. To the extent that these disciplining professions were successful, women became complicit in their own exclusion from the public economy.

Contemporary Advanced Industrial Societies

There have been major changes in patterns of family life since early industrialization. The most notable has been steep increases in labour-force participation by married women, and by mothers with pre-school-age children. What was rare in the 1950 has now become commonplace. The nuclear family homemaker/breadwinner model is also being assailed in other ways, so much so that Cherlin[5] writes of the 'deinstitutionalization' of marriage itself. Young people cohabit openly these days, both as a trial run before marriage, but also as an alternative to marriage, often continuing to cohabit after children are born, or subsequently switching partners. Divorce is also commonplace, including among couples with young children. Same-sex marriages and adoptions are now legal in Canada.

These sweeping changes raise new concerns about how to insure proper caregiving. Homemaking and caregiving work remain as central to the efficient functioning of advanced industrial economies as it was under the conditions described by Donzelot. Yet this dependence remains largely obscured and unacknowledged, segregated conceptually and financially behind the public/private divide. Hence, we explore first the nature of this dependence as a base for looking more deeply at how caregiving work gets done, as well as the continuing role of the State and social sciences in disciplining the social.

Families in Corporate Service

Low-income families absorb the stress and misery generated by insecure and low-waged work at the bottom of the stratified labour force. When money is tight, homemakers do the work of struggling to make do, make over, substitute, and do without, that is essential to keeping a home pleasant and family members physically healthy and feeling reasonably happy. Homemakers strive to keep angry and discouraged workers returning to work year after year because their families depend on their income.[6] They absorb the rage and frustration that workers experience when cyclical recessions, euphemistically referred to as 'economic restructuring,' downsizing, and productivity improvements, push them to the margins of the paid economy. They absorb the stress of unemployed youth, cut off from the promise of luxury and consumer goods incessantly displayed in mass media. This emotional labour is not infrequently done at the cost of domestic violence, an experience far more common within low-income families than among the better-off.[7] It is this homemaking and caregiving work that employers depend on to continually reproduce and make available the supplies of docile, low-waged labour that their businesses require.

Homemakers in financially better-off families perform different kinds of work under very different conditions, but their work is nonetheless essential to the public economy. It is their work that sustains the pinstriped image of men in corporate managerial and professional occupations. They make it possible for corporate bosses to sustain their constant demands for greater productivity, tighter deadlines, more overtime, and commitment of one-hundred-and-ten-percent to the enterprise.[8] Such workaholic lives can only be maintained when someone else is available to do all the work of bodily care and maintenance, and the bulk of childcare work. When women enter high-powered professional occupations, they are expected to keep up with male colleagues, and indeed to exceed them in order to prove their commitment to their work. Otherwise they are considered corporate failures.[9]

Childcare

The dependence of the public economy on homemaking work extends far beyond servicing workers, to the longer-term reproduction of a disciplined and talented labour force. Obscured within the privatized term "childcare" is the complex and long-term work of developing middle-class children for future corporate labour. Qualified professional and managerial labour is not simply available, ready-made, to be purchased by human resources personnel in the public economy. Skilled labour is necessarily produced over many years of work—much of it done for free by parents.[10] Intensive parenting work goes into producing children who are 'school ready'—who have already been drilled in the bodily disciplines of sitting still, attending to adult authority figures, answering questions when asked, and knowing how to think in abstract category terms required by schools.[11] Without such preparation, teachers 'waste' months of teaching time in elementary classes getting sufficient bodily discipline in young charges to be able to teach them. The time that teachers save when children arrive already conforming to the behavioural norms of schools is the time that middle-class mothers have invested in training their children from birth.

This work of preparing children for school continues throughout their school careers. It is part of middle-class parenting work to ensure that homework is routinely done, is neat, and is turned in on time, and that children are sufficiently rested and alert for school each morning. It is part of parenting work to continually motivate children for school work, encouraging them, getting them back into school when they are discouraged, failing, bullied, or alienated from school. Parents who aspire to middle-class careers for their children must do the sometimes enormously stressful emotional work involved in breaking resistance to the regimes of schooling. New school conduct codes passed in Ontario in 2001[12] require that pupils arrive in school punctually, appropriately dressed and well groomed, and that they be polite and respectful to people in authority. Rule infractions are punishable by suspensions and expulsion. Such conduct codes, Raby argues, are designed "to cultivate a certain *kind* of self, one that is restrained, docile, and firmly located within hierarchy, property relations, equality, gender and age."[13] It is the responsibility of middle-class parents to reproduce these codes in their children. What is at stake here is their children's careers and future middle-class status.A study of wives of Japanese executives working in Toronto[14] documents the intense work that these women are expected to do as mothers to prepare their sons for a series of examinations that are entrance requirements for good kindergartens, good primary schools, good high schools, and eventually good universities, from which young men will be recruited by top Japanese corporations. If sons fail to do well at any stage in this sequence of examinations mothers feel they have failed as mothers. In effect, these mothers are engaged in intensive, unpaid work for years to produce the labour force that corporations demand. Embedded in this description of what mothers do is the moral prescription that mothers *ought* to do such work, and that it is virtually a full-time occupation. Some of Ueda's respondents acknowledged that girls could themselves become corporate executives these days, but only as an alternative to becoming wives and mothers. Being a wife and mother in a Japanese corporate executive family is a full-time job in itself.

Parenting work may not end even when children leave home to take up work. Families are increasingly called upon to absorb the risks and insecurities produced by unstable labour markets. As employers shift from tenured employment to contract work, even highly-skilled young people return to stay with parents in between contracts, often with children in tow. [15] These parents may find themselves part of the 'sandwich' generation, still caring for children while their own parents are growing elderly and infirm, and requiring care. In short, homemaking and parenting work are profoundly and inextricably tied into public economy. If such work were not carried out, or not done adequately, the labour-market conditions that capitalists rely upon would not exist.

The Gender of Homemakers: The 'Stalled Revolution'

Who does this homemaking and childrearing work? It is no secret that profoundly gendered labour is hidden behind gender-neutral terms like 'homemaker' and 'parenting.' But why is this so? And what are the active practices that keep women as mothers doing the bulk of unpaid homemaking, caring, and parenting work? A widely shared prediction in studies of family life in the 1960s and 70s was that as wives entered the paid labour force, routine housework would become more equitably shared between spouses.[16] This has not happened.

Housework in twentieth-century Canada is far lighter than under the horrific conditions of backstreet Montreal in the 1800s, but nonetheless is still tiring, time-consuming, and emotionally demanding work.[17] Meg Luxton identifies major components of housework as all the activities of maintaining the house and servicing members, including planning and preparing meals, cleaning and maintaining the house, its contents and members' clothing, budgeting and shopping to obtain materials and supplies needed to meet the daily needs of family members, often on limited money; managing all the daily rhythms of coping with pregnancy, birth and infancy, training preschoolers and supporting school-age children and managing the multiple and often conflicting schedules of children and other adults in the family; and the emotional labour of tension-management work involved in repairing the damage done to members by stresses at school and work.

All this work remains largely unnoticed when done by mothers—until husbands begin to feel pressured into doing some of it. Hochchild's[18] striking ethnographical study of housework focuses on how women working full-time in paid employment struggle to get husbands to participate in housework routines, and the lengths to which husbands often go to minimize their involvement. The major explanation that Hochschild and others put forward to explain this stalled revolution is the tenacity of the gender ideology that 'housework is naturally women's work'—work that girls, but not boys, are socialized to do from early childhood. The model of a full-time homemaker-wife-and-mother may no longer be the statistical norm for families in Western societies, but it is still normative in the sense of an idealized expectation of how things should be.[19]

Changes have occurred over time, with some husbands doing far more housework than others. Sullivan argues that this increase is more likely to occur in families where women have 'acquired greater relational resources'[20] from occupational training, and know how to manipulate their husbands by gender strategies that include retraining, coaching, praising, and open confrontation, carried on over long periods of time. Fox [21] counters with the view that the experience of pregnancy and caring for infants tends to reverse previously more egalitarian sharing of housework between spouses. New mothers often strive to encourage more 'daddy-time' between her husband and her infant by leaving daddy free to play with the infant when he returns from work, while mothers get a break from her infant, and time to do all the other routine features of housework like shopping, cooking, and cleaning. Housework again becomes the undervalued work that mothers simply 'do.' By the time that children are older and mothers think of returning to paid employment, the pattern of expectations are set. Daddy spends time after work playing with the children while mommy gets dinner.

The application of exchange theory in microeconomics to housework makes explicit how devalued housework is.[22] The challenge is to explain how wives can routinely do so much more housework than husbands do and yet both wives and husbands describe their exchange as 'fair.' It is easy to explain how loading all housework on unemployed women can be conceptualized as 'fair' since they do not bring any income into the household and are dependent on subsistence allowances from breadwinners. However, it is less easy for exchange theory to account for the apparent 'fairness' of wives in full-time employment still doing the bulk of housework. The argument goes that their financial contribution to family well-being is still so much less than that of the primary male breadwinner that they might as well not be working. Some husbands may even lose money, he suggests, if the combined earnings of both spouses pushes them into a higher tax bracket. In the context of unstable marriages, women who pressure husbands into housework risk facing divorce. If he walks out of the marriage, most women still do not earn enough to support themselves and their children, without a sharp drop in their standard of living. It is common knowledge that males with good incomes fare better on the re-marriage market than lower-paid ex-wives with children.

The exchange theory argument explicitly considers homemaking work to be of minimal exchange value; but even at this minimum, the theory does not account for the fact that shows husbands earning less money than their wives. Exchange theory would predict these husbands should do more housework than higher-earning husbands, but the evidence suggests that they actually do *less*.[23] An alternative explanation favoured in feminist theory focuses on the tenacity of gender ideology. As a resistant husband in Hochschild's 1989 study expressed it, he felt he had already given up enough in self esteem by accomodating his wife in her higher-income professional job. Expecting him to do low-status housework on top of this was too much. His wife agreed and carried more of the load without complaint. Managing the double shift of paid work and housework was seen by both of them as her exclusive responsibility. If she could not manage she should cut back on her paid work.

The focus on gender ideology, and how couples negotiate or fight over housework, is itself limited, in that it implies that attitude change by husbands would be sufficient to resolve gendered inequalities in housework. This focus risks obscuring how strongly the conditions of doing housework are tied to exploitative labour relations within the wider economy. When workers are subject to unrelenting pressures on their job to be more competitive, more productive, to speed up, to take work home, to be available to employers or clients by fax, telephone, and email on evenings and weekends, they have limited time or energy to devote to housework , even if they are willing to do it. Quality 'daddy-time' may get squeezed in around job demands but with no time left for much else.[24] For men who do take up the challenge to be equal homemakers and parents, the cost is commonly a stalled career, loss of promotion, and lower pay.

Women who compete with men in professional and corporate careers are expected to play by the same rules. Many decide to forego having children altogether in order to pursue a career. Gender ideology comes into play most forcefully when women in highly pressured careers do have children. When neither she nor her male partner can find more time or energy for childcare, the responsibility, by default, falls to her. The expected and 'natural' choice for women is to give up—to join the lower-paid, slower, and lower-status 'mommy track' or to drop out altogether. Some women opt for setting up their own business to escape the corporate rat-race[25]—but they face similar workaholic pressures to succeed, especially if they are primary breadwinners for their families. The artificiality of the supposed boundary between economy and private life become even more obvious.

In effect, the bottom line for many high-pressured corporate employers is that it is cheaper and more efficient for them to push women out of the top jobs altogether than to provide flexible time schedules and shorter work weeks for all employees. Only under conditions of significant labour shortages, when employers have been clamouring to persuade women with children to re-enter the active labour force, have employers and the State been willing to pay for the caregiving responsibilities of employees. This has been cited as an important incentive behind Sweden's generous paid parenting and paid caregiving policies—policies carefully drafted to apply to both mothers and fathers, and without concern for whether they are married.[26] In the United States only during the labour shortages caused by the Second World War were a few such measures widely, if temporarily, introduced.

Marketing Housework and Caregiving Work

The option of marketing housework and caregiving is extensively available only to high-income families, and then usually under difficult conditions. Technological improvements have made keeping house vastly easier than in earlier times, and hiring out the more time-consuming parts of house-cleaning is relatively common. But help with the more complex and responsible work of child-care is more difficult to organize, more expensive, hard to find, and far more stressful. Spaces in licenced day-cares in Canada remain far below the numbers needed to meet demands. Calls for a national child-care program have so far fallen on deaf ears because the costs to taxpayers and the state are considered prohibitive—an issue explored further below. Employed mothers, already stretched to their limits, describe their hard-won struggle to get quality childcare in place continually falling apart as baby-sitters get sick, prove unreliable, or quit; or children get sick and their daycare refuses to take them; or their children drag their feet and refuse to get up, get ready, and get out the door fast enough for mommy to get them to the daycare and arrive at work on time [27] or mothers are pressed to do overtime at work and cannot leave soon enough to pick up children from daycare before punitive penalties will be exacted. Ultimately the stress and worry of managing paid caregivers still rests with mothers.[28] The option of a full-time live-in nanny is a luxury few parents can afford, and it comes with high social costs of lost privacy and exploitative working conditions for the temporary foreign domestic workers who are available to do such work.[29] Caregivers face similar struggles trying to purchase help with care of the frail elderly and the chronicly sick in their homes.

Managing the Social: The Welfare State and the Professions

Struggles around the expansion and contraction of the welfare State in Canada, as in other Western societies, make visible the paradox that caregiving work is essential, and yet expected to be without cost to the public economy.[30] From the perspective of business interests it is essential that caregiving work gets done, and done to high enough standards to ensure a skilled, disciplined, healthy, flexible, docile labour force. It is the role of the State to accomplish this efficiently at the lowest possible cost to corporate tax dollars. From the perspective of family caregivers, it is essential that the State provide extensive support to free up time and energy for mothers and fathers to carry successful careers. The shifts in family form from nuclear family homemaker/breadwinner couples, towards single parenthood, cohabitation, and high divorce rates promotes concerns among young women in particular to have autonomous careers and financial independence[31] at the same time that it heightens concerns of business and the State in disciplining families to perform caregiving work. These conflicting interests are played out in the constant struggles around the welfare state.

The State also services business interests in managing the inevitable volatility of market economies, smoothing out booms and slumps in labour force demands by offering unemployment benefits, retraining schemes and incentives, managing immigration to meet labour shortages in certain fields, as well as managing the costs associated with aging baby boomer populations. Again, such regulation is essential for the smooth functioning of capitalist markets, but at the same time is considered expensive and parasitic on business profits.

The expansion of social services during the booming post-war economy of the 1960s provided significant sources of professional employment for women in such fields as nursing, teaching, and social work, and in civil service administration, but such employment has always come under the shadow of business attitudes that view government services as inefficient, not subject to productivity controls expected in the public economy, and hence wasteful of taxpayer's money. One result of this cost squeeze has been a significant and consistent wage penalty. A comparative study of occupations that controlled for gender of workers, level of education, years of experience, and hours worked, showed that salaries for workers in social service occupations were significantly lower than in non-service occupations.[32] The authors suggest that a combination of factors account for this wage penalty. Service work is seen as a 'natural' choice for women, needing skills that women 'naturally' possess and hence not warranting higher wages. But most importantly, they suggest, social service work is considered work that 'ought' to be provided freely by mothers at home, out of love and obligation towards family members. Paying women to do it looks like a luxury that should not be overdone, lest it undermine altruistic motives within the family. People who need social services the most are also least able to pay for them, and hence not able to access services in the profitable market sector.

During periods of economic recession and heightened global competition from low-waged economies (for example, in Asia and the Southern hemisphere) business interests turn up the pressure on governments to cut welfare expenditures so as to lower the tax burden on businesses. Economists argue that social benefits for citizens constitute hidden 'rents' that businesses in the European Union must pay to employees, thus undermining competitiveness in global markets.[33] The neo-liberal view is that economies have 'no choice but to adapt' to globalization by shifting away from soft feminized 'nanny states' to hard masculine free-enterprise states in which individuals are expected to absorb the risks and instabilities of capitalism.[34] Other economists accept that welfare states remain essential to the maintenance of business-friendly environments, and so will not disappear.[35] The question therefore becomes one of how tightly expenditures can be reigned in, and how far services can be downloaded onto the unpaid economy of family caregiving work.

From the standpoint of the State, cuts to services appear as savings, but from the perspective of women who lose their salaried jobs, they constitutes an extreme form of exploitation, since many must continue to perform the services without pay.[36] When the State cuts back on hospital services, women do more convalescent care at home. When there are cuts to seniors' homes and residential homes for the disabled, women do more chronic care nursing without pay. When the State cuts funds to day-care and kindergartens, mothers do the work at home. When there are cuts in the number of teachers, and classroom assistants, mothers take up the slack with extra coaching and remedial work with their children. When families break up or descend into violence under the chronic frustration of unemployment, mothers redouble their work in stress management, trying to absorb and contain the damage done by economic insecurity. When numbers of social workers are cut, more families are left to cope without help.

As more people, especially single mothers with young children, fall back onto social assistance, states place them under increasing pressure to engage in 'workfare' by doing "volunteer" community service work as a condition of receiving welfare cheques. This arrangement can appear as fair exchange at the individual level. But at the level of the agencies themselves, the influx of workfare recipients serves to depoliticize and control the community activism of agencies who find themselves both compelled to take on welfare recipients, and required to engage in surveillance and report on their charges on behalf of the state.[37]

The Hidden Costs of Caregiving

The financial and emotional costs of caregiving to individual caregivers can be enormous. As women withdraw from full-time employment to meet demands for care of chronically sick or disabled family members and the frail elderly, they pay a price in poorer health, and higher levels of stress and depression.[38] At the same time as losing their salary, they also lose coverage by State pensions and other rights of citizenship[39]. They are pushed to the margins of society. The formal public economy benefits greatly from the combined home care, elder care, and childcare work that women do—estimated to be three to four times the financial value of paid care work.[40] Their work is worth millions of dollars in government savings and tax savings, but they are nonetheless classified as unproductive dependents of breadwinners or social assistance.

The enormity of the stress load that caregivers carry is made particularly visible in studies of families with 'special needs' or 'expensive' children, such as children diagnosed with severe forms of attention-deficit-hyperactive-disorder or ADHD.[41] Litt begins with the account of an affluent dual-income family who managed "through years of persistence, tears and thousands of dollars"[42] to provide workable supports for their son. They did so through purchasing the additional caregiving services of a full-time nanny, a tutor who would attend school daily with their son, and the support of a very expensive private school. A further advantage was the mother's profession as a free-lance journalist, able to work with flexible hours out of her home. Other parents who lack such financial and professional resources describe themselves as driven to desperation by the unrelenting demands on their time. Most mothers found they had to abandon paid work to focus all their time and energy on their child. They felt they had to acquir expertise in psychological, teaching, and medical data on their child's condition so that they could deal with the multitude of specialists from whom they needed resources for their child. They also had to become experts in advocacy work, mastering the stacks of reports and papers required to get through the bureaucracy of the social services. They volunteered in classrooms to protect their children from the wrath of frustrated teachers and bullying fellow students. At night they spent hours going over lessons their child had been unable to follow. In a typical day they found themselves constantly on call from their child's daycare or school to manage their child's misbehaviour - forced to be ready to turn up at a moment's notice when teachers phoned to say they could not manage their child. Such interruptions were sufficient grounds for regular employers to fire the mothers for disrupting work by bringing their private stress into the office. Mothers in these accounts describe themselves as buckling under the stress, reduced to yelling at their children and weeping. The stress load not infrequently pushed families to the point of divorce.

Many single mothers found themselves forced to seek social assistance in order to cope. Yet rarely are children who exhibit the symptoms of ADHD diagnosed as 'disabled' to the point of qualifying for any extra support. Litt recounts that in 1996 the U.S. government tightened restrictions on eligibility for cash assistance under the *Aid to Families with Dependent Children* programme and cut over 135,000 children off welfare rolls, 80 percent of them with mental disorders. Mothers cried as they described their living conditions without this extra income, and without any resources to find help with their children. The final humiliation was that virtually all the mothers with hyperactive children found themselves routinely condemned as bad mothers for failing to better manage and discipline their children. Similar stories can be told by parents of children suffering from autism. Parents are faced with costs of over $36,000 a year for the intensive one-on-one tutoring considered the best care available. Yet while it is considered essential for their child, it is classified as outside the responsibilities of public welfare, medical or educational services, and far too expensive to be considered for assistance.

Policing Families: Keeping Caregivers Working

The crucial question for the State is how to ensure that family members continue to do the intensive caregiving work for the long term, without pay, and with minimal resources, and especially how to ensure it under conditions of uncommitted cohabiting parenthood, single parenting, divorce, unemployment and poverty. The growing concern is that young women, who have seen the struggles and sacrifices that their mothers have made to raise families, will reject it for themselves.[43] Faced with the option of being a homemaker in a traditional family or having autonomous careers, adolescent women overwhelming favour autonomy.

The active practices employed by the State are essentially similar to those described by Donzelot[44]—a combination of intensive mothering ideology backed up with surveillance and compulsion. The central discourses that have emerged within social science disciplines, and the helping professions that draw on them, are all complicit in promoting the ideology of motherhood as the natural and centrally defining characteristic of being a woman. Overwhelmingly, it has been women as mothers, rather than men as fathers, who are targeted. The support role of husbands and fathers as breadwinners is emphasised and their helpful presence in childcare honoured, but in the crunch it is mothers who are policed to care. Emphasis on caregiving expectations for fathers would potentially undermine the strategic separation of productive labour, or breadwinning, from family caregiving and the availability of male workers for super-exploitation.

The ideological pressure towards motherhood begins even before conception, with states increasingly worried that young women will choose to forego having children altogether, in favour of careers and leisure. Such choices threaten future capitalist labour markets, leaving states dependent upon immigration.[45] Mothers are blamed for opting for a kind of 'free-ridership'—their selfish consumption choices resulting in insufficient younger people to carry the burden of an aging population.[46]

Once the baby is born, an increasingly strident discourse extols breastfeeding as the only good choice for women, no matter how incompatible it might be with her other responsibilities or employment demands.[47] Literature on breastfeeding has evolved over time from information on the values and joys of breastfeeding, to identifying it with the moral constitution of a good mother. Breastfeeding is being linked in developmental psychology with the 'new brain science,' the stimulation of skin-to-skin contact extolled as an important part of infant brain development. Embedded in the literature is an ever-growing list of prescriptions for how mothers ought to manage and discipline their maternal bodies to provide pure breast milk.

Breastfeeding discourse merges with a wider discourse of intensive mothering in which mothers are enjoined to be available 24/7 for their babies, to attune themselves to the natural rhythms of the baby, to sleep when baby sleeps, and to offer the breast whenever baby becomes fussy.[48] Such intensive mothering both requires the consent of fathers or partners to support the new mother, and at the same time sets the pattern that mother is the primary caregiver, and coincidentally the primary house-worker, while father 'helps.' The involvement of grandmothers often adds to the message that childcare is and ought to be women's work. The financial conditions under which breastfeeding could succceed, and the obligations of employers and the State to ensure adequate, paid maternity leave, is generally muted or absent from the promotional literature.[49]

Once the infant is old enough for daycare outside the home, another set of promotional discourses stress that even the best child-care centre is a poor substitute for mother, and risks developing insecurity and emotional attachment problems in children. The discourse both helps to excuse the absence of a national child care programme in Canada, and promotes an aura of guilt among mothers who do resort to nannies or childcare centres.[50] Mothers often go to extreme lengths to provide more 'quality time' that exceeds or trumps their child's time with other caregivers, while other caregivers themselves learn to fade into the background when mothers appear.

As children grow to school age, yet another burgeoning discourse associates school success unequivocally with intensive mothering.[51] Should the child appear anything less than perfect, mothers carry the blame. Mothers of children with attention-deficit disorders have found themselves subject to an entire gamut of professionals who pervasively and repeatedly assigned guilt to mothers.[52] Teachers, activity leaders, day-care workers, family physicians, psychologists, psychiatrists, and social workers, along with school-bus drivers, other mothers and family members all blamed the mothers. Mothers find their lives under intensive professional scrutiny, especially whenever they seek social assistance of any kind.

In this professional discourse the conditions under which caregiving takes place disappear from view. When fathers abandon the family, they disappear from social-work records. It is mothers, not fathers, who are held responsible for the well-being of children, and who are criminalized as neglectful or 'bad' mothers, and who are policed to care.[53] A mother may be alone, living in great poverty, with chronic health problems, depression, and addictions, but none of this excuses her from caregiving work. In the worst cases of neglect, children may be temporarily re-moved, and then returned to the mother under more intense surveillance. Mothers must be forced to care, because there is no one else to do the work. Foster mothers may be used by the state for temporary mothering, but the essential and emotionally extremely stressful work of foster-mothering for the state is itself done for limited money and under strict surveillance.[54]

Conclusion

This morally-loaded discourse of intensive mothering is difficult to resist because any challenge sounds like opposition to motherhood itself. The discourse incorporates much feminist literature that defends mothering as an antidote to sterile capitalist values of making money and spending it. The problem is that it feeds into a regime for managing social life that enforces strongly gendered boundaries separating caregiving from public economy. The real need is for an alternative vision of the economy that reintegrates producing and consuming, and a vision of caregiving as a communal responsibility inseparable from our understanding of what economy is about.

Notes

1. Bradbury, Bettina, *Working families, Age, Gender and Daily Survival in Industrializing Montreal* (To-ronto: McClelland and Stewart 1993), chap. 1.

2. Smith, Dorothy E, "Feminist reflections on Political Economy," in *Feminism in Action: Studies in Polit-ical Economy,* ed. Maureen P. Connelly and Pat Armstrong (Toronto: Canadian Scholars Press,1992), 1-23.

3. Donzelot, Jacques, *The Policing of Families* (New York: Pantheon Books 1979).

4. Parr, Joy, *The Gender of Breadwinners* (Toronto: University of Toronto Press 1990).

5. Cherlin, Andrew J., "The Deinstitutionalization of American Marriage," *Journal of Marriage and Family* 66 (Nov 2004):848-861.

6. Luxton, Meg, "Family Coping Strategies: Balancing Paid Employment and Domestic Labour," in *Family Patterns: Gender Relations. 2nd ed.*, ed. Bonnie Fox (Toronto:Oxford University Press 2001), 318-337.

7. McKendy, John, "The Class Politics of Domestic Violence," *Journal of Sociology and Social Welfare* 24,3 (1997):135-155.

8. Menzies, Heather, *No Time: Stress and the Crisis of Modern Life* (Vancouver/ Toronto /Berkeley CA: Douglas & McIntyre 2005).

9. Gazso, Amber, "Women's Inequality in the Workplace as Framed in News Discourse: Refracting from Gender Ideology," *Canadian Review of Sociology and Anthropology* 41,4(2004): 449-473.

10. Griffith, Alison I. and Dorothy E. Smith, *Mothering for Schooling* (New York and London: Routledge Falmer 2005); Malacrida, Claudia, "Motherhood, Resistance and Attention Deficit Disorder: Strategies and Limits," *Canadian Review of Sociology and Anthropology* 38,2(2001):141-165.

11. Noble, Joey, "Social Class and the Under-Fives: Making the "Differences" Visible," *Our Schools/ Our Selves 2,2 (April 1990):42-61.*

12. Raby, Rebecca, "Polite, Well-Dressed and on Time: Secondary School Conduct Codes and the Production of Docile Citizens," *Canadian Review of Sociology and Anthropology* 42,1(2005):71-91.

13. Ibid. p. 75.

14. Ueda, Yoko, "Corporate Wives: Gendered Education of their Children," *in Knowledge, Experience, and Ruling Relations: Studies in the Social Organization of Knowledge,* ed. Marie Campbell and Ann. Manicom (Toronto: University of Toronto Press 1995), 122-134.

15.Mitchell, Barbara A., Andrew V. Wister and Ellen M. Gee, "Culture and Co-residence: An Exploration of Variation in Home-Returning among Canadian Young Adults," *Canadian Review of Sociology and Anthropology* 37, (2000):197-221.

16. Cherlin, Andrew J, "The Deinstitutionalization of American Marriage," *Journal of Marriage and Family* 66(Nov. 2004):848-861.

17. Luxton, Meg, *More Than a Labour of Love: Three Generations of Women's Work in the Home* (Toronto: Women's Press 1980).

18. Hochschild, Arlie, *The Second Shift* (New York: Avon 1989).

19. Smith, Dorothy E., "The Standard North American Family: SNAF as an Ideological Code," in Dorothy Smith, *Writing the Social: Critique, Theory, and Investigations* (Toronto: University of Toronto Press 1999), 157-171.

20. Sullivan, Oriel, "Changing Gender Practices Within the Household. A Theoretical Perspective," *Gender and Society* 18,2(2004):207-222, page 217.

21. Fox, Bonnie, "The Formative Years: How Parenthood Creates Gender," *Canadian Review of Sociology and Anthropology* 38,4(2001):373-390.

22. Parkman, Allen M, "Family Harmony and the Home. Bargaining Over Housework: The Frustrating Situation of Secondary Wage Earners," *The American Journal of Economics and Sociology* 63,4 (2004):775-793.

23. Bittman, Michael, Paula England, Nancy Folbre, Liana Sayer and George Matheson, "When Does Gender Trump Money? Bargaining and Time in Household Work," *American Journal of Sociology* 109,1(2003) July:186-214.

24. Luxton, Meg, "Family Coping Strategies: Balancing Paid Employment and Domestic Labour," in *Family Patterns: Gender Relations. Second Edition* ed. Bonnie Fox, (Toronto:Oxford University Press

2001), 318-337; Hochschild, Arlie, "The Third Shift." in *Family Patterns: Gender Relations. Second Edition,* ed. Bonnie Fox. (Toronto:Oxford University Press 2001),338-351.

25. Arai, A. Bruce, "Self-Employment as a Response to the Double Day for Women and Men in Canada," *Canadian Review of Sociology and Anthropology* 37,2(2000):125-142.

26 Baker, Maureen, *Canadian Family Policies: Cross-National Comparisons* (Toronto: University of Toronto Press,1995).

27. Hochschild, Arlie, "The Third Shift." in *Family Patterns: Gender Relations. Second Edition,* ed. Bonnie Fox. (Toronto:Oxford University Press 2001),338-351; Menzies, Heather. *No Time: Stress and the Crisis of Modern Life.* (Vancouver/Toronto/Berkeley CA: Douglas & McIntyre 2005).

28. Crittenden, Danielle, "The Mother of All Problems," *Saturday Night* (April 1996):44-54.

29. Arat-Koc, Sedev, "The Politics of Family and Immigration in the Subordination of Domestic Workers in Canada," in *Family Patterns, Gender Relations. Second edition,* ed. Bonnie Fox. (Toronto: Oxford University Press 2001), 352-374; Arat-Koc, Sedev, "In the Privacy of Our Own Home: Foreign Domestic Workers as Solution to the Crisis in the Domestic Sphere in Canada," *Studies in Political Economy* 28(Spring 1989):33-55.

30. McDaniel, Susan A, "Women's Changing Relations to the State and Citizenship: Caring and Intergenerational Relations in Globalizing Western Democracies," *Canadian Review of Sociology and Anthropology* 39,2(2002):125-150.

31. Gerson, Kathleen, "Moral Dilemmas, Moral Strategies, and the Transformation of Gender: Lessons From Two Generations of Work and Family Change," *Gender and Society* 16,1(2002):8-28.

32. England, Paula, Michelle Budic and Nancy Folbre, "Wages of virtue: The Relative Pay of Care Work," *Social Problems* 49,4(2002):455-473.

33. Turner, Stephen, "The Third Way," *Society* (January/February 2005):10-14.

34. McDaniel, Susan A., "Women's Changing Relations to the State and Citizenship: Caring and Intergenerational Relations in Globalizing Western Democracies," *Canadian Review of Sociology and Anthropology* 39,2(2002):125-150; 2002; Marchak, Patricia, *The Integrated Circus: The New Right, and the Restructuring of Global Markets* (Montreal and Kingston: Queens University Press, 1991).

35.Clarke, John, "Turning Inside Out? Globalization, Neo-Liberalism and Welfare States." *Antropologica* 45,2(2003):201-219.

36. Armstrong, Pat, *Labour Pains* (Toronto: The Women's Press 1984); Armstrong, Pat and Hugh Armstrong, *Thinking it Through: Women, Work and Caring in the new Millennium* (Halifax: Nova Scotia Advisory Council on the Status of Women,2002).

37.Michaud, Jacinthe, "Feminist Representation(s) of Women Living on Welfare: The Case of Workfare and the Erosion of Volunteer Time," *Canadian Review of Sociology and Anthropology* 41,3(2004):267-290.

38. Herd, Pamela and Madonna Harrington Meyer, "Care Work: Invisible Civic Engagement." *Gender and Society* 16,5(2002):665-688.

39. McDaniel, Susan A., "Women's Changing Relations to the State and Citizenship: Caring and Intergenerational Relations in Globalizing Western Democracies," *Canadian Review of Sociology and Anthropology* 39,2(2002):125-150.

40. Benoit, C. M., *Women, Work and Social Rights: Canada in Historical and Comparative Perspective* (Scarborough,ON :Prentice Hall Allyn and Bacon Canada 2000).

41. Litt, Jacquelyn, "Women's Carework in Low-Income Households. The Special Case of Children with Attention Deficit Hyperactivity Disorder," *Gender and Society* 18,5(2004):625-644; Malacrida, Claudia, "Motherhood, Resistance and Attention Deficit Disorder: Strategies and Limits," *Canadian Review of Sociology and Anthropology 38,2(2001):141-165.*

42. Litt. Ibid.,625.

43. Gerson, Kathleen, "Moral Dilemmas, Moral Strategies, and the Transformation of Gender: Lessons From Two Generations of Work and Family Change," *Gender and Society* 16,1(2002):8-28.

44. Donzelot, Jacques, *The Policing of Families* (New York: Pantheon Books 1979).

45. Brown, Jessica Autumn and Myra Marx Ferree, "Close Your Eyes and Think of England. Pronatalism in the British Print Media," *Gender and Society* 19,1(2005) February: 5-24.

46. Turner, Stephen, "The Third Way," *Society* (January/February 2005):10-14.

47. Wall, Glenda, "Moral Constructions of Motherhood in Breastfeeding Discourse," *Gender and Society* 15,4(2001):592-610, p. 202.

48. Fox, Bonnie, "The Formative Years: How Parenthood Creates Gender," *Canadian Review of Sociology and Anthropology* 38,4(2001):373-390.

49. Singley, Susan G. and Kathryn Hynes, "Transitions to Parenthood. Work-family policies, gender, and the couple context," *Gender and Society* 19,3(2005):376-397; Wall, Glenda, "Moral Constructions of Motherhood in Breastfeeding Discourse," *Gender and Society* 15,4(2001):592-610, p. 202.

50. MacDonald, Cameron L, "Manufacturing Motherhood: The Shadow Work of Nannies and Au Pairs," *Qualitative Sociology* 21,1(1998):25-53; Murray, Susan B., "Child-care Work: Intimacy in the Shadows of Family Life," *Qualitative Sociology* 12,2(1998):149-168.

51. Griffith, Alison I. and Dorothy E. Smith, *Mothering for Schooling* (New York and London: Routledge Falmer 2005).

52. Malacrida, Claudia, "Motherhood, Resistance and Attention Deficit Disorder: Strategies and Limits," *Canadian Review of Sociology and Anthropology 38,2(2001):141-165.*

53. Swift, Karen J., *Manufacturing 'Bad' Mothers: A Critical Perspective on Child Neglect* (Toronto: University of Toronto Press 1995).

54. Swartz, Teresa T., "Mothering For the State: Foster Parenting and the Challenges of Government-Contracted Carework," *Gender and Society* 18,5(2004):567-587.

ChapterTwo

$7/Day, $7/hour and 7 Days a Week: Juggling Commutes, Low-waged Shift Work and Child Care in a Changing ("New") Economy

Patrizia Albanese

THE CANADIAN welfare State has been labeled by many as liberal or residual,[1] and its family policies follow an "individual responsibility model" or set of assumptions.[2] This means that there is a commitment on the part of the Canadian State to the basic assumption that the public has very little responsibility for the economic well-being of a family or for the provision of care and support, unless a family is in dire need, and only then has access to temporary aid.[3] While this has been found to be true of Canada as a whole, there is considerable variation across provincial borders, with Quebec, identified by some as being more "social democratic" in its policy goals and spending, and seemingly closer to a social responsibility model of family policy.[4] This approach to families assumes that the public shares the responsibility with parents for the basic care of its members, especially dependent children, with the cost of care expected to be shared by families and the state. One of the key policy areas where the Canadian welfare State obviously differs from the Quebec model is in the provision of affordable non-parental childcare, where Quebec stands out as a leader, well ahead of other provinces in government commitment to universality of access and cost. Childcare has been deemed by many to be of particular importance to families today, for a number of reasons—some of which will be the focus of this chapter.

To begin with, many studies have identified the benefits of quality, affordable childcare on children.[5] Affordable care has also been recognized as a way to deal with child poverty in this country, especially enhancing employability of mothers.[6] My research set out to assesses the impact of Quebec's $7/day childcare program on the lives of women, families, and a community located in an economically disadvantaged region of Quebec. While conducting my first phases of research, I found that having $7/day childcare proved to be highly advantageous for employability and the general well-being of women, somewhat improved family stability, and was effective in a community's economic development.[7] On the other hand, families were having a difficult time juggling long commutes, shift work, characteristic of low-paying peripheral labour markets, and childcare centre hours of operation. They reported that commutes and shift work made drop-off/pick-up of children complicated and often required the support of friends, extended family and sitters. Welcome to Canada's "new economy," I thought. Welcome to the "post-industrial society."[8]

Researchers and residents of Canada are increasingly aware of the sweeping economic changes linked to globalization that are taking place across this country (and parts of the rest of the world, for that matter). While global in nature, economic change has meant different things for different individuals, families and communities. Because of geographic location, the nature of a region's economy, and different levels of social support to families, women across provincial borders struggle with different kinds of challenges connected to combining work and family. This chapter will identify some of the economic changes and challenges encountered by families living in small-town Quebec, near the Ontario border. The chapter begins with an overview of the important and growing need for childcare in this country. It also presents some of the economic shifts occurring at the national and local level. In presenting some of the key preliminary findings from a qualitative study on childcare in a small Quebecois community, this chapter hopes to link what seem to be micro changes and challenges that affect the everyday lives of women and families to provincial-level policy decisions and even larger national and global economic shifts.

This chapter aims to show the importance of universal, affordable childcare in light of women's often low-wage, service-sector employment in a region hard-hit by the decline of the lumber industry and the decline and disappearance of (predominantly) men's primary and secondary sector jobs. In doing this, the chapter hopes to show that some of the seemingly inevitable challenges created by broader economic change can be buffered by universal social programs geared at helping families in economic transition.

The Study

The overall goal of my study was to assess of the impact of $5/day ($7) childcare at the community and inter-personal levels using a series of qualitative interviews with mothers and childcare providers, and one year later, fathers, living in a community located on the Quebec/Ontario border. The study was conducted in a community made up of two adjoining towns that were established in 1888. In 2001, the larger of the two conjoined communities (472.85 square km), a canton, had 2,007 inhabitants, and the smaller of the two (3.19 square km), a village, had a population of 1,661 inhabitants.[9] The communities were predominantly Francophone, with an Anglophone minority (12.8% Anglophone in the smaller of the two and 16.4% in the larger). The towns were located on the Ottawa River, an ideal location for the logging industry. They were part of a prosperous logging community until quite recently, with the last log run on a second nearby river dating to1982. Many of the town's men still work in the economically hard-hit (soft-wood) lumber industry, in one of the few remaining paper and lumber mills in the region (most recent mill closure in August 2005). Many women work in traditional service sector jobs, including retail sales, food services, health, beauty/hair dressing and childcare; others commute to jobs in neighbouring towns or Ottawa/Hull/Gatineau, between a half hour and an hour and a half away. One of the fastest growing employers in the region is customer service call centres, that benefit from the region's abundant, relatively cheap, bilingual population. A disproportionate number of people in the towns are on some form of social assistance or disability insurance.

My specific research objectives were to assess the economic and social impact of $7/day childcare on the community and on domestic relations. I hoped to assess the impact on children, indirectly, by asking mothers and child care providers about the school readiness of children before and after attending childcare. I was also interested in understanding the impact of this provincial program on domestic relations, specifically, its impact on (husband/wife; common-law) conjugal relations. I sought to establish the effects on the community by assessing the impact on the employability of mothers and the effect on household income; employment opportunities in the childcare "industry"; and other spin-off jobs created by the program. Some of these findings will be presented below.

The Quebec Initiative

For decades many Canadian women have been fighting for the creation of a national childcare strategy,[10] with relatively few concrete, positive results. Things appeared to be improving under a Federal Liberal minority government (2004-2005), with the launch of a new large-scale childcare initiative, whereby provinces would have the power to forge their own unique paths towards improved childcare, with an infusion of federal dollars. Following a Liberal defeat and the election of a Conservative minority government in early 2006, the national childcare plan was shelved, replaced by a "Universal Childcare Benefit," which proposed to give families "more choice in childcare" with a taxable $100 monthly payment for each child under six. While this may seem generous to some, given the cost of care and the very limited number of childcare spaces available, this plan offers no relief to families in need of non-parental childcare. Only Quebec has seen substantial growth in the creation of childcare spaces (still under-serviced) and the proportion of children in childcare.[11]

In 1997, Quebec's new family policy included the implementation of $5 per day childcare for all four-year-olds who used childcare at least three days a week, regardless of their family's household income and employment status. The program was extended to include three year olds in 1998, two year olds in 1999, and by the year 2000, all children regardless of age or financial need would have access to the program. Bill 145, set up a network of early childhood and childcare agencies out of non-profit childcare centres and family care agencies, for children ages 0-12.[12] In implementing the program, the Parti Quebecois hoped to promote social democracy, protect Quebec language and culture, assist working-class families, promote gender equality, fight poverty, and improve school readiness of children.[13] Struggling with the high cost of the program, on November 13, 2003 Carole Theberge, the minister responsible for the family, tabled a new child-care bill in the Quebec legislature proposing to increase the cost from $5.00 per day to $7.00. It is estimated that the Quebec (Liberal) government would save $52 million for every extra dollar charged to parents. The program costs Quebec more than $1 billion a year, but over 168, 000 children are covered by the program.[14]

Despite reports and evidence of welfare State decline,[15] from this example, we see that welfare states vary internally in the emphasis they place on service provision. The Quebec government, for instance, appears (despite problems) committed to implementing public policies aimed at supporting families with children—again, a characteristic of the social democratic/responsibility model of family policies. At the same time, parts of Quebec are vulnerable to American pressures surrounding trade in general and softwood lumber, in particular, global economic restructuring, the high cost of fuel, the exchange rate for the Canadian dollar and environmental constraints (eg. effects of clear-cutting, etc.). So, while we see fragmentation in policy goals and practices on the one hand (diversity across provincial borders), there are homogenizing broader global trends and challenges touching the lives of average Canadians. This chapter sets out to assess the impact of provincially-funded childcare on Quebecois families experiencing changes associated with the "new economy."

Canada's "New Economy"—The Prediction

In 1973 and again in 1976, Daniel Bell welcomed the West to the "post-industrial society." In his theorizing, he outlined the changes, in progress and expected, towards an information society, where the main sources of innovation are derived increasingly from the codification of theoretical knowledge. He argued that value, in Adam

Smith's and Karl Marx's sense, is fundamentally increased not by labour, but by knowledge, with the last revolution of the twentieth century being in telecommunications. With this, he predicted a fundamental shift from goods-producing to a service economy and the pre-eminence of the professional and technical classes. Put very simply, we would see a shift from dirty jobs to clean jobs, from "dumb" jobs to "smart" jobs, or from blue-collar to white collar jobs.

Bell identified a new axis of social organization and stratification, with increased interdependence of the world economy and the rise of the "world business corporation," facilitated by new telecommunication and jet transport.[16] Bell explained that while the industrial revolution was an attempt to substitute nature with machines, the post-industrial revolution, in contrast, was an attempt to substitute machines with increased reliance on people. As a result, he optimistically concluded that:

> political ethos of an emerging post-industrial society is communal, insofar as social goals and priorities are defined by, and national policy is directed to, the realization of these goals. It is sociologizing rather than economic..., insofar as the criteria of individual utility and profit maximization become subordinated to broader conceptions of social welfare and community interests-particularly as the ancillary effects of ecological devastation multiply social costs and threaten the amenities of life.[17]

The Canadian Reality

It is well documented that over the past three decades we have seen a fundamental restructuring of the Canadian economy, driven by global economic change. We find ourselves in "a digital economy, an information economy, an internet economy, an innovation economy, a high-tech economy, a real-time economy, and a global-economy."[18]

There is no question that there has been a decline in the manufacturing sector, with the locus of economic activity shifting to the service sector. In Canada's new economy the "ability to create wealth is increasingly dependent on the effective management of knowledge...the organizational capability to create, acquire, accumulate, disseminate, and exploit information and knowledge."[19] The share of employment accounted by knowledge workers has increased in all regions of the country, and knowledge workers have become "a highly-prized commodity."[20] Many of the leading growth industries in Canada, between 1986 and 1991 were linked to communication technology and services, followed by business and community/social/personal services. In contrast, there was industrial decline in textile, wood/wood products/furniture, and other manufacturing and heavy industries.[21]

While we have seen an increase in the demand for knowledge workers, it is also well documented that there is a bifurcation within the service sector, and a polarization of jobs and earnings.[22] That is, while some of the new jobs are high-skilled and knowledge-based, many of the new jobs being created in Canada's new economy are low-paid, low status and part-time—or what some have colloquially termed "McJobs." For example, between the 1991 and 1996 Census, the number of people who reported that they worked part-time throughout the year increased by nearly 20%, with women still more likely than men to do so.[23] Furthermore, by 1996, of the 10 broad occupational categories in Canada, the sales and services category was the largest, with a labour force of 3.6 million or 26% of Canada's total employment. That year, retail sales clerk/person was the leading job group for both men and women, among all workers in the four largest census metropolitan areas in Canada. The top 10 most frequent jobs for men in Canada, in 1996 were truck driver (#1), retail sales person, janitor, retail trade managers, farmers, sales representatives (whole sale trade), motor vehicle mechanic, material handler, carpenter and construction trades helper (#10). For women they were, retail sales person (#1), secretaries, cashiers, registered nurses, accounting clerks, elementary school teachers, food servers, general office clerks, babysitters and (#10) receptionists.[24]

As a result of all this, family earnings instability and inequality grew throughout the 1990s.[25] There was, and continues to be, widespread worker displacement and increased worker alienation.[26] Furthermore, part-time and casual labourers, who are often women, are experiencing increased stress levels, and other physical and emotional problems due to work conditions.[27] As a result, some have argued that the more appropriate terms to characterize the new economy would be organizational cost-cutting, restructuring and downsizing,[28] leading to instability and increased inequality.

In this new economy, there is a growing emphasis on education, in general, and lifelong learning, in particular. However, there is talk of boys' potentially lower success in the knowledge economy, as girls generally outperform boys in school achievement, report more positive attitudes towards school, are less likely to be early school leavers compared to boys and are more likely to enroll and remain in full-time undergraduate studies.[29] On the other hand, women still earn less than men, gender-blind, market-based individualist approaches to education ignore gendered work conditions, and the ongoing work-family conflict is still experienced by many women today.[30]

Smaller communities traditionally dependent upon industries in the primary and secondary sector of the economy are interesting and important case studies for understanding the actual changes touching the lives of real Canadians. For example,

Miewald and McCann (2004) conducted a study of the recent changes in the coal min-ing industry in the Appalachian coalfields. In a recent article, they document the im-pact of the decline in the traditionally male-dominated mining industry and increase in female-dominated service sector jobs. They document the gender struggles over appropriate gender roles that result from this transformation.[31] My own research at-tempts to do the same in Pontiac County, Quebec, where I try to show that universal, affordable childcare acts as a buffer to some of the most hard-hitting changes and challenges brought on by Canada's new economy.

The "New Economy" in Pontiac County (A view from the trenches)
The Pontiac's 15,000 square kilometers is located in the Outaouais region of Western Quebec, and is made up of 20 villages, and 15 736 inhabitants. The Pontiac Tourist Guide boasts of it 4,000 lakes, 7 rivers, 2,000 kilometers of country roads and only one traffic light—"*un secret bien conserve*" (a well kept secret).[32] Two of its rivers enve-lope the community under investigation—a community struggling under the weight of the economic shift from primary/secondary to tertiary sector jobs in the new, post-industrial economy, but at the same time, experiencing the benefits of Quebec's universal, affordable childcare program.

The Declining Wood Products Industry
In 1999, the wood product industry accounted for only 1.1% of the jobs in Canada.[33] On the other hand, Quebec has the largest number of workers in this industry (49,500), followed by BC (41,900), and Ontario (30,000),[34] with entire communities re-lying primarily on wood. A Statistics Canada report revealed that the "processing of forest resources in Quebec anchors the economies of more than 250 municipalities, providing 100% of the manufacturing jobs in 135 towns and villages."[35]

The importance of the lumber industry was apparent in my own preliminary findings. My first wave of interviews with mothers and childcare providers revealed that of fifteen mothers interviewed who had partners, nine, or sixty percent, had partners or husbands who, at the time of the interviews, worked in the lumber industry. Of the sixteen childcare providers who were married or cohabiting, eleven, or 68.8% had partners in the lumber in-dustry. A second round of interviews, one year later, with fathers, revealed that of the ten fathers in the study (summer 2005), two were working at a nearby paper mill, two were re-cently laid off from a saw mill, two left the sawmill (one for construction and one for truck driving) and one was on disability insurance after a back injury acquired while working in the sawmill. While this was not a representative sample, study participants were not se-lected because of their links to lumber, pulp or paper mills.

The lumber or wood products industry has received some economic blows over recent years. Between 1987 and 1999, the GDP growth rate for the wood industry was lower than that of the Canadian economy and of all manufacturing industries.[36] In Quebec, the second largest lumber-producing province, production has declined by over ten percent between 2000 and 2001.[37] Ironically, Statistics Canada recently reported that wholesale sales of lumber and millwork advanced 11.7% in January of 2004, a gain attributed in part to rising prices and solid performance of the construction and renovation sector in both Canada and the United States.[38] On the other hand, the industry was hard hit by the ongoing soft-wood lumber dispute with the United States, rising energy costs, the high Canadian dollar, and environmental restrictions on cutting implemented and enforced by the provincial government in Quebec. The impact of all this was clearly felt in this community that experienced its second mill closure (in August 2005) in as many years. To make matters worse, employees in the larger wood and furniture group had a relatively low rate of training (21%) compared to other industries in the country (39%),[39] making finding new, "good-paying" jobs much more difficult.

When the second mill closed in this community in the summer of 2005, almost every adult resident was heard echoing "there will be five jobs lost in town for every job lost in the mill"–jobs in the bush, truckers, mechanics, etc. Some anticipated major job losses in restaurants, the community's major grocery story and other local services. Local businesses seemed to have slowed somewhat, but many of the low-paid, part-time jobs seem to have been spared, and continue to be held, for the most part, by local townswomen, who now, more than ever, seem to depend on $7 per day childcare, while holding their minimum wage (or so) jobs.

The Importance of Women's (Service Sector) Employment

Not all of the local townswomen I interviewed worked in minimum wage jobs, to be sure. There was clearly a bifurcation of jobs, with about half of the women I interviewed holding jobs in somewhat better-paid, yet still traditional female-dominated service industries, including nursing/health, adult care (social work-type jobs), and administration or civil service/government jobs. All of these jobs however, required the women to commute to towns and cities located between a half-hour and one-and-half hours away. The other half worked in lower-paid, local retail sales, food service, child care, hair/beauty and secretarial jobs. Despite the low wages of some and long commutes and/or irregular hours of others, most saw their jobs as absolutely necessary for their own and their family's economic well-being.[40]

In line with recent findings on women's levels of education in the new economy,[41] a large number of women interviewed had significantly higher levels of education (some college or higher, on average) than their male partners (high school or some college). Many of the women pursued some post-secondary education, knowing that many of the jobs in the more lucrative lumber industry were closed to them (53.3% of all workers in this industry receive an income of between $30,000 and $79,000, compared to 36.9% for Canadian industries as a whole).[42] Men, in contrast, often anticipated following their fathers and grandfathers into the relatively better-paid jobs in the lumber/mill industry. Unfortunately, as the two mills closed, many men turned to mining (requiring week-long absences from families), trucking (also often absent from families) and construction, for employment.

Now, more than ever, it was obvious that women's employment was extremely important for the overall wellbeing of families. One father, who lost his job due to the second mill closure, in August 2005, explained that they were very fortunate because his wife's well-paying job (a one-and-a-half hour commute away) and (un)employment insurance allowed them to continue to live, with only minor cuts to expenditures, as they had in the past. He was hopeful that he could find employment or retraining before the (un)employment insurance ran out. This couple decided to keep their child in daycare despite the family's lower household income.

The Importance of Universal, Affordable Childcare in the Pontiac's New Economy

During my second round of interviews, as the second mill was closing, I asked mothers and fathers of children in $7 per day childcare if they anticipated a loss of jobs in the childcare industry—would parents be forced to pull their children out of care, to save the $35 per week? Only a few anticipated that families would be forced to take their children out of daycare, explaining that $35 per week was better spent on groceries and paying bills. Interestingly, those most affected by the closures seemed to be the most likely to say "no, daycare will not be affected" or "no, we decided not to take our child out of daycare–for now." Some explained that the affected men needed to devote their attention to applying for (un)employment insurance, finding a new job or enrolling in retraining programs, and could not assume new childcare responsibilities. Others explained that it was obviously clear now that daycare was essential as a first step to better prepare their children for a "new world of work" (the new economy) outside of the wood industry. Others still noted that $35 per week for daycare, where meals were served and included in the cost, was still cheaper than feeding and caring for children at home.

Some mothers explained that to a certain extent, Quebec's childcare program has improved domestic relations because they are experiencing less financial stress, and therefore less conflict at home. Mothers were only now able to seek or return to paid work, improving family income, but they could justify and "afford" working part-time, or taking minimum wage jobs. Some explained that if childcare were more costly, low-paid or part-time employment, most of the jobs available to them in within the town, would not cover the cost of care.[43]

While many had to look for jobs out of town, some mothers mentioned that this program kept them residing in Quebec, or mentioned that while one or both partners worked in Ontario, they could not afford to live there due to the high cost of childcare. One gave an example of a friend who, while vowing never to return to Quebec after leaving the province, moved back because of affordable childcare and cheaper housing. At least 5 women interviewed either worked in Ontario, or their husbands/partners worked there. Three speculated on how they could not afford to leave Quebec, because of childcare, even if job opportunities came up in Ontario.[44]

Almost all the mothers interviewed mentioned that this program has created jobs for the town and made it possible for people, but especially women, to find paid work, even if it were low-paid and/or part-time. In fact, I found that, approximately 35 women were employed in the local childcare centres on a full or part-time basis. Most of them began working in this area since the introduction of $5 ($7)/day childcare.[45]

The two conjoined towns had a total of 12 childcare centres in operation in the summer of 2004 when I interviewed childcare providers. Eleven of them were home/family childcare centres and one was a large, newly built centre. The home childcare centres were typically in a woman's basement, and run as independent small businesses. Home centres that had one owner/operator (adult woman) were allowed to care for six children, ranging in ages from a few months to four years of age. Home centres with an owner/operator and an assistant were allowed to care for nine children. All but 3 home centres had two adult women working in each. Many childcare providers preferred having an assistant for the adult company, to share the work and responsibilities, and to make routine things like temporarily leaving the room to attend to their own or individual children's needs, possible. They were required to remain open for a minimum of 10 hours per day, and working alone meant having virtually no breaks for the full 10 hours.[46]

The large center was newly built and opened in March 2004. It employed 11 women, in mostly full-time care positions. It had a general manager who operated and supervise this centre and two others in neighboring towns in the county. There was also a local manager/supervisor, a cook, five full-time ECE teachers, three part-time ECE teachers who relieve the other workers or are available if child to teacher ratios require it and one cleaner who washed floors and cleaned every evening after the centre closed. Almost all the early childhood educators at this centre had college-level training. This larger centre was also required to remain open 10 hours per day.[47]

The Ongoing Challenges—Juggling Shift Work, Commuting and Care

I asked mothers how they selected their childcare providers and if they had a preference for home versus larger centre care. Often, the centre's hours of operation was the main determining factor for selecting one centre over another. That is, while all centres had to stay open for 10 hours, individual centre operators could choose when to open and close (example 7am-5pm or 6:30-4:30 pm). Centre hours of operation were a serious concern for most mothers, as all mothers interviewed had to contend with their own and their partners (where applicable) shift work and/or commuting. Not surprising, it was often still mothers, and not fathers, who organized the complex juggling of people and schedules needed to make their childcare arrangements work.

I did not anticipate being drawn into the intricate web of support required to make childcare and paid employment work. It happened nonetheless. During the time I was conducting interviews, I received an unexpected phone call and request from a neighbour. Could I be on stand-by, ready to pick-up her son at daycare, if her husband was forced to work overtime? Her own shift finished one hour after the daycare closed, and her parents, who she usually relied on in these situations, were not available. Of course, I agreed, but did not have to step in on that occasion. I did however step in on two other occasions, when the shifts of four adults (two parents and two grandparents) did not coincide with daycare hours of operation. After experiencing this first hand, I learned by talking to others that this was not an unusual occurrence. Researchers remind us that in the face of economic pressures and other inequalities, individuals form formal and informal networks or collectives, especially in light of increased reliance by the State on the provision of informal care.[48] Informal networks have been used by women in particular, to challenge various forms of marginalization that ensue from the intersection of local and global forces that shaped their lives.[49] What the community under study here experienced was but one concrete example of this.

The new economy, with commutes, shift work, comparatively low wages, job insecurity, part-time hours, holding multiple jobs and working overtime, was not easy to navigate. Having universal, affordable childcare certainly made working under these conditions a little more manageable for most families. However, even this was clearly not without its share of new challenges.

Conclusions

The goal of this chapter was to present some of the sweeping economic changes affecting Canadian families today. I hoped to show that despite declines in primary and secondary sector jobs (often, traditionally men's jobs), growing economic insecurities, and the rise of lower-paid jobs (especially for women) in the service sector, with State support in the form of affordable childcare, families can better cope with the inevitable challenges. Many families in small-town Quebec experienced severe economic blows and increasingly relied on women's/wives' employment for economic stability, but this would not have been possible, for many, without affordable childcare.

Quebec's $7 per day childcare program has produced a few of the better-paid managerial and administrative jobs and many more of the lower-paid, traditionally female-dominated care and other service jobs (cleaning and food services). At the same time, the program has made it possible for many women to find employment at a time when some of their husbands and partners are losing better-paid primary and secondary sector jobs. Families are forced to look further away from home for employment, resulting in longer commutes. Some are forced to work shifts, or hold multiple jobs, with unusual or part-time hours. As a result, families and especially women, find themselves planning and implementing complex drop-off and pick-up schedules that rely on a network of family and friends. But despite the challenges, both mothers and fathers generally agree that $7 per day childcare is a basic necessity of life as they live through the changes brought on by "the new economy." In fact, many wondered out loud how other Canadians manage without it. And that got me wondering, too. So, the next phase of my research will have me looking at women across borders, provincial borders, to see how parents residing in a comparable logging town, across the Ottawa River, in Ontario, cope with changes and challenges brought on by the new economy, when affordable childcare is not available.

Notes

1. Esping-Andersen, G. "Women in the New Welfare Equilibrium" *The European Legacy*. 8.5 (2003):599-610; Esping-Andersen, G. "Citizenship and Socialism: Decommodification and Solidarity in the Welfare State," in G. Esping-Andersen and L. Rainwater (eds.), *Stagnation and Renewal in Social Policy: The Rise and Fall of Policy Regimes*. London: Sharpe, 1987; Baker, M. *Restructuring Family Policies: Convergences & Divergences*. Toronto: University of Toronto Press, 2006.

2. Eichler, M. *Family Shifts: Families, Policies and Gender Equality*. New York: Oxford University Press, 1997.

3. Ibid., 14.

4. Albanese, P. "(Under)Valuing Carework: The Case of Child Care Workers in Small-Town Quebec" *International Journal of Early Years Education*. 15.2 (2007): 125-139; Baker, *Restructuring Family Policies*.

5. Stahmer, A. and C. Carter. "An Empirical Examination of Toddler Development in Inclusive Childcare" *Early Childhood Development & Care*. 175.4 (2005): 321-333; Lamme, L. L., D. Sabis-Burns and J. Gould. "Project Booktalk: Library Books and Lap Reading in Childcare Homes" *Early Childhood Education Journal*. 32.1(2004), p. 45-50.

6. Bainbridge, Meyers and J. Waldfogel. "Child Care Policy Reform and the Employment of Single Mothers." *Social Science Quarterly*. 84.4 (2003): 771-791; Baker, M. *Restructuring Family Policies: Convergences & Divergences*. Toronto: University of Toronto Press, 2006; Baker, M. "Child Care Policy and Family Policy: Cross-National Examples of Integration and Inconsistency," in G. Cleveland and M. Krashinsky (eds.). *Our Children's Future: Child Care Policy In Canada* (pp. 275-295). Toronto: U of T Press, 2001; Brown, G., J. Roulston, B. Ewart M. Schuster, J. Edwardh and L. Boily. "Investments in Comprehensive Programming: Services for Children and Single-Parent Mothers on Welfare Pay for Themselves Within one Year" in G. Cleveland and M. Krashinsky (eds.). *Our Children's Future: Child Care Policy In Canada* (pp. 334-346). Toronto: U of T Press, 2001; Cleveland, G. and M. Krashinsky. "Special Arrangements for Lone-Parent Families," in G. Cleveland and M. Krashinsky (eds.). *Our Children's Future: Child Care Policy In Canada* (pp. 315-333). Toronto: U of T Press, 2001; Friendly, M. "Subsidized Child Care Delivers Future Payoffs." *National Post*, March 31, 2003, FP 15, 2003; Mulroney, C. "Affordable Day Care Can Ease Child Poverty." *Toronto Star,* Jan. 13, 2003; Han, W. and J. Waldfogel. "Child Care Costs and Women's Employment: A Comparison of Single and Married Mothers With Pre-School-Aged Children" *Social Science Quarterly*. 82.3 (2001): 552-568; Te Velde, E.R. "Is Women's Emancipation still Compatible with Reproduction in this Country?" *International Congress Series*. 1279 (2005): 58-67. Statistics Canada. "Parental Work, Child-care use and Young Children's Cognitive Outcomes," *The Daily* of October 23. Ottawa: Statistics Canada, 2003; Toroyan, T., I. Roberts, A. Oakley, G. Laing, M. Mugford and C. Frost. "Effectiveness of Out-of-home Day Care for Disadvantaged Families: Randomised Controlled Trial." *British Medical Journal*. 327.7420 (2003): 906-909; Waldfogel, J. "Child care, Women's Employment, and Child Outcomes" *Journal of Population Economics* 15 (2002): 527-548; Willms, D. J. (ed.). *Vulnerable Children: Findings From Canada's National Longitudinal Survey of Children and Youth*. Edmonton: University of Alberta Press, 2002.

7. Albanese, P. "Small Town, Big Benefits: The Ripple Effect of $7/day Child Care. *Canadian Review of Sociology and Anthropology*. 43.2 (2006): 125-140.

8. Bell, D. "Welcome to the Post-Industrial Society" *Physics Today*. 28.2 (1976): 46-49; Bell, D. *The Coming of Post-Industrial Society: A Venture in Social Forecasting*. New York: Basic Books, 1973.

9. Statistics Canada. 2001 Community Profile—M-et-P. Ottawa: Statistics Canada, 2004 (http://www 12.statcan.ca/english/profil101/Detials/details1.cfm?...); Statistics Canada. 2001 Community Profile—F-C. Ottawa: Statistics Canada, 2004a (http://www12.statcan.ca/english/profil101/Detials/details1.cfm?...).

10. See the 1970 *Report of the Royal Commission on the Status of Women in Canada*. Bird, F. J. Henripan, J.P. Humphrey, L. Lange, J. Lapointe, E.G. MacGill and D. Ogilvie. *Report of the Royal Commission on the Status of Women in Canada*. Ottawa: Crown Copyrights, 1970.

11. Roy, F. "From She to She: Changing Patterns of Women in the Canadian Labour Force." *Canadian Economic Observer*. Catalogues No. 11-010. Ottawa: Statistics Canada, 2006, pp. 3.1-3.10; Bushnik, T. *Child Care in Canada*. Children and Youth Research Paper Series (Cat. No. 89-599-MIE-No.003).

Ottawa: Statistics Canada, 2006; Stafford, J. *A Profile of the Childcare Services Industry*. Ottawa: Statistics Canada, Catalogue no. 63-016-XPB, 2002.

12. Bégin, L., L. Ferland, G. Girard, C. Gougeon. *School Daycare Services*. Québec: Gouvernement du Québec. Cat. No. 2002-02-00121, Quebec: 2002; Tougas, J. "What we can Learn From the Quebec Experience" in G. Cleveland and M. Krashinsky (eds.). *Our Children's Future: Child Care Policy In Canada* (pp. 92-105). Toronto: U of T Press, 2001; Tougas, J. "Quebec's Family Policy and Strategy on Early Childhood Development and Childcare" *Education Canada*. 39.4 (2000): 20-22.

13. Ibid."Quebec's," 20.

14. Canadian Press. "Quebec Hikes Cost of Day Care to $7 from $5." *Toronto Star*, Nov.13/03, 2003.

15. Evans, P., D. Rueschemeyer and T. Skocpol (eds). *Bringing the State Back In*. Cambridge: Cambridge University Press, 1985; Esping-Andersen, G. "Citizenship and Socialism," 1987.

16. Bell, 1973, 484.

17. Ibid., 481

18. Statistics Canada. "Update on Economic Analysis" Cat. 11-623.XIE. Ottawa: Statistics Canada, 2004b (www.statcan.ca/english/freepub/11-623-XIE/2003001/trdescrip.htm).

19. Gera, S. and K. Mang. "The Knowledge-Based Economy: Shifts in Industrial Output" *Canadian Public Policy*. 24.2 (1998): 149-184, 150.

20. Statistics Canada, 2004b.

21. Gera and Mang, 1998, op. cit. (footnote 19).

22. Hughes, K. and G. Lowe. "Surveying the "Post-Industrial" Landscape: Information Technologies and Labour Market Polarization in Canada" *Canadian Review of Sociology and Anthropology*. 37.1 (2000): 29-53; Lowe, G. *The Quality of Work - A People-Centred Agenda*. Toronto: Oxford University Press, 2000; Myles, J. "The Expanding Middle: Some Canadian Evidence on the Deskilling Debate." *The Canadian Review of Sociology and Anthropology*. 25.3 (1988): 335-364.

23. Statistics Canada. "1996 Census: Labour Force Activity, Occupation and Industry, Place of Work, Mode of Transportation to Work, Unpaid Work" *The Daily* of March 17. Ottawa: Statistics Canada, 1998.

24. Ibid.

25. Morissette, R. and Y. Ostrovsky. "The Instability of Family Earnings and Family Income in Canada, 1986 to 1991 and 1996 to 2001" (11F0019MIE – No. 265). Analytical Studies Branch Research Paper Series, Ottawa: Statistics Canada, 2005

26. White, M. "Retraining Programs for Displaced Workers in the Post-Industrial Era: An Exploration of Government Policies and Programs in Canada and England" *Compare* (Journal of British Association for International and Comparative Education). 33.4 (2003): 497-505; Menzies, H. "Umbilical Cords and Digital Fibre-Optics: Communication and the Disembodiments of Digital Globalization" *Gazette* 62.3-4 (2000): 271-280.

27. Zeytinoglu, I.U., B. Seaton, W. Lillevik and J. Moruz. "Working in the Margins: Women's Experiences of Stress and Occupational Health Problems in Part-Time and Casual Retail jobs" *Women & Health*. 41.1 (2005): 87-107.

28. Silver, S., J. Shields and S. Wilson. "Restructuring of Full-time Workers: A Case of Transitional Dislocation or Social Exclusion in Canada? Lessons from the 1990s." *Social Policy & Administration*. 39.7 (2005): 786-801; Lowe, G. *The Quality of Work;* Krahn, H. and G. Lowe. *Work, Industry and Canadian Society*. Toronto: Thomson, 2002.

29. Fenwick, T. "What happens to the girls? Gender, work and learning in Canada's "new economy." *Gender and Education* 16.2 (2004): 169-185.

30. Ibid.

31. Miewald, C. and E. McCann. "Gender Struggle, Scale and the Production of Place in the Appalachian Coalfields" *Environment & Planning*. 36.6 (2004): 1045-1064.

32. Corporation de dévelopment économique du Pontiac, "Bienvenue chez-nous: Guide touristique" Campbell's Bay: Pontiaction, n.d.

33. Human Resources and Skills Development Canada (HRSDC). "Wood Products Industry" Government of Canada. Ottawa, 2005. (www.hrsdc.gc.ca/en/hip/hrp/sp/industry_profiles/woods.shtml).

34. Ibid.

35. Dufour, Daniel. *The Lumber Industry: Crucial Contribution to Canada's Prosperity-.Manufacturing Overview Research Papers*. (Cat. No31F0027XIE-No.01). Ottawa: Statistics Canada, 2002, p.2.

36. HRSDC. "Wood Product,",op. cit. (footnote 33).

37. Statistics Canada. "Sawmills and Planing Mills," *The Daily* of March 5. Ottawa: Statistics Canada, 2002.

38. Statistics Canada. "Wholesale Trade" *The Daily* of March 21. Ottawa: Statistics Canada, 2005.

39. HRSDC. "Wood Product."

40. Albanese, P. "Small Town, Big Benefits," op. cit. (footnote 7).

41. Fenwick, T. "What happens to the girls?" op. cit. (footnote 29).

42. HRSDC. "Wood Product,",op. cit..

43. Albanese, "Small Town, Big Benefits," op. cit.

44. Ibid.

45. Ibid.

46. Ibid.

47. Ibid.

48. Pfau-Effinger, B. "Welfare State Policies and the Developments of Care Arrangements" *European Studies* 7.2 (2005): 321-347; McDaniel, S. "Women's Changing Relations to the State and Citizenship: Caring and Intergenerational Relations" *Canadian Review of Sociology and Anthropology*. 39.2(2002): 125-149

49. Skocpol, T. and J. L. Oser. "Organization Despite Adversity" *Social Science History* 28.3 (2004): 367-437; Purkayastha, B and Subramaniam, M. (eds).*The Power of Women's Informal Networks: Lessons in Social Change From South Asia to West Africa*. Lanham, MD: Lexington Books, 2004; Stack, C. *All Our Kin*. New York: Basic Books, 1974.

Chapter Three

Ripping in Half: A Political Economy of Women's Everyday Lives

Susan Bryant

THIS CHAPTER explores the boundaries faced by women with respect to the nexus between paid and unpaid labour in contemporary times. Particularly within the context of the digital age, women are being told through various discourses that they can now 'have it all'—both career and family life. The chapter contributes to the political economy of women's lives by analyzing the discourses related to new technologies—and the promise of flexibility associated with these—in relation to the empirical evidence with respect to women's experiences with paid and unpaid labour. Existing research is used as a foundation for a small study of young women's attitudes and expectations about their futures, and the argument is made that important challenges remain for the next generation of women to negotiate in terms of these issues.

A number of years ago, while I was carrying out my dissertation research for my Ph.D. in Communication, I came across a quote in Arlie Hochschild's preface to *The Second Shift*[1] that struck a chord with me. She writes about her experiences with having a child while working as a full-time academic in an American university, and describes her experiences with bringing her baby to work with her in order to continue breastfeeding. (Women in the United States are typically only permitted six weeks of maternity leave from their paid work, a fact which makes breastfeeding extremely challenging and which surely contributed to Hochschild's decision to bring her infant to work with her.) She explains how torn she felt by her own relief that this experience did not seem to have compromised her professional status and yet her resentment that what she had done was such a complete anomaly in her workplace. She refers to the "smooth choicelessness" of her male colleagues' careers and writes,

> I felt it…when I saw wives drive up to the building in the evening, in their station wagons, elbow on the window, two children in the back, waiting for a

man briskly walking down the steps, briefcase in hand. It seemed a particularly pleasant moment in their day. It reminded me of those summer Friday
evenings, always a great treat, when my older brother and I would pack into
the back of our old Hudson, and my mother, with a picnic basket, would drive
up…to Washington, D.C., at five o'clock to meet my father, walking briskly
down the steps of the government office where he worked, briefcase in hand.
We picnicked at the Cherry Basin…my parents sharing their day, and in that
end-of-the-week mood, we came home. When I see similar scenes, something
inside me rips in half. For I am *neither and both* the brisk stepping carrier of a
briefcase *and* the mother with the packed picnic supper (italics mine).[2]

I was between two and nine months pregnant with my first child while carrying out
my dissertation research, and I was feeling confident about my future as both mother
and academic. However, Hochschild's expressions, that something inside her "rips in
half" and the notion of being "neither and both," brought tears to my eyes as I pon-
dered the possibility that combining the two roles was going to be much, much more
complex than I could possibly imagine.

That was over ten years ago. Since then both my personal experiences and my
scholarly research on women's experiences with the nexus between unpaid and
(many types of) paid work have led me to conclude that women are, in many ways, indeed being 'ripped in half' by the choices and compromises they continue to have to
make. This chapter examines the discourses related to so-called flexibility and equality we are presented with in the digital age, considers some of the realities being experienced by women in both the unpaid and paid realms, and documents the
attitudes and expectations of some of today's young women. I am taking up Dorothy
Smith's[3] call to generate a political economy of the every day/every night with respect
to women's experiences. I wish to pose the question: what, then, does all this 'ripping in half' tell us about the challenges for feminism in the early part of the 21st century? What types of 'roadblocks' do women—even relatively privileged Western/
Northern women—still face as they negotiate the terrain of their everyday lives?
And, if these relatively privileged women face ongoing inequality, what concerns
ought we to have about their counterparts in other socio-economic categories and/or
in other parts of the world? As my use of the Hochschild quote indicates, I am particularly interested in analyzing the subject of gendered labour through a focus on
women who are in an on-going relationship with a male partner, and, in particular,
those who may choose to have children.

In constructing a political economy of everyday life, we need to be careful not to romanticize earlier periods in time with respect to the choices and opportunities women had available to them. The above quote from Hochschild should not be taken as an indication that she, or anyone else, is looking back on women's past experiences to argue that times were necessarily better for women—or their families—in past decades (perhaps, for example, the 1950s, '60s, or '70s). The more clearly defined, highly gendered division of labour in most (at least North American) homes offered women few choices about how their lives would play out with respect to who performed the paid and unpaid labour in a household. And, more to the point, it also presented few questions as to where economic (and often other forms of) power lay within the family. However, we need to think critically as we assess the qualitative and quantitative changes we have witnessed with respect to the division of labour between the sexes. Women certainly seem to have more choice–but are the choices *meaningful*? In other words, do they get to choose *between* activities, or do they simply have to add the new activities to the ones they already have been assigned in our culture?

For several decades feminists in Canada and elsewhere called for governments to begin collecting data on time spent on unpaid domestic work and child care as part of national census-taking programs.[4] Finally, in 1996, the Canadian census included for the first time a series of questions about the number of hours spent per week in unpaid domestic work and unpaid child care—with the findings being divided by sex. To date we have data from the 1996 and 2001 Canadian censuses to give us a very clear idea what is going on in Canadian homes. Not surprising to many of us, these data confirm what we see anecdotally all around us amongst heterosexual couple households with respect to the kinds of 'choices' available to women.

In the 1996 census, among women who were engaged in paid work for thirty or more hours per week (considered full-time by Statistics Canada), fifty-one per cent reported spending fifteen or more hours/week in unpaid housework. On the other hand, among women with no paid employment seventy per cent did fifteen or more hours of unpaid housework. The contrast between these numbers and those reported by men is striking. Among men with full-time employment, twenty-three per cent spent fifteen or more hours/week engaged in housework, while for men with no paid work the proportion was thirty-six per cent. When these findings are sorted according to the presence of children in the home (Statistics Canada includes any household with at least one child under the age of fifteen), the data are even more gender differentiated. For women in full-time paid employment and no children, thirty-seven per cent reported spending fifteen hours or more per week on house-work. This figure increased to sixty per cent for those with children. For men in full-time paid work and no children, nineteen per cent did fifteen or more hours/week of housework, while amongst those with children, twenty-six per cent did as much. The census asks questions about unpaid care of children as well. Among women with full-time paid work, sixty-four per cent spent fifteen or more hours/week looking af-ter children. For men in paid employment full-time, this figure was thirty-nine per cent. For those without paid employment, the numbers were seventy-nine per cent of women and only forty-two per cent of men spent fifteen or more hours on child care activities per week.[5] The quick shorthand to take away from all of these numbers (and the others presented by Statistics Canada) is that in almost all categories related to unpaid housework, women are doing about *twice* as much unpaid work as men, even when they are also working for pay full-time. When it comes to unpaid child care men seem to be doing a little better, but these duties are in no way shared evenly, even when the children's mother works full-time for pay. Given the gross inequities con-firmed by these findings, feminists were eager to ascertain whether the 2001 census data would reveal any improvements to the status quo.

The 2001 and 2006 census data, unfortunately, provide relatively little evidence that major change is in the works. Once again, the federal government included census questions regarding unpaid domestic work and unpaid child care and once again clear gender imbalances were uncovered. The data for the 2001 census reveals virtually the same gender differentiation with respect to unpaid housework and unpaid childcare as did the 1996 study. Much like in the 1996 data, approximately twice as many men as women reported doing either no unpaid work or less than five hours per week. On the other hand, for unpaid housework almost exactly twice as many women as men report doing over fifteen hours per week. The 2006 census data shows small improvements to the contributions being made by men, and these are certainly not to be disregarded. However, the bulk of unpaid domestic work and unpaid child care is still being carried out by women, even when they work for pay outside the home.[6]

A political economy of the everyday world of women's experiences helps to un-pack some of the complexities underlying the numbers revealed by the census data. To this end, the *discourses* of everyday experience are a good place to begin. If dis-courses are, at the most general level, the stories we tell ourselves and are told about the world,[7] then much is revealed by examining the discourses about women and work in this, the digital age. Over the past few decades we have been told time and again—both explicitly and implicitly—that women have made great strides toward equality in our society. So much so that some have observed that the feminist move-ment may be in decline of late due to a sense of satisfaction with how far we have come.[8] There are backlash elements of popular discourse that repeatedly tell us that women have become so completely equal that something called 'reverse discrimina-tion' exists. And yet, the Canadian census data reveal that at the very least the *politics of the home* have not changed anywhere near as much as we might have hoped. One element of this relative absence of change that should be considered alongside the discourses about gender equality are those of another sort that became dominant in the mid-1990s: the discourses related to technological change and a promise of flexi-bility. I became very interested in some of the discourses related to women, work, and technology in the mid-1990s when a new incarnation of the stories about women and work was appearing on the popular (and in some cases the academic) scene—one that was particularly related to notions of so-called technological prog-ress. We need to recall that there is a well-entrenched set of assumptions within Western/Northern cultures with respect to the relationship(s) between technology and progress. Part of the long-standing, liberal, progressivist tradition of Western thought is a firm commitment to the idea that technological change necessarily brings with it social progress, that technological change *is* indeed progress.[9] James Carey describes the more recent manifestation of this type of thinking as that which

> ...identifies electricity and electrical power, electronics and cybernetics, com-puters and information with a new birth of community, decentralization, eco-logical balance, and social harmony.[10]

One aspect of the triumphant discourses related to technology that was—and still is—relevant for analyzing women's work usually invokes the amorphous and ubiqui-tous notion of *flexibility*. In the 1980s and 1990s we started to hear more and more about 'flexible corporations,' 'flexible production,' 'flexible banking,' and 'flexible employment.' Flexibility, for both organizations and individuals, became something to aspire to, with technology ostensibly making it all possible.

During the same decades in which flexibility was becoming a major buzz-word in our culture, women were continuing to enter the paid workforce in large num-bers.[11] Faced with the many challenges related to the so-called 'home-work balance,' the discourses I was monitoring in the 1990s must have been particularly appealing to many women. We began to see the suggestion that workers, and particularly women, had much to gain by adopting computer-networked technologies in order to make their paid work more 'flexible.'

Stories in newspapers and popular and business magazines began to feature stories about workers using technology to make their lives more flexible. Headlines such as: "Flexible workstyles: in the future workplace, fewer workers will have full-time permanent jobs"[12]; and "On their own: more and more Canadians are finding that the most secure job is the one they make themselves."[13] The adoption of then-fairly new networking technology was presented as offering individuals more flexibility, more autonomy, and even a means of escaping urban life. In addition to all of this, it was also presented, time and again, as offering the opportunity to harmonize paid work and family responsibilities. Headlines such as: "Home-based business offers flexibility: gives parents more time to raise kids and keep house,"[14] and "Home base: work and family under one roof."[15] One article in the well-respected *Financial Post* promises that home-based work "...provides flexible working arrangements for families and allows parents to see more of their children."[16] Many of the visual images accompanying such articles, including two in the *Globe and Mail,* featured parents working at their home computers with their children close at hand. One image featuring a content-looking woman in her home office with her smiling pre-schooler colouring at her feet was an inset in the article entitled "Canadians flocking to Home-Sweet-Home Businesses."[17] The stories about the world being presented in these mainstream discourses were consistent with positive ideas about the relationships between technology and society. In the case of home-based information work, the promise of reconciling the challenges of paid and unpaid work were (and continue to be) directed heavily toward women.

My research at that time explored the ways in which the adoption of this flexibility mantra played out for men and women who chose to do information work from home. I interviewed thirty-eight workers, twenty-four women and fourteen men, who had recently begun to do the bulk of their paid work from a home office using computer networking for connections to employers and/or clients. Twenty-three of these were independent contractors and fifteen were employees from both the private and public sector. The most common motivator for wanting to work from home was the need and/or desire to spend more time looking after their children and/or the search for a more flexible way of reconciling the demands of paid and unpaid responsibilities.[18]

Important gender differences were revealed in the ways in which men and women dealt with domestic responsibilities. The vast majority of women I met with reported doing "half," "most" or "all" of the unpaid domestic work for the family —even when their paid work was on a full-time basis. Also worth considering is that regardless of what proportion of the unpaid work they took on, men tended to keep it as separate as possible from their paid labour. Men were more likely to have a completely separate workspace (complete with a door) and to do the bulk of their work in what would be considered regular business hours. Women, on the other hand, tended to have less of a physical division of space between their paid and unpaid lives,[19] and tended to have to intersperse housework and child care with their paid work. If this resulted in not getting all their paid work done in the day time, these women carried on their paid work well into the late evening, often after children were in bed, in order to get everything accomplished.[20] The promise found within the popular discourses of 'balancing' or 'harmonizing' paid and unpaid labour seemed rather elusive for many of the women participants. Rather, family life seemed to have morphed into a scene in which not only were women expected to 'do it all,' but now there seemed an assumption, as one of my participants observed, that they could do it all *simultaneously*.[21]

One of the strategies used by some of my participants to deal with the huge list of expectations they were faced with was the adoption of part-time paid work. Sixteen of my thirty-eight participants worked part-time, and all but one of these were women. These women, for the most part, chose to do their paid work on a part-time basis in order to continue caring for the household without the full load of the proverbial 'double day.' As Ann Duffy and Norene Pupo have argued,[22] part-time work appears to be both promise and problem in that it could present a challenge to the traditional gendered division of labour or it could reinforce existing inequalities. They suggest that for women with a lifelong, relatively equitable relationship and a high standard of living, part-time work may be a positive choice. Conversely, for other women part-time work may provide a short-term solution while solidifying their long-term dependency.[23] This analysis of part-time work seems one that might be even more aptly applied to part-time paid work when it is accomplished from the home.

In spite of the inequities I discovered during my research, I was also surprised to find how many of the women I interviewed expressed considerable satisfaction with their choice to do paid work from home. It seemed to me that it was extremely important to question the degree to which capital's flexibility was translating into a positive, flexible experience for individuals. And yet, despite the complexities and challenges of their new work arrangements, most of the women I met with seemed to be *somewhat* satisfied with the new work arrangements. It seemed to me that perhaps they were using home-based information work as a means of taking some degree of increased control over the rhythm of the everyday lives.[24] The issue of control, one strongly related to power, is of tremendous import for women's lives. Since, as the Statistics Canada data bear out, women continue to have placed upon them the bulk of the domestic burden, adopting home-based work may be seen as constituting an attempted refusal "to accept male working patterns for themselves."[25]

One could argue, as I have, that we *might* understand women's adoption of home-based information work as a rejection of the legitimacy of the public-private divide and the related temporal and spatial patterns related to paid and unpaid labour.[26] The notion that paid work is something that happens in the 'public' realm and that unpaid labour occurs in the 'private' realm is a problematic—even fictitious—divide that has been bad for women. This divide has made unpaid labour in the domestic sphere virtually invisible for the purposes of public policy analysis related to economic, cultural, and social issues. *However*, while working from home may offer women somewhat more control over the *rhythm* of their daily lives—that is, when and how they take care of their seemingly endless 'to do' list—it does not seem to have meant a shortened list of responsibilities. Additionally, there are questions of visibility and credibility associated with home-based work that may also make women more precariously placed in terms of their position in the labour market and more economically reliant upon their spouse. In spite of such alternative work arrangements as home-based work, there does not appear to have been any major shift in the expectations placed upon women with respect to unpaid labour. In terms of the division of labour, the traditional politics of the home remain intact. Indeed, my qualitative work confirms and complements the quantitative data collected by Statistics Canada. Meaningful gender equality, then, seems yet a long way off.

While the women in my study chose home-based information work as a means to accommodate both their paid and unpaid responsibilities, other women have made, and continue to make, other types of choices in order to deal with the obstacles to equality placed before them in our culture. Once again, the discourses telling women that they can 'have it all' and 'be anything they want to become' promise women any career they might wish to embark upon. However, research on the subject of women's career tracks uncovers the fact that women are negotiating the terrain of their careers by making difficult and often life-altering choices in order to succeed in their paid work lives.

Judy Wajcman's important study of British executives presents some disturbing findings with respect to the choices women have been making.[27] Wajcman's research is on senior managers within high-technology (oil, chemicals, and computing) private sector firms that were known to have progressive equal opportunity policies. She ze-roes in on how the nexus between work and home is central to what she calls the "…formation of particular gender regimes."[28] She takes issue with the argument that men and women are differently oriented to their work, and her findings show that the executive-level men and women she studied had similar career paths and the same motivation levels with respect to their paid work. She notes, however, that men and women differ very clearly in terms of their relationships to the domestic sphere as well as with respect to some fundamental choices to be made.

In terms of their domestic arrangements, Wajcman found that eighty-eighty per cent of women managers had spouses who also worked full time while only twenty-seven per cent of the men fell into this category (and of the other men, forty per cent had a spouse who was a full-time homemaker).[29] Over two thirds of the men had children living with them, while over two-thirds of the women did not. And, when there were children on the scene, only fifteen per cent of men reported having primary responsibilities for their children compared to ninety-four per cent of the women with children. The data Wajcman presents support the census findings for Canada discussed above. And, she argues that in the majority of cases women manag-ers have achieved their occupational status at the cost of motherhood while male managers live in families with children and a traditional division of domestic labour. Some of the women interviewed in the study spoke frankly about choosing *between* children and a managerial career. When women in the study did have children, they attributed their success to carefully managing domestic labour and child care through hiring the work out—a choice that Wajcman points out is highly problem-atic because it "…lays bare the material differences between women, particularly those based on class and race."[30] For women to succeed at the upper levels of man-agement, they can either choose childlessness or have children and rely on the cheap domestic labour of other women. Neither of these options confronts the imbalance of power within domestic relationships, Wajcman argues.

Wajcman is also very clear that her analysis of the study's data is not merely about the need to improve the range of choices available to women. She argues that Carol Pateman's 'sexual contract'[31] that frees men to hire out their labour because they have a wife to take care of the domestic scene is good for neither women nor men. Within the traditional arrangements, men are not afforded the opportunity to participate fully in their families' lives. Indeed, many men with busy careers see very little of their children or their spouse. She suggests that the dominant model of orga-nizational work life is "inimical to family life,"[32] and argues that our entire way or organizing paid work is flawed—for both women and men. This analysis echoes that of Arlie Hochschild.[33] The personal comments quoted at the outset of this chapter are a preface to her study of women and men's paid and unpaid labour. She notes that "…the long hours men devote to work and to recovering from work are often taken from the untold stories, unthrown balls, and uncuddled children left behind at home."[34] Hochschild also argues that the way we structure work as a culture is in need of change. A better balanced set of expectations placed on employees could allow women *and* men to have more time for other commitments; and, provided that labour were divided more equitably than the status quo, women *might* have more meaningful choices before them.[35]

The imposed need to make difficult choices related to career and family are evident in other professional career paths as well. Within the academic world, anecdotal observations reveal a world in which a significant portion of women in full-time faculty positions do not have children. This anecdotal evidence is supported by path-breaking research presented by the Canadian Federation for the Humanities and Social Sciences (CFHSS). In their annual 'Ivory Towers: Feminist and Equity Audits' they present data on equity issues related to the academe. In 2002, the proportion of women academics in Canada was just under thirty-four per cent, with only approximately one-third of all full-time appointments going to women in the 2001-2002 academic year.[36] The study also reveals what it calls the "academic women's 'baby gap.'" Looking at academic women aged thirty-five to thirty-nine, it reports that forty-nine point six percent had no children under the age of twelve living with them in 2001, and that this number was forty-five point six for all women doctorate holders.[37] Other professionals mentioned in the study, primarily as a point of comparison with respect to the 'baby gap,' are lawyers and physicians. Using the same age categories, the data show that forty-two point three percent of women lawyers and thirty-two point nine per cent of women physicians do not have children under twelve living with them. Wendy Robbins, one of the compilers of the CFHSS study makes this plea, referring to academic women: "How will we reproduce ourselves? We aren't having children and we are neither diverse nor ideal role models for our students."[38] Robbins also notes that academic women are more likely than their male peers never to marry and much more likely to divorce.[39]

Not unlike Wajcman's findings, the data on women academics quantify what anecdotal observations suggest: women academics seem to be choosing *between* their careers and having children. With only half of women academics in the later portion of their child-bearing years reporting that they have children under twelve living with them, one wonders whether these women would consider themselves to have had truly *meaningful* choices available to them. As well, the CFHSS data count as academics anyone employed by a university as a professor, whether on a part-time or full-time basis. While more detailed research has not been done, I feel quite confident suggesting that a large proportion of the women who report having children may be in the part-time ranks. Academic work, like executive work, constitutes another career track that, for women, is relatively incompatible with family life. Indeed, women cannot really 'have it all.'

Other research demonstrates that life in the digital age is not making life any more flexible for men or women. Heather Menzies writes about the variety of ways in which our sped-up world of digital, asynchronous connections have brought with them lives of multi-tasking, over-work, fragmented family relationships and immeasurable stress levels for adults and children alike.[40] And, I would suggest that the expectations placed upon women are even higher with all the contemporary connectivity available to us. The promise of 'flexibility' in the digital age has come to mean something other than convenience, meaningful options, and control over one's daily rhythms, as the early uses of the term seemed to imply.

One of Arlie Hochschild's optimistic conclusions about the future of gender equity back in 1989 was that more and more couples will achieve a meaningful balance. She notes that the 'lucky' couples in her study were those where "they shared the role between them….Making it to the school play, helping a child read, cooking dinner in good spirit….these were the silver and gold of the marital exchange." And, she argues that "…as government and society shape a new gender strategy, as the young learn from example, many more women and men will be able to enjoy the leisurely bodily rhythms and freer laughter that arise when family life is family life and not a second shift."[41] The question is, are there enough role models, enough 'lucky couples'? What are young women to look to as their example of how to change the politics of the home?

During in-class discussions with my undergraduate students over the past several years I have been struck by their reticence to discuss, even in academic let alone in personal terms, the issues I raise herein. In a course on communication, culture, and paid labour I include a section on gender and labour, and we discuss the challenges facing women in trying to negotiate the nexus between paid and unpaid work. I show them the Statistics Canada gender breakdowns on unpaid housework and child care, and we discuss the ways in which women are disadvantaged by the enormous burden of unpaid labour place upon them. Students, both men and women, have almost always seemed at least somewhat if not very uncomfortable with the subject. In relatively small classes in which students had been informal, comfortable, and even outspoken on other topics, the discomfort with this subject is often palpable. When I introduce the notion of a political economy of the household and begin to analyze the politics of the home, they have difficulty articulating how they see their future roles playing out. Women students assert that they definitely do not want their future reality to be that of the status quo I am presenting to them. However, when asked what they might do to ensure that they experience equity with respect to their paid and unpaid work lives they seem at a loss. I suggest to them that, should they choose a long-term (heterosexual) relationship, they ought to choose their partner carefully, ensuring that he will take on his share of the unpaid duties related to the home and/or children. When asked if they ever discuss these matters with people they are dating, one woman raised her hand immediately. She mused that she would like to know a man's values on this subject as early as possible, and yet if she were to explore the topic very early in a relationship she could find herself going on an awful lot of first dates! We all laughed and agreed with her humourous yet succinct analysis. However, what concerns me most is that the dilemma she identified seems to be dealt with primarily by avoidance.

These classroom discussions as well as other conversations with my students have led me to worry that today's young women may not be on the road to a very different future from the 'ripping in half' experienced by their older counterparts. In order to explore this question further, and to ask the question 'what might a political economy of women's everyday lives look like for the next generation?,' I engaged in focus groups and interviews with young women between the ages of eighteen and thirty and asked them about their expectations with respect to their careers, family life, the negotiation of paid and unpaid work, and what they see as the greatest challenges for women of their generation. The women were recruited from the university population and were therefore all in the process of gaining a higher education. The career goals they mentioned included becoming an artist, entertainment lawyer, politician, film-maker, journalist, and video game producer.

All of the women had grown up in homes where their mother worked outside the home full-time, either as part of a two-income family or as the single parent of the household (in two cases). In one case the woman's father had become disabled early in her lifetime and had been home full-time while his wife worked outside the home. It was striking how much this age category of women feel that having a career is to be the norm, not only for their own career fulfilment, but also because they generally expect to have the lifestyle afforded by two incomes. When asked how unpaid labour was divided in the family when they were growing up, most of the women said that their mothers did more, although none said that they believed that their mother did twice as much as their father. In the case of Kelly[42] whose parents both worked full-time shift work and divorced when she was ten years old, her mother is described as "a formidable woman" who worked hard for pay, did everything at home (both before and after the divorce) and never complained about it. In Sandra's family, her father went on long-term disability when she was two years old and her mother worked as a full-time teacher thereafter. Her mother also took care of most things at home at least in the early years, since her father was physically unable to manage these tasks for many years. Most of the women describe the children helping more and more with household tasks as they grew into their teens, and a number of them describe their homes currently (several are still living at home) as ones in which "everyone pitches in to help out." However, both Marissa and Anna also explain that in their families they are expected to do more domestic work, while their brothers of a similar age are "let off the hook" much of the time. Interestingly, in some cases the balance of unpaid labour has shifted slightly later in the parents' careers. Juliet explains that although her mother did most of the unpaid work when she was younger (with a grandmother also helping before and after school), her mother has had a promotion recently and travels frequently for her job. Juliet describes her father as having taken on much more domestic work now. Of course, the intensity of domestic labour changes as the children in the home grow and this may partly explain the adjustments being made in Juliet's home.

The key questions that I had for the participants related to how they foresee organizing their lives in the future (with respect to paid and unpaid labour) and whether this is on their minds and in their conversations with friends and, more importantly, with people they date. Overall, the replies were much like the other conversations I have had with young women both one on one, and those that have occurred during seminar discussions described earlier. Emily seems to sum up the young women's expectations with respect to their future relationships, when she says that her husband would need to be "someone who has great respect for their mother or who has had positive female influences in their family." Almost all of the women say that they want to have children 'some day,' although they find it hard to even imagine right now. These women are thinking a bit about what sorts of compromises will be made to have the careers they want and the family they may also choose to have. However, they all explain that it is very difficult to discuss these issues when they are in a relationship. Juliet describes her long-term boyfriend's parents as having a "very traditional relationship" wherein the father does very little domestic work. When asked if she is worried about this role model and whether she raises the issue of having different expectations with her boyfriend, she says "only jokingly." She feels he understands that their life would be different, but finds it a touchy subject to raise in a serious or direct manner. She just has to hope that he understands that she would not accept that type of relationship. Marissa, who says she doesn't plan to have children, doesn't discuss these issues with her long-term boyfriend. She feels that the expectations are more or less understood.

Jordan has been with her boyfriend for seven years and he talks about marriage and children now. She says they do talk about how things will be organized somewhat, and says that he likes to clean and she likes to cook. However, she worries a considerable amount about how it will all fit in—going to law school, getting established professionally and then having children. Referring to the research by Judy Wajcman, she says that it is "not surprising that high-powered career women have to choose between being a mother and their careers." She also has health issues that *may* make it more difficult for her to conceive a child and is therefore quite concerned about waiting until her thirties to try to have children. However, she wants to be well on her way in her career first. On the other hand, she also acknowledges that once she does have children "there's a very real possibility that [she'll] want to be home with [her] children." Although Kelly is not dating anyone presently, she does think about these issues and says that she feels they should be discussed early on. She sees a lot of her friends in relationships in which the women are doing more, "making more effort, doing more mental work." She acknowledges as well that it is hard to get these things "on the table," to be sure you are "on the same page." Kelly astutely comments that most couples wouldn't make a long-term commitment to one another without discussing their expectations related to whether or not they want to have children. However, once this is agreed upon, they carry on without discussing much else related to their care or what parenthood will mean for each of their careers. She notes that this is considered to be unnecessary or too difficult a subject to broach.

One of the women in the study fell into the age range, but was married with two young children. The inclusion of her case has provided some interesting contrasts to those of the other young women. Leah is pursuing a B.A. currently and is also the mother of a five year-old and a seven-month old. She explains that she has a very supportive husband who shares the unpaid labour with her equitably and makes it possible for her to succeed in her studies and also be a good mother. She acknowledges that she has done things quite differently from most of her student peers who are getting their higher education first and may then "settle down." She feels that this is working well for her and her husband and will free her up to focus more fully on her career in her thirties, already having had her children. This optimism is in spite of the fact that one of her female art professors told her that "women with children can't be successful artists because they don't have enough time to live and breathe their art." With respect to whether things are changing overall for women in their relationships, she notes that her marriage is unusual and that when she gets together with other young mothers they talk a lot about how little housework and child care their husbands do.

These women for the most part come from relatively privileged backgrounds and look forward to middle-class careers. And yet, in spite of the all the flexibility they have been promised in our digital age, they have complex boundaries to negotiate in terms of the political economy of their everyday lives. They seem to be aware of the difficulties ahead of them—some more explicitly than others—and yet they do not know what to do about the challenges they will face. Many of the women express a clear desire to be mothers as well as career women, and to do a good job in both roles. However, they do not have clear role models in their own families to look up to that will help them to expect an equitable division of responsibilities in their home lives. Their fathers and their boyfriends' fathers do less unpaid work than their female counterparts and they do not know for sure what their own future partners' values and everyday practices will be like in this regard.

Whether or not young women will feel 'ripped in half' in the future will depend upon many factors. One of the challenges for feminism in the early part of the 21st century is to continue to raise awareness and foster action related to this aspect of inequality. We need to continue to demand more and more detailed data on unpaid labour such as that provided by Statistics Canada, and to fight for institutional changes that will provide women (and men) with meaningful choices related to their careers. Along with this, however, constantly deconstructing the discourses around us related to all aspects of women's labour and being willing to include this topic in our everyday conversations would be a good start. The more prepared younger women can be for the challenges and choices they will face, the more able they may be to contribute to change within the political economy of women's everyday lives.

Notes

1. Hochschild, Arlie, *The Second Shift: Working Parents and the Revolution at Home* (New York: Viking, 1989).

2. Hochschild, Arlie, *The Second Shift: Working Parents and the Revolution at Home* (New York: Viking, 1989): ix-x.

3. Smith, Dorothy, *Writing the Social: Critique, Theory and Investigations* (Toronto: University of Toronto Press, 1999).

4. See for example: Waring, Marilyn, *Who's Counting: Marilyn Waring on Sex, Lies and Global Economics*. (Montreal: National Film Board of Canada, 1995).

5. Statistics Canada, *The Daily: Labour Force Activity, Occupation and Industry, Place of Work, Mode of Transportation to Work, Unpaid Work* (Ottawa: Supply and Services Canada, March 17, 1998).

6. Swain, Sandra, Personal communication with Statistics Canada Methodologist, January 31, 2006 (by telephone).

7. Winner, Langdon, 1996. "Who Will Be in Cyberspace?," *The Information Society* 12,1, (1996): 63-72.

8. Wolfson, Monica, 2005. "Feminists Urged to Form Alliances," *The Windsor Star,* (October 14, 2005): A2.

9. See for example: Kumar, Krishan, *Prophecy and Progress: The Sociology of Industrial and Post-Industrial Society* (New York: Penguin, 1978); Kumar, Krishan, *From Post-Industrial to Post-Modern Society: New Theories of the Contemporary World* (Oxford: Blackwell, 1995); Leiss, William, *Under Technology's Thumb* (Montreal: McGill-Queen's University Press, 1990).

10. Carey, James, *Communication as Culture: Essays on Media and Society* (New York: Routledge, 1989): 114.

11. Statistics Canada, *Women in Canada: Work Chapter Updates* (Ottawa: Supply and Services Canada, August, 2001).

12. Canada and the World Backgrounder (CWB), "Flexible Workstyles: In the Future Workplace, Fewer Workers Will Have Full-time, Permanent Jobs," 60,5 (March, 1995): 20-24, p. 20.

13. Canada and the World Backgrounder (CWB), "On their Own: More and More Canadians Are Finding the Most Secure Job is the One They Make Themselves," 59,3 (November, 1993): 18-21, p. 20.

14. *Montreal Gazette*, 1997. "Home-based Business Offers Flexibility: Gives Parents More Time to Raise Kids and Keep House," (March 15, 1997): F1.

15. *Today's Parent*, 1994. "Home Base: Work and Family Under One Roof," 11,1 (February, 1994): 34-37, p. 32.

16. *Financial Post*, "Survey Finds Telecommuting Brings Benefits," 10,46 (November 15/17, 1997): IT27.

17. *Globe and Mail*, "Cottage Industry: Wither Merging Technologies and Falling Prices, More and More People are Surrounding Themselves with Technology...," (July 2, 1996): C1, C12.

18. Bryant, Susan, "The Cottage or the Sweatshop: Gender and Home-based Work on the Information Highway," in *Women, Work and Computerization: Charting a Course to the Future*, ed. Ellen Balka and Richard Smith (Boston: Kluwer, 2000): 276-283.

19. See also: Gurstein, Penny, *Wired to the World, Chained to the Home: Telework in Daily Life* (Vancouver: University of British Columbia Press, 2001).

20. Bryant, Susan, "The Cottage or the Sweatshop: Gender and Home-based Work on the Information Highway," in *Women, Work and Computerization: Charting a Course to the Future*, ed. Ellen Balka and Richard Smith (Boston: Kluwer, 2000): 276-283; Bryant, Susan, "At Home on the Electronic Frontier: Work, Gender and the Information Highway," *New Technology, Work and Employment* 15,1 (2000): 19-33. See also: Christensen, Kathleen, *Women and Home-based Work: The Unspoken Contract* (New York: Henry Holt and Company, 1998); Phizacklean, Andrea and Carol Wolkowitz, *Homeworking Women: Gender, Rascism and Class at Work.* (London: Sage, 1995); Haddon, Leslie and Roger Silverstone, *Teleworking in the 1990's: A View From the Home.* SPRU CICT Report Series, Number 10 (Sussex: Science Policy Research Unit, University of Sussex, 1993).

21. Bryant, Susan, "The Cottage or the Sweatshop: Gender and Home-based Work on the Information Highway," in *Women, Work and Computerization: Charting a Course to the Future*, ed. Ellen Balka and Richard Smith (Boston: Kluwer, 2000): 276-283; Bryant, Susan, "At Home on the Electronic Frontier: Work, Gender and the Information Highway," *New Technology, Work and Employment* 15,1 (2000): 19-33.

22. Duffy, Anne and Norene Pupo, 1992. *Part-time Paradox: Connecting Gender, Work and Family* (Toronto: McClelland and Stewart, 1992).

23. Duffy, Anne and Norene Pupo, 1992. *Part-time Paradox: Connecting Gender, Work and Family* (Toronto: McClelland and Stewart, 1992).

24. Bryant, Susan, "The Cottage or the Sweatshop: Gender and Home-based Work on the Information Highway," in *Women, Work and Computerization: Charting a Course to the Future*, ed. Ellen Balka and Richard Smith (Boston: Kluwer, 2000): 276-283.

25. Phizacklean, Andrea and Carol Wolkowitz, *Homeworking Women: Gender, Rascism and Class at Work.* (London: Sage, 1995), p. 83.

26. Bryant, Susan, "The Cottage or the Sweatshop: Gender and Home-based Work on the Information Highway," in *Women, Work and Computerization: Charting a Course to the Future*, ed. Ellen Balka and Richard Smith (Boston: Kluwer, 2000): 276-283.

27. Wajcman, Judy, *Managing Like a Man: Women and Men in Corporate Management.* (Cambridge: Polity Press, 1998).

28. Wajcman, Judy, *Managing Like a Man: Women and Men in Corporate Management.* (Cambridge: Polity Press, 1998), p. 3.

29. Wajcman, Judy, *Managing Like a Man: Women and Men in Corporate Management.* (Cambridge: Polity Press, 1998).

30. Wajcman, Judy, *Managing Like a Man: Women and Men in Corporate Management.* (Cambridge: Polity Press, 1998), p. 164.

31. Pateman, Carol, *The Sexual Contract* (Cambridge: Polity, 1988).

32. Wajcman, Judy, *Managing Like a Man: Women and Men in Corporate Management.* (Cambridge: Polity Press, 1998), p. 157.

33. Hochschild, Arlie, *The Second Shift: Working Parents and the Revolution at Home* (New York: Viking, 1989).

34. Hochschild, Arlie, *The Second Shift: Working Parents and the Revolution at Home* (New York: Viking, 1989), p. xi.

35. Hochschild, Arlie, *The Second Shift: Working Parents and the Revolution at Home* (New York: Viking, 1989).

36. Canadian Federation for the Humanities and Social Sciences (CFHSS), *Ivory Towers: Feminist and Equity Audits 2005.* http://www.fedcan.ca/english/issues/issues/ivoryaudit2005.

37. Canadian Federation for the Humanities and Social Sciences (CFHSS), *Ivory Towers: Feminist and Equity Audits 2005.* http://www.fedcan.ca/english/issues/issues/ivoryaudit2005.

38. Robbins, Wendy, "Tenure Track and Reproductive Track on Collision Course," *CAUT Bulletin*, (October, 2004): A4/A6, p. A4.

39. Robbins, Wendy, "Tenure Track and Reproductive Track on Collision Course," *CAUT Bulletin*, (October, 2004): A4, A6.

40. Menzies, Heather, 2005. *No Time: Stress and the Crisis of Modern Life* (Vancouver: Douglas & McIntyre, 2005).

41. Hochschild, Arlie, *The Second Shift: Working Parents and the Revolution at Home* (New York: Viking, 1989), p.270.

42. Pseudonyms have been used throughout this document to protect the anonymity of my participants.

WOMEN AND THE CULTURE INDUSTRY

The chapters within this section explore how women are represented in the media and in advertising, the gender gap in global communications, and pornography and the question of men's responsibility. —*Jeffery Klaehn, editor*

There are things you tend to notice as a woman. These 'things' are especially noticeable as a young woman living in a university town. For instance, the way you attract or, on the flipside, don't attract men—all interaction with men is fiercely noted—by yourself and your peers. Some of the most important concerns young females face in Kitchener- Waterloo are those of gender, sexuality, body image, and the question of what to do about them.

It's not easy being female, to paraphrase Kermit the Frog. And it's not easy dealing with those aforementioned issues. The ideals of beauty are relatively linear and *Cosmo* and *Maxim* magazines are good examples of media that exhort those ideals. Both magazines focus on stereotypical ideas of heterosexuality, of femininity, masculinity—despite *Cosmo's* mandate of encouraging and empowering women, an overwhelming number of their cover stories feature pleasing men, looking your best, and finding ways to attract men.

Perhaps you're wondering what I'm talking about—I'll offer some me-dia-related examples: on the importance of body image—the reality show, *The Swan*; on the conflict between messages for young girls—the movie, *Cruel Intentions*, and the list goes on; men competing for sex—the movie, *Wedding Crashers*. I'll qualify these examples now. The reality show *The Swan* was based on contestants being made over with the aid of plastic surgery for the end goal of competing in a beauty pageant. In the movie *Cruel Intentions*, a young male seduces young women for fun and then decides to seduce one particular girl just because of the challenge she presents as someone who wants to wait until marriage. In *Wedding Crashers*, the idea of men wracking up notches on their bedposts is taken even further—they have guide-lines and rules for who to talk to at weddings and other emotional events where women would be, conceivably, the most emotionally and socially vulnerable.

I suppose the reason that this topic engages me so deeply is because as a young female myself, I can understand the struggle that, I imagine, most females go through—I constantly have male friends questioning me about my romantic and sex-ual life—and while I'm not bothered discussing it with them, they seem confused at why I'm not in a relationship. Moreover, when I occasionally complain about my body woes, they chide me for not being more confident—but Kitchener-Waterloo is rife with girls who more closely fit the North American beauty ideals and I'm bombarded on a daily basis why even they, and definitely me, are just not good enough, not thin enough. To be honest, it's enough to make a girl throw up.

Natalie Dias, Student, Sociology and Global Studies, Wilfrid Laurier University, Age: 20

Chapter Four

Consuming Desires: Reflections On Women And Advertising

Michèle Martin and Kathleen Gotts

TO BEGIN to understand the connections between production, consumption, advertising, and women, do any of the following: flip through the pages of a glossy magazine or newspaper; watch out for product placement in movies and television shows; observe the commercials that break into television and radio programming; notice how advertising banners and sidebars increasingly frame information on the Internet. The mass media are channels of information, education, and entertainment, as well as disseminators of social values, beliefs, and expectations. They also represent a market place, with opportunities for making profit. In this respect, the history of the mass media can be read as a history of advertising, their origins and trajectories are intertwined and interdependent. Within these histories women have been targeted, marketed to, and represented in various ways. Throughout the last century and into the present one, women have been seen as a market opportunity, a target audience, and a means of selling dreams, aspirations, fantasies, and, at the profane root of it all, products.

Despite their prominence as a target audience, market and source of representation, women tend not to have been positioned as the focal point in histories of the mass media and advertising. Trends in academic scholarship have shifted the focus from "great men" to the "common man" and then onto "absent others," such as women.[1] In many areas of life and scholarship, feminist activism has criticized how women have been overlooked, marginalized, or objectified. Feminist scholarship has focused attention on the lost, forgotten, unspoken, or undocumented contributions, roles, reflections, and stories of women. "At first, the very act of discovering sexism in scholarship was revolutionary… it was radical simply to study women."[2] With this chapter, we contribute to the rich feminist tradition of woman-centred research and ongoing efforts to make women's experiences and perceptions visible, audible, and documented. Using scholarship on history, communication and gender, this chapter reflects on how women have been perceived by advertisers, represented in advertising, and how some women have responded to those perceptions and representations to advocate change.

In this chapter we set the scene with a brief history of the origins and development of advertising and its relationship with women. This first section on women *and* advertising, provides an overview of the links between production, consumption, advertising, the mass media, and gender. It also indicates how advertisers have perceived women consumers since the late nineteenth century. From this initial scene setting, the chapter proceeds with a consideration of advertising representations of women. In this second section, on women *in* advertising, we explore the recurring stereotypes that have been used to represent women for over a hundred years. We also consider the implications and marginalizing effects of these representations. Women have reacted and responded to advertising in a variety of ways. This is the focus of the chapter's third and final section: women *on* advertising. In it we consider the potential and limitations of consumer action, political activism, and attempts to effect changes from within the advertising industry. Throughout the chapter our reflections draw together diverse sources that consider women across borders of time, place, and perception, as we try to understand how the relationship between women and advertising today has been shaped by the past.

Women and Advertising: A Brief History

Advertising as a commercial enterprise developed with the advent of the industrial revolution, both as an outgrowth of, and support for, mass production and the already well-developed capitalist economy. Technological advances gained momentum from the 1860s onward, during the second stage of the industrial revolution, with developments in electrical power, machinery, and production capacity.[3] During this period, industrial advances in the making of glass, electricity, and colour influenced promotional and advertising techniques and transformed commercial spaces such as the department store.[4] Changes in the technologies of mass production were also accompanied by developments in the mass media techniques of printing, engraving, layout, and photography in the early twentieth century.[5] The confluence of industrial, commercial, and promotional developments tightened the interdependence of mass production, the mass media, the advertising industry, and the market place.

The decades from 1860 to 1920, when the second stage of the industrial revolution unfolded, were also a time of tremendous social flux. During this time the traditional status of women and other social 'minors' was contested, and the public face of society began to change.[6] The "first wave" of feminists demanded educational, legal, and professional equality with men, and began to secure women's right to vote, with New Zealanders leading the way in 1893. Women became more and more visible as producers and workers. With greater independence and personal income they began to participate in the increasingly conspicuous practice of consumption. Reflecting the growing visibility of women in public and the anxieties that this provoked for traditionalists, consumerism at that time was often represented as female and the consuming woman associated with capriciousness, hedonism, and modernity.[7] Although both men and women engaged in the practice, shopping was regarded as a female and urban form of amusement.[8]

On the one hand, the proponents of consumerism in the 1870s worked to identify shopping with middle-class women and respectability, to counter opposition to the new commercial innovation of the department store. On the other, critics of consumerism described women's shopping as immoral, insatiable, lacking control and self-restraint, an addiction that threatened to disrupt family life.[9] Then, as now, women were popularly depicted as prone to the seductive powers of advertising,[10] (mis)represented as dupes of commercialism rather than agents of self expression. Developments in production, retailing, mass communication, and advertising at the cusp of the nineteenth and twentieth centuries along with these social changes made the practice of consumption more widely accessible, broadening it from a pastime of the elite to a habit of the masses.[11] Mass-produced household goods and clothing became widely accessible "for the first time [to] women of nearly any economic bracket."[12] By 1915, women were responsible for up to ninety-five per cent of consumer purchases in the United States.[13]

Mass Media and Advertising: Changing Values and Shifting Attitudes
Mass production depends on mass consumption. Advertising in the mass media links producer and consumer by creating needs and desires for the products on sale. Integral to the mass distribution system, advertising helped to create the mass consumer and the mass market. Women have long been the focal point of advertising on signs and billboards in public spaces, in mass-circulation magazines, newspapers, supplements, and direct-mail catalogues, on commercial radio, television, and, most recently, on the Internet.[14] In the late nineteenth century, producers and their advertisers recognized that women made, or influenced, the vast majority of purchases in the home. For this reason, they regarded women as the target consumer for many of their mass-produced goods and tried to develop their advertising with her in

mind. Interestingly, the use of the mass media as tools for advertising messages was initially resisted in North America. It was seen as inappropriate and opportunistic commercialism that would sully the private sphere of the home. Although women's magazines were first published in the United States in the 1820s they resisted advertising revenue until the 1880s. Similarly, radio was initially rejected as a mass medium for advertising, partly due to its small audience sizes in the 1920s, and to the perceived unsuitability of commerce intruding into the home.[15] With improvements in technology, reductions in cost, and increases in audience, commercial breaks became a regular part of radio programming in the 1930s.

The shift in social perceptions from opposition to the acceptability of commercial advertising in the domestic sphere was complete by the 1950s when the television set became a permanent fixture in the middle-class home. Producers and advertisers capitalized on the commercial potential of television as a mass medium to target women consumers.[16] The mutually dependent economic objectives of the mass media and advertising industries transformed resistance into acceptance of the commercial accompaniment to entertainment. This relationship was underwritten by the increasing dependence of mass media on advertising revenue, whereby the entire communication system became driven by the "economic engine" of advertising.[17] Another attitudinal shift precipitated by the mass industries of production, media, and advertising was the transformation of social values from the promotion of thriftiness to the valorization of spending and conspicuous consumption. Following the Second World War the shift from "pay as you go" to "buy now pay later" habits of spending resulted in increased standards of living and consumption at the cost of unprecedented levels of consumer debt.[18] With the emergence of the consumer debt society, families began to spend and live beyond their means, a reality that many people continue to struggle with today.[19]

Selling New Products to "New Women"

Fuelling consumer debt and the interdependent cycles of production and consumption are the principles of newness and planned obsolescence.[20] Advertising seeks to stimulate and maintain a desire for the new rather than encouraging the ability to fix and make do with the old. Products are associated with modernity and newness, promoted as "cutting edge" and "indispensable."[21] These objects quickly become outdated and are replaced by other more modern products. Michèle Mattelart calls this continuous process of renewal the principle of planned obsolescence[22]: the technological aging of a product is associated with the appearance of a new object. Newness and obsolescence drive the fashion industry's changes in colour and design with every passing season. Imprints of the latest styles are sold to the masses with photographs of celebrities in popular magazines and with designer "knock-offs" in high-street stores. In contemporary society, nothing beats the electronic industry for applying the concept of planned obsolescence. Within months of purchasing the latest cell phone, personal computer, digital camera, or MP3 player, the technology has moved on and your purchase is too outmoded to warrant technical support. Buying a new product is easier and more cost-effective than trying to fix the "old" one. New products are replaced by newer products even before the latter have deteriorated or become obsolete. Without sufficient thought given to their safe disposal, they add to our growing landfills.

The cheapness of mass-produced goods and fascination with newness and technology have displaced and discredited the traditional skills of mending and fixing. A common tactic used by advertisers has been to associate new products with modernity. By depicting the consumer as the modern "new woman" advertisers have bound her to consumerism in the process. Advertisers of the past—and into the present—have sent women consumers mixed messages of emancipation and traditionalism, encouraging them to embrace modernity and newness with timesaving products while restricting their social role primarily to the home.[23] In the late nineteenth century, products that "women formerly made at home and in private" were made publicly available to them in the form of mass-produced foods, clothing, soap, and cosmetics.[24] With the development of convenience foods, the "new woman" of the 1950s was encouraged to become the consumer of mass-produced commodities rather than the producer and maintainer of domestic goods.[25] This advertising trend continues today, at the expense of traditional food knowledge, nutritional value, and health. The growing interest in organic produce, "slow food,"[26] and local farmers' markets is a partial reaction to this trend.

Targeting Women: Worthy Consumers

The targeting of women by advertisers is not new. Since the late nineteenth century, advertisers have used the mass media to communicate product information to women. Women have long been regarded as worthy consumers who represent market opportunities. In the 1930s, when radio began to be seen as a viable advertising medium, women consumers were regarded as an important target audience. The "soap opera," commercially sponsored programming, was first developed for women in 1933.[27] Sponsored by the manufacturers of household cleaning products such as

Procter and Gamble, Pillsbury, American Home Products, and General Foods, "soaps" were regarded as a "woman's genre."[28] By 1940, these serialized radio dramas made up about ninety per cent of commercially sponsored daytime broadcasting; in 1948, listeners' top ten programs were all soap operas. The highly popular broadcast format of serialized programming was transplanted to the new medium of television in the early 1950s. Television producers and advertisers recognized that women influenced the purchase of high-end products.[29] They designed their advertising and programming accordingly: first reflecting the conventions of radio broadcasting with live, fifteen-minute, week-daily episodes then, in 1956, the TV soap came into its own with the debut of *As the World Turns*, a half-hour week-daily show.[30] Then as now, marketers and advertisers targeted their commercial breaks at women of means, those with disposable income, who represented opportunities for growth in market share and profit.

Despite historical evidence of the targeting of women, some contemporary female marketers and advertisers frame this practice as new knowledge that they divulge to help producers "decode" women consumers,[31] understand "female gender culture,"[32] and tap into their market potential. Women have been (re)conceived as "a worthwhile market,"[33] a "new consumer class of [the] economically empowered" with "unprecedented buying power,"[34] representing "the most significant and profitable opportunity in marketing today."[35] Women are also (re)defined as worthy consumers: "big spenders," the "consumers of big ticket items,"[36] with "incredible buying power: [who] purchase, or influence the purchase of 80% of all consumer goods."[37] This 'knowledge' is used to define women—or rather those with purchasing power—as a viable market, an under-tapped audience, worthy of the attention of advertisers.

As we have seen, contrary to the suggestions of some contemporary marketers, the act of perceiving women as a viable market has a long history. The targeting of women, as both producers and consumers, was intimately connected with the development of the market economy and the industries of mass production, the mass media, advertising, and consumption. Over time, advertising has developed into a form of communication that has capitalized on every new mass medium to diffuse its commercial messaging.[38] The mass media as products for consumption and vehicles for advertising enhance the links between capital, production, communication, and consumption. The woman consumer with disposable income has long been a target of the capitalist production cycle, sought by the advertiser. Equally, advertising has long used the woman as a representational object to transmit certain cultural meanings in order to sell products.

Women in Advertising: The Power of Representation

The mass media, as the main disseminators of informational and commercial messaging in our society, are makers of meaning and sources of socialization.[39] Media content and the advertising messages that accompany it, reflect, represent, and act as the carriers of certain cultural values that exclude alternatives or obscure unsightly social realities.[40] Prescriptive rather than descriptive,[41] advertising sells "cultural representations of success,"[42] by creating a "mythical... world in which no one is ever ugly, overweight, poor, toiling, or physically or mentally disabled."[43] Thus, the product is only part of the message that is used to communicate social values and cultural representations.[44] In this respect, advertising has been perceived as an "interpreter of culture," a means of framing consumer choices that defines "life as a series of problems to be solved."[45] The power of advertising lies in its ability to persuade us to make that purchase, by tapping into our collective fears and anxieties and associating products with meaningful social values and the promise of improvement, efficiency and fulfillment.

Advertising is premised on the promise of progress. It feeds the culture of aspiration by "reflecting people's needs, desires, and anxieties [rather] than depicting their actual circumstances and behavior."[46] Hence, by associating products with social values and the means to overcome human deficiencies, advertisers seek to persuade the consumer that by buying the product "one also buys social respect, health, beauty, success, and control over one's environment."[47] Luxury and celebrity have long been combined in advertising to demonstrate what is "in vogue," yet beyond the purse of most women. In the late nineteenth century, "by purchasing imitation jewels, artificial silk and furs, cheap perfume...women could partake of both the luxury and the theatrical behavior of the rich."[48] Today's high-street stores continue to capitalize on the consumer desire for designer fashion at an affordable price. The one-off collaboration of fashion designers Karl Lagerfeld and Stella McCartney with fashion outlet Hennes & Mauritz (H&M) in 2004 and 2005 recognizes the pull of the designer brand and the practicality of a price that won't break the bank. In the words of one advertiser, "advertisements give us clues to help us determine what that better version of life will be," by suggesting that "buying the product transforms us into a better version of ourselves."[49] Besides their potential to transform, the intention of advertising, she recognizes, is also "to sell products [and] build brands."[50]

How does advertising persuade us that we would indeed be happier, healthier, more efficient, and generally a better person by making that specific purchase? To sell products, "advertisements present brief dramatic stories with a message."[51] Advertising choices, who is targeted, with what medium, and how, influence the content of the message. To reach their target consumers, advertisers "generate… categories and create subject positions" that help to define the focus of their messaging.[52] Advertisers use stereotypes to "convey characters and images quickly and clearly" and set the stage for the advertisement's message.[53] If stereotypes work, it is because they are "reassuringly familiar" and communicate cultural meaning.[54] Representations of women are used to advertise a vast array of products. However, the women represented in advertisements tend to be created from traditional feminine stereotypes and a narrow ideal of femininity.[55] These images represent "culturally sanctioned ideal types of masculinity and femininity."[56] They inform women on "how they should look, feel, and act, and how they will be seen by others."[57]

(Re)Creating the "New Woman"

Recurring representations of women as savvy consumer, good wife, caring mother, high-powered professional, and her foil, the independent, carefree good-time girl, have been invoked by advertisers for well over a century. Despite the different guises, advertising representations of women have tended to promote the "white, heterosexual, middle-to upper-middle class woman that dominant culture held (and continues to hold) as ideal."[58] The forerunners of the contemporary "new women" were cast by advertisers and their illustrators in the late nineteenth century. Cover girl illustrations have been described as the "first mass media stereotypes of women."[59] The practice of using representations of idealized women to articulate cultural meaning through public artifacts such as statues, coins, and flags has a long tradition. Whereas the symbolism of womanhood in public art was used to sell ideals, in advertising it was (and still is) used to sell products and lifestyles with the help of ideal types. From the 1890s to the 1920s, the social anxieties and commercial opportunities that accompanied the expansion of consumerism, first wave feminism, and women's increasingly public visibility as producers and consumers, were represented in cover girl illustrations and advertisements.[60]

In the late nineteenth century, advertisers appropriated the political concept of the New Woman to reformulate women's rights and freedoms in the traditional terms of marriage, motherhood and consumption.[61] The "new women" of that time were represented in advertising as beautiful wives, doting mothers, and civic housekeepers whose responsible purchases would preserve the family's health and well-being. Less traditional images of the independent "new woman" reflected the contradictory tensions of the time with representations of the masculinized outdoor sportswoman[62] and the feminine, glamour girl.[63] Profitability rather than advocacy for the rights of women is what guided these representations. The progressiveness of these images was undercut by the advertising subtext that exercising and being fashion-conscious were the means to become "fetchingly attractive" and land a husband.[64]

The commercial appropriation of the political concept of the New Woman diluted its radicalism and marked a "'return to normalcy' after a culturally and politically intense, if brief, period" of feminist activism.[65] Decades later, women's liberation, the second wave of feminist activism in the 1960s and 1970s, was also identified as a market opportunity to be tapped for its commercial potential. The third wave's politics of difference in the 1990s opened up "niche" markets that advertisers have tried to capture by representing some of the social diversity that lies beyond the white, heterosexual, middle-class ideal type. Advertising to lesbians is an example of niche marketing.

Since the 1980s, marketers have sought out homosexual consumers. While some advertisers have targeted an exclusively gay audience, most mainstream advertising has adopted a "dual-marketing" approach, using the same advertisements and ambivalent depictions of sexuality to send different messages to homosexual and heterosexual consumers.[66] Advertising supports the production needs of the capitalist economy and tends to reflect the social trends that it can capitalize on as market opportunities, recasting the New Woman as shopper, wife, mother, and homemaker, office worker, the "superwoman" who successfully juggles career and family, or the sexually liberated good-time girl.[67] Since the 1880s, advertisers have recycled these stereotypes of women, to represent what women could or should be rather than who they really are.

Advertising and Female Sexuality

Studies of how women are stereotyped in advertising have drawn attention to the sexual representations that objectify and fragment women's bodies, turning them into the decorative means to sell products. Using female sexuality as the "bait" for selling products,[68] advertising images seek to attract both the male and female "gaze,"[69] with the intention of seducing the male consumer and persuading the female consumer to emulate the style or look that could secure the "male gaze" for her. Premised on heterosexual attraction, these two-dimensional representations use the promise of female sexuality to sell products targeted at men and women. As an example, advertising for alcoholic drinks often uses attractive, hip, young people, a congenial social setting, and the promise of sex as their primary selling features.

Advertisements rarely challenge traditional gender relations or question "dominant representations of female sexuality."[70] In this respect, how women are represented in advertising is often both a reflection and reinforcement of cultural traditions and social inequalities.

Advertising commonly invokes female sexuality with a disembodied hand, foot, leg or some other body part, a "fragment" rather than her whole body.[71] Adverts for shoes or hosiery often depict the model's shapely, elongated legs and little else. A voluptuous bosom and plunging cleavage cut off from the rest of her body is the frequent focus of adverts for bras. This "fragmentation" or "dismemberment" is criticized for dehumanizing and objectifying women.[72] It occurs more frequently to women's bodies in advertising than to men's.[73] Equally, women tend to be portrayed more decoratively in advertising, although decorative representations of men are on the increase.[74] In decorative portrayals the model is "passive and disengaged," used to enhance the product rather than to communicate its function.[75] Decorative passivity is often evident in advertisements for perfume, where the model's beauty is used to communicate taste, luxury, sensuality, sexuality—to confer meaning rather than to demonstrate the product. Ironically, the highest proportion of decorative depictions of both men and women appear in women's fashion magazines.[76] Decorative representations perpetuate patriarchal associations of women with passivity and reinforce gender stereotypes that undermine women's abilities and achievements.[77]

Advertising and its Marginalizing Effects

Beauty, youth, and seduction, in both female and male models, are the attributes most commonly sought and represented by advertisers.[78] This practice has been criticized for promoting narrow ideals and unrealistic standards of beauty.[79] We know that these images are "constructed through cosmetics, photography, and airbrushing techniques."[80] As supermodel Linda Evangelista states, "I don't look like I do in the pages of *Vogue*.... it's work being me. It's a lot of upkeep!"[81] She is open about the cosmetic procedures that she has used to retain her looks. "[I]t's just for enhancement, like hair color or makeup or any other tricks you can do to make yourself feel better."[82] Despite our knowledge of the effort (cosmetics, on top of cosmetic surgery, and photo manipulation on top of that) that goes into transforming natural beauty into stunning visual images, women still, consciously or subconsciously, hold ourselves up against these two-dimensional, constructed beauties and find ourselves failing to make the mark.

Why? Because we live in a consumer-based "patriarchal culture that constantly reminds us that we will be judged on the way we look"[83]—and that products can help to improve how we look. Advertising deploys the techniques of persuasion to trigger our individual needs, failings, and faults. Advertisements seek to persuade us by first raising our anxiety level and then offering a solution.[84] Explicit in this messaging is that we are not good enough as we are. For example, "You, Only Better" offers the advertisement for a Clairol hair colour product, inviting us into a "world of fantasy where we can all achieve the ideal if we only have the product."[85] The advertising image plays into and preys upon women's low self-esteem and appearance anxiety. Although the perfection represented in advertising images is a constructed and "commodified ideal,"[86] it is a factor that contributes to women's body image problems, appearance anxiety, and eating disorders.[87] Advertisers reject the causal link between exposure to advertising and eating disorders, arguing that, "such diseases cannot be attributed solely to advertising."[88] True, but advertising clearly plays a central role in how women perceive themselves and seeks to exploit their anxieties for commercial gain.

By promoting particular cultural ideals of beauty, efficiency, and perfection, the advertising image silences real social conditions and inequalities. The illusory representations imply universal access—offering up a world of possibility that is priced beyond the reach of many. Certain criteria need to be met for marketers to decide to develop a target audience; the population segment must be "(1) identifiable, (2) accessible, (3) measurable, and (4) profitable."[89] Society's marginalized groups rarely fit these criteria, profitability above all. As a result their realities are not represented, nor are their needs met, in a world driven by commerce and consumption. For example, advertising images tend to over-represent female professionals and under-represent the "low-wage, low-skilled jobs that the majority of women perform."[90] Women in advertisements still tend to be "young, thin and white,"[91] heterosexual and able-bodied.[92] By majoritarily excluding women of colour and variations in age, size, and sexuality, the advertising industry continues to cling to traditional social values and a narrow idealization of beauty. The power offered to women through advertising is the "ability to attract" members of the opposite sex, "not real political or emotional power, the type … that might lead to equality in the long run."[93]

Women On Advertising: Responses and Reactions
Consumer Choice: Consumer Action

Consumers can choose to reward companies that respect women's strengths, abilities, and diversity in their labour relations, work safety practices, and advertising images. Consumers are active participants in the decoding of advertisements and decision-making about purchases, rather than passive recipients of commercial messaging.[94] It is overly simplistic, however, to suggest that consumers are "in control"[95] and have the "ultimate power"[96] to decide the fate of products in the market place. Although ninety per cent of new products fail in an average year,[97] consumer choice is just one factor, albeit significant, in the production cycle. Different readings of advertising and the choices made are shaped by the complex interaction of who we are (gender, age, race, class, employment status, income, life experiences) in our socio-cultural context with its influences and pressures coming from all directions. Consumers are "active but ... not fully autonomous," as the acts of interpretation and choice are influenced by the structural constraints that shape our experience of the world.[98]

The suggestion that consumers wield power by creating meaning and communicating identity through their purchasing decisions is used to counter the criticism that advertising is a manipulative force.[99] More nuanced perspectives consider the ambiguities, complexities, and exclusions inherent in the relationship between production and consumption. Women's consumption, particularly in relation to fashion, is marked by ambiguities: a source of pleasure yet anxiety; a means of both subverting and reinforcing dominant modes of representation; a mechanism of social control with the potential to test the boundaries of conventional femininity.[100] The rise of consumer organizations and assertion of the rights of the "consumer-citizen"[101] suggest a shift in the balance of power between consumers and producers, offering a means of recourse or protection to the consumer. They also indicate the extent to which consumerism has become a "central organizing feature of Western societies"[102] and how, accordingly, the concept of citizenship has changed. The citizen now makes an "active contribution to the national community" by having the "potential to engage in processes of consumerist recognition, exchange and choice."[103]

Political Activism: Feminist Critiques of Advertising
The reframing of individual rights and freedoms in terms of consumerism empowers those who have the means to make choices while it further excludes those who are socially marginalized and disempowered, recasting them as dependents or beneficia-

ries rather than active citizens.[104] Feminist critiques of the role of consumption in society have drawn attention to the ambiguities and exclusions of this feature of our society, calling into question the association of consumerism with empowerment. Critical consumerism, however, can be a source of meaningful political action, social change, and, in this respect, genuine empowerment. Feminist critiques of advertising are concrete examples of how women have actively rejected stereotypical representations and lobbied for progressive social change.[105]

The "No Comment" feature in the original feminist *Ms.* magazine provided readers with a space to "identify [advertising] images from mainstream media and 'expose' their underlying sexism."[106] Offerings from *Ms.* readers included responses and reactions to overt sexism, such as an advert for men's shoes in *Playboy* magazine.[107] A naked blonde lies gazing adoringly at a shoe. The tag line reads "Keep her where she belongs…"—the implication being naked, submissive, and happy at her man's feet. Readers also submitted advertising images and newspaper articles that explicitly or implicitly restricted women to the traditional occupations of wife and mother or to support roles in the workplace.[108] The collective act of exposing sexism and rejecting restrictive or demeaning representations of women helped to build the oppositional identity and discourse of feminism, to raise consciousness of social inequalities, and support the demand for change.[109]

In Canada, women's groups were the first to lobby the government to act against offensive gender portrayals and sexual stereotyping in media advertising. In 1969, the Royal Commission on the Status of Women condemned the use of sexual stereotypes in media representations of women. The Council on the Status of Women reported on the sexism of television advertising on Radio-Canada (the francophone public broadcaster in Canada) in 1978. In the next year, the Council followed up its findings by defining sexist advertising "as that which rigidly divides social roles and functions along gender lines" and successfully argued that such representations oppress women and constrain their potential.[110] At that time, women's groups successfully lobbied the Canadian Radio-Television and Telecomunications Commission (CRTC) to take up the issue of sexism in Canadian advertising. A task force was struck to explore "Sex-Role Stereotyping in the Broadcast Media," develop guidelines for advertisers, and establish a program to monitor sexism in the media, particularly in advertising. The CRTC guidelines opted for voluntary self-regulation by the advertising industry, making this a condition of licensing. In 1990, the CRTC declared that "*most* of the concerns about sex-role stereotyping had been *largely satisfied*" and disbanded the task force.[111]

Advertising: Change from Within

By failing to represent equitably the diversity of women and society, the advertising industry tends to uphold the status quo rather than using its creative talents to make progressive social statements. Paid to attract consumer attention, develop brand recognition, and build loyalty, advertising is not in the business to promote social change. However, some advertisers have used their position within the industry to try to do just this. Half of the people working in most major advertising agencies today are women.[112] Some of these women are working "through the market to achieve feminist ends,"[113] by celebrating womanhood, promoting female empowerment (usually sporting, professional or commercial rather than political), and using more responsible and realistic representations of women in their advertisements.

Advertisements for sports equipment have communicated women's strength and independence,[114] not as elite athletes but as healthy women. Turning traditional feminine hygiene advertising on its head, the brand *Always* has tried to reframe menstruation with the claim that "the world is better when women can embrace and celebrate their period."[115] *Dove's* Campaign for Real Beauty set out to challenge the narrow idealization of beauty in advertising by representing and celebrating the diversity of women in colour, age, and size. Using "real women with real bodies and real curves," the campaign "aims to change the status quo and offer in its place a broader, healthier, more democratic view of beauty."[116] By looking to the "huge variety of people on the street during any given day," advertisers can present more complex, realistic, and diverse images of society and women.[117] If they choose to listen, marketers and advertisers can learn that women want to see images of other "multifaceted, multidimensional women," with more positive and realistic representations of their strengths, humour, sensuality, and sexuality.[118] They want to see these images asserted for their own pleasure—and humour—rather than someone else's.[119] What women do not want to see is "images they can't live up to."[120]

Conclusions

An analysis of women and advertising must consider the paradoxes that this relationship involves. Indeed, advertising entails contradictory feelings: the pleasure induced by looking at a beautifully designed, clever, or thought-provoking ad and the guilt at feeling that pleasure! In some ways, advertising allows a temporary means of escape from a dull and miserable life and the chance to dream of another more glamorous one. This is what Michèle Mattelart calls "the democracy of desires."[121] We know that the dream is illusory and beyond the reach of many of us, yet we are surrounded and influenced by the images and illusions of advertising. With studies that consider historical and contemporary perspectives of communication and gender, this chapter has reflected on women and advertising across the borders of time, place, and perception to consider how the relationship between women and advertising today has been shaped by the past. As a contribution to the feminist tradition of woman-centred research, the chapter has drawn together diverse sources to focus attention on some of the different ways women figure in the histories of advertising and the mass media. We have considered how women over time have been perceived as a market, how they have been represented in advertisements, and how they have responded to these representations with calls for change.

Despite the gains and successes made by feminist activists, sex role stereotyping remains a feature in advertising today; women are still used as decoration to enhance the products on display; and the diversity of women continues to be both under-represented and inadequately represented. Some advertisers have responded to the call for women to be represented in more positive, active, and relevant ways. Cynics might suggest that attempts by advertisers to contest traditional stereotyping are just another strategy to increase market share and profit. Whatever the case, more meaningful, respectful, and diverse representations of women should be encouraged. We must be alert to the assumptions behind advertising choices and their implications for women. We must also be prepared to take action and lobby for change when women are represented in harmful, demeaning, or unrealistic ways. More fundamentally, though, we need to open our eyes to the broader social and environmental impacts of our consumer society.

Notes

1. Bruce Curtis, *The politics of population: State formation, statistics, and the census of Canada, 1840-1875*, (Toronto, ON: University of Toronto Press, 2001), 16.

2. Reinhartz (1992) cited in Liesbet Van Zoonen, *Feminist Media Studies* (Sage Publications, 1994), 15.

3. Daniel Delis Hill, *Advertising to the American Woman 1900-1999* (Columbus: Ohio State University Press, 2002).

4. William R. Leach, "Transformations in a Culture of Consumption: Women and Department Stores, 1890-1925," *The Journal of American History*, 71, no. 2 (1984), 319-342; Erika D. Rappaport, "'The Halls of Temptation': Gender, Politics, and the Construction of the Department Store in Late Victorian England," *The Journal of British Studies*, 35 no. 1 (1996), 58-83.

5. Liz Ini Conor, *Spectacular Modern Woman* (Indianapolis: Indian University Press, 2004); Hill, *Advertising to the American Women*; Carol Kitch, *The Girl on the Magazine Cover* (Chapel Hill and London: University of North Carolina Press, 2001).

6. Conor, *The Spectacular Modern Woman*; Kitch, *Girl on the Magazine Cover*; Leach, *Transformations in a Culture of Consumption*.

7. Anne M. Cronin, *Advertising and Consumer Citizenship* (New York: Routledge, 2000).

8. Leach, *Transformations in a Culture of Consumption*; Rappaport, *Halls of Temptation*.

9. Ibid.

10. Cronin, *Advertising and Consumer Citizenship*.

11. Cheryl Buckley and Hilary Fawcett, *Fashioning the Feminine. Representation and Women's Fashion from the Fin de Siècle to the Present* (London: I. B. Tauris & Co, 2002); Leach, *Transformations in a Culture of Consumption*.

12. Leach, *Transformations in a Culture of Consumption*, 327.

13. Leach, *Transformations in a Culture of Consumption*.

14. Hill, *Advertising to the American Woman*.

15. Ibid.

16. Ibid.

17. Michèle Martin, *Communication and Mass Media: Culture, Domination and Opposition* (Scarborough: Prentice Hall Allyn and Bacon Canada, 1997), 201.

18. Angela, R. Record, "Born to Shop: Teenage Women and the Marketplace in the Postwar United States," in *Sex & Money: Feminism and Political Economy in the Media*, eds. Eileen R. Meehan and Ellen Riordan (Minneapolis: University of Minnesota Press, 2002), 182-183.

19. Canadian Broadcasting Corporation (CBC), "Buy now, pay later: Canadians and debt," by Tom McFeat, in *CBC News Indepth*, September 20, 2004, http://www.cbc.ca (accessed August 13, 2006); Maclean's, *Canadians Personal Debt at Historic Level*, by Steve Maich, December 6, 2004, http://www.thecanadianencyclopedia.com (accessed August 13, 2006); USA Today, *Consumer Debt Loads at Record*, by Barbara Hagenbaugh, 17 March, 2004, http://www.usatoday.com (accessed 13 August, 2006).

20. Cronin, *Advertising and Consumer Citizenship*; Martin, *Communication and Mass Media*.

21. Martin, *Communication and Mass Media*, 108.

22. Michèle Mattelart, *Les femmes et les industries culturelles* (Paris: Unesco, 1981).

23. Martin, *Communication and Mass Media*; Shelley Nickles, "'Preserving Women': Refrigerator Design as Social Process in the 1930s," *Technology and Culture*, 43, no. 4 (2002), 693-727.

24. Leach, *Transformations in a Culture of Consumption*, 327.

25. Martin, *Communication and Mass Media*, 106.

26. For information on the slow food movement, visit: http://www.slowfood.com/

27. Hill, *Advertising to the American Woman*.

28. Museum of Broadcast Communications, *Soap Opera*, by Robert C. Allen, (n.d.), http://www.museum.tv/archives/ (accessed October 1, 2006).

29. Hill, *Advertising to the American Woman*.

30. Museum of Broadcast Communications, *Soap Opera*.

31. Mary Lou Quinlan, *Just Ask a Woman. Cracking the Code of What Women Want and How They Buy* (Hoboken: John Wiley & Sons, 2003), 14.

32. Martha Barletta, *Marketing to Women. How to Understand, Reach, and Increase Your Share of the World's Largest Market Segment* (Dearborn Trade Publishing, 2003), 19.

33. Barletta, *Marketing to Women*, xx.

34. Cheryl Berman, Denise Fedewa and Jeanie Caggiano, "Still Miss Understood: She's Not Buying Your Ads," *Advertising and Society Review*, 7, no. 2 (2006), 3.

35. Barletta, *Marketing to Women*, xxviii.

36. Ibid, xix-xx.

37. Kim Sheehan, *Controversies in Contemporary Advertising* (Sage Publications, 2004), 92.

38. Hill, *Advertising to the American Woman*; Martin, *Communication and Mass Media*.

39. Anthony J. Cortese, *Provocateur: Images of Women and Minorities in Advertising*, second edition, (Rowman & Littlefield Publishers, 2004); Martin, *Communication and Mass Media*.

40. Cortese, *Provocateur*; Martin, *Communication and Mass Media*.

41. Kitch, *Girl on the Magazine Cover*.

42. Cortese, *Provocateur*, 24.

43. Ibid, 51.

44. Cortese, *Provocateur*; Martin, *Communication and Mass Media*.

45. Cronin, *Advertising and Consumer Citizenship*, 31.

46. Hill, *Advertising to the American Woman*, x.

47. Martin, *Communication and Mass Media*, 201.

48. Leach, *Transformations in a Culture of Consumption*, 327.

49. Sheehan, *Controversies in Contemporary Advertising*, 20.

50. Ibid, 86.

51. Ibid, 79.

52. Cronin, *Advertising and Consumer Citizenship*, 7.

53. Sheehan, *Controversies in Contemporary Advertising*, 79.

54. Kitch, *Girl on the Magazine Cover*, 191.

55. Cortese, *Provocateur*; Martin, *Communication and Mass Media*.

56. Cortese, *Provocateur*, 51.

57. Lucinda Joy Peach, ed., *Women in Culture: A Women's Studies Anthology* (Malden: Blackwell Publishers, 1998), 119.

58. Record, *Born to Shop*, 185, parentheses in original.

59. Kitch, *Girl on the Magazine Cover*, 5.

60. Buckley et al., *Fashioning the Feminine*; Kitch, *Girl on the Magazine Cover*.

61. Kitch, *Girl on the Magazine Cover*.

62. Ibid.

63. Buckley et al., *Fashioning the Feminine*.

64. Kitch, *Girl on the Magazine Cover*, 179.

65. Kitch, *Girl on the Magazine Cover*, 184.

66. Cortese, *Provocateur*.

67. Kitch, *Girl on the Magazine Cover*; Martin, *Communication and Mass Media*; Record, *Born to Shop*.

68. Martin, *Communication and Mass Media*, 205.

69. Robin Anderson, "The Thrill is Gone: Advertising, Gender, Representation, and the Loss of Desire," in *Sex & Money: Feminism and Political Economy in the Media*, eds. Eileen R. Meehan and Ellen Riordan (Minneapolis: University of Minnesota Press, 2002), 224.

70. Ibid, 233.

71. Anderson, *The Thrill is Gone*; Cortese, *Provocateur*.

72. Anderson, *The Thrill is Gone*, 232; Cortese, *Provocateur*, 38; Martin, *Communication and Mass Media*, 205; Sheehan, *Controversies in Contemporary Advertising*, 103.

73. Cortese, *Provocateur*.

74. Tom Reichert, "Men Change, Women Stay the Same: Images in Ads Targeted Toward Young and Mature Adults," in *Women and the Media: Diverse Perspectives*, edited by Theresa Carilli and Jane Campbell (Lanham: University Press of America, 2005); Sheehan, *Controversies in Contemporary Advertising*.

75. Sheehan, *Controversies in Contemporary Advertising*, 99.

76. Reichert, *Men Change, Women Stay the Same*.

77. Anderson, *The Thrill is Gone*; Sheehan, *Controversies in Contemporary Advertising*.

78. Cortese, *Provocateur*.

79. Ibid.

80. Cortese, *Provocateur*, 54.

81. Vogue, *Big Girls Don't Cry*, by Sarah Mower (August, 2006), 234.

82. Ibid.

83. Anderson, *The Thrill is Gone*, 228.

84. Cortese, *Provocateur*.

85. Anderson, *The Thrill is Gone*, 229.

86. Ibid.

87. Anderson, *The Thrill is Gone*; Cortese, *Provocateur*.

88. Sheehan, *Controversies in Contemporary Advertising*, 109.

89. Cortese, *Provocateur*, 44.

90. Peach, *Women in Culture*, 120.

91. Sheehan, *Controversies in Contemporary Advertising*, 98.

92. Peach, *Women in Culture*, 122.

93. Anderson, *The Thrill is Gone*, 231-232.

94. David Croteau and William Hoynes, *Media/Society: Industries, Images, and Audiences*, second edition (Pine Forge Press and Sage Publications, 2000); Sheehan, *Controversies in Contemporary Advertising*.

95. Sheehan, *Controversies in Contemporary Advertising*, 32.

96. Croteau et al., *Media/Society*, 268.

97. Sheehan, *Controversies in Contemporary Advertising*.

98. Croteau et al., *Media/Society*, 293.

99. Sheehan, *Controversies in Contemporary Advertising*.

100. Buckley et al., *Fashioning the Feminine*.

101. Cronin, *Advertising and Consumer Citizenship*.

102. Ibid, 27.

103. Ibid, 32.

104. Cronin, *Advertising and Consumer Citizenship*.

105. Cortese, *Provocateur*; Croteau et al., *Media/Society*.

106. Croteau et al., *Media/Society*, 286.

107. *Ms*, vol. 3, no. 4 (October 1974), 113.

108. *Ms*. vol. 2, no. 1 (July 1974), 97.

109. Croteau et al., *Media/Society*.

110. Martin, *Communication and Mass Media*, 206-207.

111. Yerza (1995) cited in Martin, *Communication and Mass Media*, 209, emphasis added.

112. Berman et al., *Still Miss Understood*.

113. Linda M. Scott, "Progressive Images of Women," *Advertising and Society Review*, 7, no. 2, (2006), 1.

114. Anderson, *The Thrill is Gone*; Scott, *Progressive Images of Women*.

115. Berman et al., *Still Miss Understood*, 10.

116. Dove, *Campaign for Real Beauty*, (n.d.), http://www.campaignforrealbeauty.com (accessed 30 September, 2006).

117. Sheehan, *Controversies in Contemporary Advertising*, 84.

118. Berman et al., *Still Miss Understood*, 8.

119. Anderson, *The Thrill is Gone*.

120. Berman et al., *Still Miss Understood*, 6.

121. Mattelart, *Les femmes et les industries culturelles*.

Chapter Five

Invisible Ink: Women and Global Communications

Nancy Snow

"Diplomats have known for many centuries…that wives are valuable auxiliaries."
—Charles W. Thayer, U.S. Diplomat, 1959

FROM 1992-1994 I worked in two international relations venues at the federal government level: the United States Information Agency (USIA) and the U.S. State Department. I was part of a fast track of young management interns now known as Presidential Management Fellows who were hot shots out of graduate school with newly minted doctorate or master degrees. Upon entering the corridors of the Foreign Service crowd, I was struck by the paucity of women I met in positions of authority, particularly at the State Department where older white men dominated. The USIA managerial staff was mostly white men too, but there were more women in higher positions of authority at USIA because the agency as a whole was majority female. One of my bosses with just a high school diploma had even worked her way up from the secretarial pool in the early 1960s to head up the entire educational exchange division at USIA. The reason for more women at USIA seemed obvious. USIA's directive, unlike State, was not to *make* foreign policy. That was men's work. No, like Charles Thayer's observation in the 1950s, USIA had an auxiliary function—to *carry out* the foreign policy of the United States through its mandate, "Telling America's Story to the World." We would do that with our public diplomacy programs in international broadcasting, exchanges, and cultural affairs. It was as if we were serving tea and crumpets in the next room over, straining our ears to hear the men talk their big ideas.

The United States was in a position in 2008 to elect its first woman president, Hillary Clinton. Though expected to be Democratic nominee for President, Clinton was ultimately defeated by Senator Barack Obama in the primary season. Nevertheless, Clinton's candidacy became as chic as the 2007 U.S. Open lady in red dress of tennis pro Maria Sharapova. Clinton said that her administration would appoint husband and former president Bill Clinton as image czar to repair America's poor reputation in the world. While the U.S seemed ready to at least consider a lady president, is it ready to open the door wide to women in negotiation and diplomacy? Not so fast.

While at USIA, I heard about an infamous class action lawsuit brought by women Foreign Service Officers in the mid-1980s. The suit alleged that women were given different measures of work performance, including gendered determinations of social likeability such as willingness to get along well with others. The women charged that they weren't getting promotions at the rate of the men and were often relegated to the less prestigious consular duties over the heavy-hitting polit-ico-economic duties normally assigned to men. Those women ultimately won their suit but the numbers of women FSOs have not increased dramatically, especially at the top. Despite the U.S. State Department's promise to make the Foreign Service re-flect women's equal number status, of the 148 posted ambassadors in 2004, 99 were career members of the Foreign Service and just 23 of those careerists were women, less than 25 percent.

Certainly things *have* gotten better. As late as 1970, women had to leave the For-eign Service after marriage, very much like the airlines of the day. In the 1920s, the State Department even proposed banning women entirely from the Foreign Service. At times women have been perceived as not strong enough either intellectually or emotionally to handle the stresses and strains of a job where one represents the na-tional security and foreign affairs of state. But government writer Shane Harris ar-gues convincingly that there remains the double bind in male and female communication styles: "Privately, women acknowledge, and bemoan, other differ-ences with their male colleagues that statistics don't capture: Men can scream; women can't. Men can throw telephones; women can't. Men can exert an assertive, commanding style of leadership. Women who do so develop, to put it charitably, rep-utations."[1] Women who exceed in global diplomatic positions must feel like Ginger Rogers at times, doing everything their Fred Astaire counterparts can do, but also backwards and in heels.

Since 9/11, women in prominent places at State have come into sharper focus, most notably in the area of public diplomacy, which was formerly the directive of the now defunct U.S. Information Agency. The world applauded the trajectory of Dr. Condoleezza Rice's ascension from national security advisor to secretary of state. An African American woman with a Ph.D., she is arguably the highest-ranked minority woman in U.S. foreign policy history. Like her Democratic predecessor, the era of Albright and Rice suggested an opening of the door to more women diplomats and greater recognition of the contributions that women in particular make to the global communication process. Along with Albright and Rice, one could add the tenure of several under secretaries of state for public diplomacy, including Charlotte Beers (2001-2003), Margaret Tutwiler (2003-2004) and Karen Hughes (2005-2008) to this list of high-profile women in the diplomatic corps.

So what is to worry that this rise in women at the top won't change the structure or process of our global communication? For one, all four of these women from Rice to Hughes have been appointed based primarily on their proximity to the presidential administration in power. Hughes is famously known, like Rice, as the having the ear of George W. Bush. Albright excepted, she having been a political science and international relations professor, the other women did not receive their posts because of any outstanding or longstanding service in foreign affairs. Also, while much press hoopla is made of Madam Secretaries and Madam Under Secretaries, the close examination of gender in diplomacy or women's leadership in diplomacy is notably absent in the academic literature. When one examines U.S. foreign policy and diplomatic history, what emerges is a well-documented accounting of male diplomats from Thomas Jefferson and Benjamin Franklin to John Foster Dulles and Henry Kissinger on their contributions to the foreign policy process. Even the State Department cannot help itself. Karen Hughes announced in the summer of 2007 that a government-funded youth enhancement program included "80 children from rural schools in Malaysia who learned about Thomas Jefferson and other U.S. heroes on an American-style camping trip with embassy staff and families."[2] We don't call them the Founding Fathers for nothing. What is striking is the almost total invisibility of female diplomats, Founding Mothers if you will, in all ranks of the diplomatic corps, including support staff and translators, the majority of whom are women but who, because of their rank, do not constitute the power centers of the diplomatic process. They are there in daily service, but their legacy is silent.

This absence of female diplomatic power and influence is due in part to the reality that women could not be admitted to the diplomatic corps until the 20th Century and their numbers didn't appreciate until the 1930s. It wasn't until 1949 during the presidency of Harry Truman that the first female ambassador was appointed.[3] But why are women still absent for the most part in the diplomatic process in the 21st Century? Why aren't their majority numbers in the general population reflected in the global communication corps? There is no simple explanation. Some women give accounts of their family obligations that absorb all their energies and prevent them from maintaining the demands of the diplomatic service corps. Another explanation has to do with a gender bias that is attached to our definitions of diplomacy. In many parts of the world, for both cultural and religious reasons, a woman ambassador is still an oxymoron. A woman is expected not to engage in the public negotiation process that will distract her from more primary and private demands such as feeding her children, caring for elderly parents, or attending to the needs of her husband, the primary bread winner in the family household. Further, obtaining plum overseas assignments is how one generally advances up the diplomatic ladder and yet such assignments are just the type to be frowned upon in a home village that isn't used to a woman in a position of political leadership. Accepting such a position may insinuate or confirm that this woman places her needs ahead of others, thereby violating an accepted social and cultural norm of her community.

What difference would it really make if women were acknowledged and represented at the levels befitting their actual numbers? Diplomacy is directly tied to representation of a nation-state. Do women make a difference in representing America to the world? Based on what we already know about how women communicate differently from men and how such communication patterns contribute to different outcomes, the answer is yes. In the public diplomacy process, there are two tracks that predominate, with one more dominant than the other. The first track emphasizes what public diplomacy can do to reinforce national security objectives. This track, the more masculine style of diplomacy, emphasizes international operations, psychological warfare, and one-way declarative mass media processes such as international broadcasting, Al Hurra and Radio Sawa, for example. The second track in public diplomacy, which is more feminine in structure and process, emphasizes cultural diplomacy, cultural mediation, multitrack approaches, and shareholder concerns. Feminine diplomacy approaches are, to put it simply, typically more consensus-based and mutual, while masculine diplomacy approaches are one-way informational and propagandistic (advantaging one side over another). Neither one is defined by sex but on gendered constructions, which means that theoretically speaking, having more women in positions of authority in public diplomacy making should reflect a more feminine approach, while continuing to have a male-dominated diplomacy perpetuates masculine approaches.

Currently the United States approach to public diplomacy favors a more masculine-defined approach—raising the volume of America's story to the world through media propaganda efforts and tweaking press stories through public relations firms that are subcontracted to reflect favorably on the U.S. mission in Iraq. Feminine approaches, like educational, cultural, and arts exchanges that promote mutuality, are rhetorically supported but not actualized to the degree of masculine approaches.

This is a consequence of a crisis and self-preservation orientation in our public diplomacy architecture in the U.S. that favors case-making as directed by President Bush after 9/11 or confronting the enemy's propaganda as asserted by Secretary of Defense Donald Rumsfeld:

> We are fighting a battle where the survival of our free way of life is at stake. And the center of gravity of that struggle is not simply on the battlefields overseas. It's a test of wills, and it will be won or lost with our publics and with the publics of other nations. We'll need to do all we can to attract supporters to our efforts, and to correct the lies that are being told which so damage our country, and which are repeated and repeated and repeated.[4]

The former undersecretary of state for public diplomacy, Karen Hughes, gave some weight to the difference that women make in international development. In a speech before the International Women's Forum for Economy and Society, Hughes said that "I have come to realize it is increasingly women who are arbiters of peace and reconciliation…All the statistics show [that] when you educate and empower women, you improve almost every other aspect of a society."[5] This statement isn't particularly newsworthy and is based on decades of research on women and development. Nevertheless, it reflects a tiny opening of the door to consider the roles that women play in not only development but also in diplomacy. These include multitrack and exchange-centered approaches to public diplomacy that are considered "nice but insufficient" measures to national security outcomes in foreign policy. The problem remains that Hughes is 100% loyal to a president who supports the masculine-defined approach in national security and foreign policy, so no matter what she professes, the actions (or inactions) are all that matter.

Feminist author Cynthia Enloe is one of a handful of American women scholars (Elshtain, Peterson, Tickner) who has considered the masculine dynamic in U.S. foreign policy and war making. In her 1993 book, *The Morning After*, Enloe analyzes the Cold War from a gendered perspective:

> The Cold War is usually spoken of in geostrategic terms: the tight bipolar balance of Power, spheres of influence, massive retaliation shading into mutual assured destruction, espionage, space races, science in schools, the Berlin Wall, containment, etc., etc. We now know that the Cold War relied on other things beyond the pale of usual IR analysis. It relied on militarized gender, on constructions of "men" and "women" that could be mobilized for the propaganda "war"—and its dirty little fighting wars—against Communism.[6]

In the post 9/11 global communication process, men remain on the frontlines promoting masculine-defined notions of freedom and democracy while women are relegated to supporting roles defending the homeland. Women are missing from making feminine foreign policy and so are the women who cover it. Think of a woman journalist who covers foreign affairs and national security. My choice in the United States is Robin Wright, no, not the wife of actor Sean Penn, but the staff writer for the *Washington Post* and author of *Sacred Rage: The Wrath of Militant Islam*. Wright is a regular guest on the Sunday morning news shows like "This Week with George Stephanopoulos" or "Face the Nation" but she lacks the global standing of foreign affairs guru Thomas Friedman, her contemporary who is at the *New York Times*. Both cut their journalistic teeth covering the Middle East in the 1970s, but it is Friedman, and not Wright, who is the quasi-Walter Lippmann of our time. A male graduate student told me not too long ago that his dream was to be the next Thom Friedman because Friedman seems to hold so much authority among politicians and the new media. My student was dazzled by the amount of ink Friedman was given to wax politic about affairs of the day. When I see the day that a graduate student, male or female, says that Robin Wright's job is a goal, then I'll know we've entered a whole new dimension of post-gender analysis.

In the United States we have no comparable woman in authority, scholar or journalist, who regularly comments on international affairs. Even Clinton Administration Secretary of State Madeleine Albright holds no gravitas to the aging Nixon Secretary of State Henry Kissinger. As honorary chair of the Pew Center Global Attitudes Survey, Madam Secretary may show up on C-SPAN to comment on yet another depressing poll about the U.S. poor standing in the world, but she's no counterweight to Kissinger or even Bush 41's James Baker in terms of setting an agenda for foreign affairs.

Does elder stateswoman roll off one's tongue as easily as elder statesman? I doubt it. The bottom line of the gender gap in global communications became all too clear when one of the elite journals of international opinion, *Foreign Policy,* published "Inside the Ivory Tower."[7] It listed the Top 20 scholars in the field of international relations and not one woman was among them. The list included Harvard scholar Joseph Nye, former undersecretary for defense in the Clinton Administration and advocate of soft power, and Harvard colleague, Samuel Huntington, author of *The Clash of Civilizations*. Connie Francis may have sung about where the boys are in terms of fun and sun, but it's where the girls aren't that may be shaping our very understanding of complex global communications and globalization issues. The report

states with no sense of concern the following: "Like much of the political and business world, the field of international relations remains dominated by men: No
women rank among the top 25 scholars with the greatest impact on the discipline
over the past 20 years." Anyone ever heard of groupthink? In the section on "leading
lights" in the field, the authors note the same old, same old nature of IR: "One thing
that stands out about these high achievers, though, is how similar they are: Nearly all
are white men older than 50. That result is even more striking as almost a third of the
field's scholars are women and half the respondents received their Ph.D.s in the past
12 years. Odds are, it won't be a men's club for much longer." I wouldn't be so san-
guine. The old boys club is likely to not go gently into that good night, especially if
the women scholars who are predicted to rise to the top challenge the masculine assumptions that dominate in international relations offerings. Should they do so,
however, it may be to the world's benefit and despite the recognition from *Foreign
Policy* magazine that they make their mark.

Notes

1. Shane Harris, "Madam Ambassador," *Government Executive*, April 1, 2005. http://www.govexec.
   com/features/0405-01/0405-01s1.htm.

2. Farah Stockman, "Diplomacy effort reaches out to Muslim youths: Strives to create positive views
   of United States," *Boston Globe, August 18, 2007.*

3. Julia Chang Bloch, "Women and Diplomacy," *The Ambassadors Review*, Fall 2004. http://www.
   americanambassadors.org/index.cfm?fuseaction=Publications.article&articleid=69

4. Donald Rumsfeld, Secretary of Defense Donald H. Speech before the Council on Foreign Relations,
   February 17, 2006. http://www.defenselink.mil/Speeches/Speech.aspx?SpeechID=27

5. Karen Hughes, "The U.S. and France: Working Together." Remarks to the International Women's
   Forum for Economy and Society. October 5, 2006. http://www.state.gov/r/us/73614.htm

6. Cynthia Enloe, *The Morning After: Sexual Politics at the End of the Cold War*. Berkeley: University of
   California Press, 1993.

7. Susan Peterson, Michael J. Tierney, and Daniel Maliniak, "Inside the Ivory Tower," *Foreign Policy*,
   November/December 2005, 58-64.

Chapter Six

Just Prudes? Feminism, Pornography, And Men's Responsibility

Robert Jensen

I START with the simple observation that I am a man, which is important because of two things it suggests regarding what I know about the world.

First, I know some things that women don't know about men. By definition, women are never in all-male spaces. Women don't directly experience what men say about them when there are no women around. Women can hear these things second-hand, but it's not the same as experiencing male-bonding/woman-hating talk directly.

Being a man also means there's a lot I don't know, that I have had to learn—and keep learning—from women and a feminist movement. This essay is rooted in the feminist critique of pornography and the feminist anti-pornography movement, from which I have learned much.[1] But in doing that, I should acknowledge the complex position of a man speaking about the feminist analysis of pornography. I am not speaking *for* women. Instead, I see my role as speaking *with* women, toward the ultimate goal of speaking about the insights of this critique *to* men.[2]

But even that is complicated, of course, because women do not speak with one voice about pornography, or any other issue. There are pro-pornography women who would contest much of what I argue. All I can do is acknowledge the women who have helped me come to understand the issue, tell the truth as I see it, and ask men to take seriously this critique of the domination/subordination dynamic that is so common in pornography and, indeed, in the world.

The minute one begins to make such a critique, one can expect this response: Feminists who critique pornography are really just prudes at heart. Pornography's opponents, we are told, are afraid of sex.

In one sense, that's true. I am afraid of sex, of a certain kind. I'm afraid of much of the sex commonly presented in contemporary mass-marketed pornography. I am afraid of sex that is structured on a dynamic of domination and subordination. I am afraid of the sex in pornography that has become so routinely harsh that men typically cannot see the brutality of it through their erections and orgasms.

I'm not against sex or sexual pleasure. I'm against the kind of sex that is routinely presented in contemporary pornography. I'm against that kind of sex because it hurts people in the world today, and it helps construct a world in which people —primarily the most vulnerable people, women and children, both girls and boys— will continue to be hurt.

Pornographic Sex

This is one kind of sex that I'm afraid of. This is a scene from the film "Gag Factor #10" released by JM Productions, which boasts that it pushes the envelope in pornography. The company website brags that this gag series, which is going on #27 as of June 2008, offers "The best throatfucking ever lensed." The website has pictures and short video clips, under the heading "this week's victim," with the promise "new whores degraded every Wednesday."

In one of the 10 scenes from "Gag Factor #10," released in 2002, a nagging wife is haranguing her husband and asking why he is so lazy. "Why can't you do anything?" she asks, going on to insult his intelligence and criticize him because he doesn't read. She asks him if he even can read, and then suggests Henry Miller, from which she starts to read. The camera focuses on her mouth as she reads, then cuts to his eyes, which look increasingly angry. The film cuts to the woman on her knees as he yells, "Shut the fuck up." He grabs her hair and thrusts his penis into her mouth. From this point on, we hear almost exclusively from him: "Your teeth feel good you little bitch. Eat that dick. … Are you OK? Are you crying? I love you. I fucking love you. Open that mouth." He slaps her mouth with his penis. "Open wide. Choke. Open wider, wider. You're so good baby. Put your mouth on my balls. You treat me so fucking good. That's why I keep you here. Give me the eyes [meaning, look up at me] while I gag you. … Do you like to gag? Beg for it. Say please. Say please gag me some more. … Your throat is so good."

At this point, she re-enters the conversation. She says, "Keep going."

He says, "Good, that's the fucking answer I was looking for."

He the flips her over, putting her on the table with her head hanging over edge. She gags several times when he thrusts into her mouth. He holds her by the cheeks, spreading her face apart. She gags but he doesn't stop. He allows her to catch her breath. Her face is unexpressive, almost frozen.

"I want those tears to come out again, baby. I want to choke the shit out of you," he says.

He grabs her hair and drives his penis into her mouth. He says: "Suck that dick. Convulse. I want to see your eyes roll back in your fucking head. Yes, I love it." He asks her if she loves it; she says yes. He ejaculates into her mouth and says, "Spit that cum out. I can't hear you. What did you say? Don't talk with your mouth full."

He walks away and says "Don't give me any more shit."

"Gag Factor" is what the industry calls "wall-to-wall" or "gonzo" pornography, which is the roughest form available in the mainstream pornography shops and also the fastest growing genre. This scene is more overtly misogynistic than some, but it is not idiosyncratic. The sex and the language in what the industry calls "features" typically is not as rough, though the message is the same: Women are for sex, and women like sex this way.[3]

Empathy

I am afraid of that kind of sex. I'm worried about the physical and emotional well-being of the woman in that scene. I'm afraid of the way in which the men who use that pornography will act in their own lives, toward women in their lives. I am afraid of the world that such sex helps to create.

I am afraid, and we all should be.

If anyone wants to dismiss these concerns with the tired old phrases "to each his own" and "as long as they are consenting adults"—that is, if people want to ignore the reality and complexity of the world in which we live—I can't stop them. But I can tell you that if you do that, you are abandoning minimal standards of political and moral responsibility, and you become partially responsible for the injuries done as a result of a system you refuse to confront.

We live in a world in which a woman can be aggressively throat-fucked to facilitate the masturbation of men. We all live in that world. We all live with that woman in "Gag Factor #10." She is one of us. She is a person. She has hopes and dreams and desires of her own.

We all live with that woman who finds herself making a living by being filmed in another kind of gonzo film called a "blow bang," in which a woman has oral sex in similar fashion with more than one man.

In one of these films, "Blow Bang #4," released in 2001, a young woman dressed as a cheerleader is surrounded by six men. For about seven minutes, "Dynamite" (the name she gives on tape) methodically moves from man to man while they offer insults such as "you little cheerleading slut." For another minute and a half, she sits upside down on a couch, her head hanging over the edge, while men thrust into her mouth, causing her to gag. She strikes the pose of the bad girl to the end. "You like coming on my pretty little face, don't you," she says, as they ejaculate on her face and in her mouth for the final two minutes of the scene.

Five men have finished. The sixth steps up. As she waits for him to ejaculate onto her face, now covered with semen, she closes her eyes tightly and grimaces. For a moment, her face changes; it is difficult to read her emotions, but it appears she may cry. After the last man, number six, ejaculates, she regains her composure and smiles. Then the narrator off camera hands her the pom-pom she had been holding at the beginning of the tape and says, "Here's your little cum mop, sweetheart—mop up." She buries her face in the pom-pom and the scene ends.

Dynamite is one of us. She is a person. She has hopes and dreams and desires of her own.

The women in the movement to end men's violence have helped society understand that we have to empathize with the victims of sexual assault and domestic violence. We also need to extend that empathy to the women in pornography and prostitution.

Because we live in a world in which it is so easy to detach, to isolate ourselves from others, we have to practice empathy, that most fundamental of human qualities. We have to remind ourselves to exercise our ability to connect our humanity with another, to travel to that person's world and to try to feel along with another human being.

Think of that scene with Dynamite. One woman and six men. After she has performed oral sex on six men, after six men have thrust their penises into her throat to the point of gagging, after six men have ejaculated onto her, the camera is turned off. Close your eyes and think not about the sex acts but about the moment after the sex, when the camera shuts off. The men walk away. Someone throws her a towel. She has to clean the semen of six strangers off her face and body and from her hair. This woman, who is a person, who is one of us, who has hopes and dreams and desires of her own, cleans herself off.

Imagine that the women in that scene is your child. How you would feel if the woman being handed a towel to wipe off the semen of six men were your child, someone you had raised and loved and cared for. How does that feel?

Imagine that woman is the child of your best friend, or of your neighbor, or of someone you work with. Then imagine that women is the child of someone you have never met and never will meet. Imagine that women is just a person, one of us, with hopes and dreams and desires of her own. Forget about whether or not she is your child. She is a person; she is one of us.

Imagine that you are the one handing her the towel. Could you dare to look into her eyes? We need to dare to look into her eyes and try to understand what she might be feeling. We can't know for sure what she is feeling. But we can try to imagine how we might feel if we were in her position. That's empathy, and it's a virtue.

We are constantly told pornography is about fantasies. Those scenes I just described are not fantasy. They are real. They happened. They happened to those women. Those women are not a fantasy. They are people. They are just like us.

And after those scenes were put on videotape, the films were sold and rented to thousands of men who took them home, put them into VCRs or DVD players, and masturbated to orgasm. That also is real. Men fantasize when they masturbate, but the men who are masturbating are not a fantasy. Thousands of men have climaxed to the recording of those women being aggressively throat-fucked. Those orgasms happened in the real world. Those men's sexual pleasure was being conditioned to images of women being aggressively throat-fucked, in the real world.

Those specific women and those specific men are part of the world we live in. And that idea of what a woman is, and that idea of what's men's sexuality is—those ideas are also part of the world we live in. None of it is a fantasy. All of it is as real as we are.

So, a simple question: What do we owe those women? What do we owe Dynamite? What is our responsibility to her, to her hopes and dreams and desires?

Choices, Hers and Ours

At this point, some will say: "Whatever you or I may think of those activities, she chose to do that. She's an adult. Who are we to condemn her choice?" I agree; we shouldn't condemn her choice, and we shouldn't condemn her. We should empathize with her. And we should think not just about her choice but about the choices of the men who pay for the tape and create the demand for aggressive throat-fucking.

From research and the testimony of women who have been prostituted and used in pornography, we know that childhood sexual assault (which often leads victims to see their value in the world primarily as the ability to provide sexual pleasure for men) and economic hardship (a lack of meaningful employment choices at a livable wage) are key factors in many women's decisions to enter the sex industry. We know how women in the sex industry—not all, but many—routinely dissociate to cope with what they do. We know that in one study of 130 street prostitutes, 68 percent met the diagnostic criteria for post-traumatic stress disorder.[4] We also know that pimps often use coercion and violence to keep women working as prostitutes. In the words of one team that reviewed research from nine countries, prostitution is "multitraumatic."[5]

We know that any meaningful discussion of choice can't be restricted to the single moment when a woman decides to allow herself to be sold sexually, but must include all the background conditions that affect not only the objective choices she faces but her subjective assessment of those choices. What matters is not just what is available but how she perceives herself in relation to what is available. We know that in anyone's life, completely free choices are rare, that every choice is made under some mix of constraint and opportunity.

I know, for instance, that in my large lecture classes when I give a multiple-choice exam, virtually none of the students believes that such exams are an accurate or meaningful way to measure their learning. I know that many of them find such exams to be ridiculous, as do I. But all of my students "choose" to take a test they know to be virtually useless (except for the data it provides me in a large class so that I can assign grades at the end of the term). They choose to take that exam because if they chose not to—no matter how sensible and compelling their analysis of the exam's flaws—they will not pass the course, and they will be denied something that is important to them, a college diploma. They could choose to reject the institution, and thereby give up that asset, but it would cost them. Their choice is free, but it is not made under conditions of complete freedom, given their limited power in the system. So, let us not be naïve about choice.

But, for the sake of argument, let's assume that the specific woman who was used in that aggressive throat-fucking movie made a completely free and meaningful choice to participate, with absolutely no constraints on her. That could be the case, but it does not change the fact that many women in the industry choose under dramatic limitations. And so long as the industry is profitable and a large number of women are needed to make such films, it is certain that some number of those women will be choosing under conditions that render the concept of "free choice" virtually meaningless. When a man buys or rents a videotape or DVD, he is creating the demand for pornography that will lead to some number of women being hurt, psychologically and/or physically.[6] That is a fact in the world in which we live.

So, men's choices to buy or rent pornography are complicated by two realities. First, at any given moment, the consumer has no reliable way to judge which women are participating in the industry as a result of a meaningfully free choice. And second, even if the men consuming pornography could make such a determination about specific women in specific films, the demand for pornography that their purchase creates ensures that some women will be hurt.

Given that conclusion, there is only one decision that men who claim to have even minimal standards of moral and political responsibility can make: They must not buy or rent pornography. We must not create the demand that creates the industry that creates a world in which vulnerable people will be hurt.

If we buy or rent pornography, we bear some responsibility for that world. We can try to pretend we don't know that, but we can't avoid that responsibility.

Justice and Self-interest

That's the argument from justice. It's an argument that men, and the women who buy or rent pornography, should take seriously unless they want to abandon minimal moral and political standards.

But arguments from justice do not always move people who are in positions of power and privilege. Maybe such arguments from justice should be enough to change people, but they often aren't. So, arguments from self-interest are important, too. Men should stop buying and renting pornography because it is the right thing to do. They also should stop because it is in their self-interest.

To explain that, I tell a story from my experience at the 2005 convention of the pornography industry, the AVN Adult Entertainment Expo, which I attended as part of a team working on a documentary film called "The Price of Pleasure." At the end of our first day filming at the convention, the film's director, Miguel Picker, and I walked out of the Sands Expo Center in Las Vegas without saying much. We had just spent the better part of the day together on the exhibition floor, which featured about 300 booths visited by thousands of people. Miguel had been behind the camera, and I had been interviewing pornography performers, producers, and fans about why they make, distribute, and consume sexually explicit media.

We had spent the day surrounded by images of women being presented and penetrated for the sexual pleasure of men. All around were pictures and posters, screens running endless porn loops, and display tables of dildos and sex dolls. I had listened to young men tell me that pornography had taught them a lot about what women really want sexually. I had listened to a pornography producer tell me that anal sex is popular in pornography because men like to think about fucking their wives and girlfriends in the ass to pay them back for being bitchy. And I interviewed the producer who takes great pride that his "Gag Factor" series was the first to feature exclusively aggressive throat fucking. "We don't follow trends," he said confidently. "We set them."

Miguel and I had spent the day surrounded by sex for sale, immersed in the predictable consequence of the collision of capitalism and patriarchy. We had talked to dozens of people for whom the process of buying and selling women for sex is routine. When that day was over, we walked silently from the convention center to the hotel. The first thing I said was, "I need a drink."

I don't want to feign naivete. As a child and young adult, I used pornography in fairly typical fashion. I have been working on the issue of pornography since 1988. I have talked to a lot of people about pornography, and in very short and controlled doses, I have watched enough of it to understand how corrosive it is to our individual and collective humanity. But I had never been to the industry convention before; I had always found a reason to avoid it. As Miguel and I left the hall, I understood why.

"I need a drink," I said, and we stopped at the nearest hotel bar (which didn't take long, given how many bars there are in a Las Vegas hotel). I sat down with a glass of wine. Miguel and I started to talk, searching for some way to articulate what we had just experienced, what we felt. But all I could do was cry.

It's not that I had seen anything on the convention floor that I had never seen. It's not that I had heard something significantly new or different from the people I had interviewed. It's not that I had had some sort of epiphany about the meaning of pornography. It's just that in that moment, the reality of the industry, of the products the industry produces, and the way in which they are used—it all came crashing down on me. My defenses were inadequate to combat a simple fact: The pornographers have won. In the short term, the efforts of the feminists who put forward the critique of pornography, the sex industry, and men's violence have failed. The pornographers, for the time being, have won. The arguments from justice lost. The pornographers not only are thriving, but are more mainstream and normalized than ever. They can fill up a Las Vegas convention center, with the dominant culture paying no more notice than it would to the annual boat show.

And as the industry has become more normalized, paradoxically, the content of their films becomes ever crueler and more overtly degrading to women.[7] The industry talk is dominated by talk of how to push it even further. Make it nastier. Make it, in the terms of one industry observer, "brutal and real." That's the way the pornographers and the customers like it: Brutal. Because brutal is real. And real sells. It is real, and that's at the heart of the sadness. What was reflected on the convention floor was not just a truth about pornography, but a truth about gender and sex and power in contemporary culture, as well as a truth about the brutality of capitalism. At the end of that day, I was more aware than ever that the feminist critique of pornography is not simply a critique of pornography but about the routine way we are trained to be sexual, about the eroticization of domination and subordination. The feminism that I learned, both in the classroom and through participation in a movement, has to be a full-bore attack on systems of illegitimate authority, of which male dominance is one, along with white supremacy, capitalism, and imperialism.

And at that moment, all I could do was cry. It was a selfish indulgence, because at that moment, my tears were not for the women who are used and discarded by the industry, or the women who will be forced into sex they don't want by the men in their lives who use pornography. The tears were not for girls and young women who bury their own needs and desires to become sexually what men want them to be. I wish I could honestly say that was front and center in my mind and heart at that moment. But the truth is that my tears at that moment were for myself. Those tears came because I realized, in a more visceral way than ever, that the pornographers have won and they are helping to construct a world that is not only dangerous for women and children, but also one in which I have fewer and fewer places to turn as a man. Fewer places to walk and talk and breathe that haven't been colonized and pornographized. As I sat there, all I could say to Miguel was, "I don't want to live in this world."

At that moment Miguel didn't quite know what to make of my reaction. He was nice to me, but he must have thought I was going a bit over the top. I don't blame him; I was a bit over the top. After all, we were there to make a documentary film about the industry, not live out a melodrama about my angst in a Las Vegas hotel bar. The next day Miguel and I hit the convention floor again. At the end of that day, as we walked away, I made the same request. We sat at the same bar. I had another glass of wine and cried again. Miguel, I think, was glad it was the last day. So was I.

Two days after we left Las Vegas, Miguel called me from New York. This time he was crying. He told me that he had just come to his editing and recording studio and had put on some music. Miguel is not only a director and editor, but a very talented musician. He's one of those people who understand the world through music. He told me that he had put on music that he finds particularly beautiful, and then the floodgates opened. "I understand what you meant in the bar," he said.

I tell that story not to glorify two sensitive new-age men. Miguel actually is a sensitive person, though not very new-age. I'm not new-age, and I don't feel particularly sensitive these days. I feel harsh and mean. I feel angry most of the time. I spend most of my days on political organizing not writing poetry. I'm from North Dakota. People from North Dakota don't write a lot of poetry. We shovel snow.

I tell that story because it's never been clearer to me that in the struggle over pornography, the sex industry, and men's violence, it is not enough to be right and to make arguments solely about justice. The central insights of the feminist critique of pornography are, I believe, right. It remains the most compelling way to understand the issue. If anything, that critique of pornography is truer today than it was when the founding mothers of the movement first articulated it in the late 1970s.

But we live in a society in which the pornographers have won, in the short term. Their products are more widely accepted and available than ever. Much of the culture has bought the "pornography is liberation" and "pornography is freedom" lines. To the degree that an anti-pornography position can get traction in the dominant culture, it comes from right-wing groups that have co-opted the language of feminism —the political language of harm—as a cover for a regressive moralism that rejects the values of feminism. Those same right-wing groups typically resist a critique of the capitalist commodification of everything, an analysis crucial to understanding pornography.

At this moment, being right is not enough. We have to find ways to tap into the humanity of people, a humanity that is systematically diminished and obscured by capitalism and patriarchy, as well as by the explicit racism in pornography. That's the argument from self-interest that men must hear. Men get something very concrete from pornography: They get orgasms. For most men, it's an extremely effective way to gain physical pleasure. But it comes at a cost, and the cost is our own humanity. To be a man in this sense is to surrender some part of your humanity. I speak from experience here: It's a bad trade-off; no orgasm is worth that much.

That's why the experience that Miguel and I had on the floor is important. On that day, the concentrated inhumanity of the pornographic world overwhelmed us. I went onto the convention floor knowing a lot about pornography. I left the floor feeling it more deeply than ever before. We know a lot about the pornography industry and its effects. We know there is a compelling critique. We have to be willing to feel it, as well.

Feeling and Thinking Our Way Forward, Together

It is not an easy task, to help men understand the depravity of their own pleasure. Men have to feel a sense of desperation about that, but we have to make sure it leads people to action not paralysis, hope not despair, resistance not capitulation. We have to face what pornography does to us all, men and women. For men, we have to face that to be a pornography user is to be a john, to be someone who is willing to buy women for sex, someone who sees sex as a commodity, someone who has traded his own humanity for an orgasm.

Those realities are not easy for women to face either. I can't speak for women, of course, but I assume that it is not easy to be a woman and understand how pornography portrays women and their sexuality, and to know that men like it. Put bluntly, in pornography, women are reduced to three holes and two hands. In pornography, women are reduced to the parts of their bodies that can sexually stimulate men. Women are not really sex-objects (which at least implies they are human) but more fuck-objects, simply things to be penetrated. I imagine that is not an easy thing to confront when surrounded by pornography. I imagine it is not easy to realize that this is the world in which women learned to be sexual.

Men have some difficult realities to face. So do women. I understand how painful those realities can be because I continue to struggle with them, and I have talked to many other people about their struggles. Sometimes I feel that I know too much. Sometimes I wish that I didn't have all these pictures in my head. Sometimes I wish I had never heard the stories of women's pain that I have heard.

But I never wish I were back where I was 20 years ago, because 20 years ago I also was in pain, albeit a very different kind. In some ways, that old pain was easier to mask, but it was impossible to escape. This newer pain might be more intense at times, but it is a necessary part of the process that has changed my life for the better. I don't really like it, but I accept the need for it, because this pain can lead somewhere. It can lead to a long and difficult, but ultimately rewarding, process of trying to revise the way we see sexuality. It can lead to involvement in a political movement to change the world that, even if not successful in the short term, holds out the hope for not just personal but societal transformation. Confronting the violence and pain of the world, both outside and inside me, has led me to meet many amazing people whose friendship and love has sustained me through difficult times.

When we talk like this, one of the predictable rejoinders is that we are trying to impose strict sexual rules on others. As one prominent pro-pornography feminist scholar, Linda Williams, put it in an interview, "Really, who are [anti-pornography activists] to tell us where our sexual imaginations should go?"[8]

I agree. No one can tell others where their sexual imaginations should go. Imaginations are unruly and notoriously resistant to attempts at control. But our imaginations come from somewhere. Our imaginations may be internal in some ways, but they are influenced by external forces. Can we not have a conversation about those influences? Are we so fragile that our sexual imaginations can't stand up to honest human conversation? It seems that pro-pornography forces live with their own fear of sex, the fear of being accountable for their imaginations and actions. The defenses of pornography typically revert to the most superficial kind of liberal individualism that shuts off people from others, ignores the predictable harms of a profit-seeking industry that has little concern for people, and ignores the way in which we all collectively construct the culture in which we live.

I have no interest in telling people where there sexual imaginations must end up. But I would like to be part of a conversation about the direction in which we think our sexual imaginations can move. While I am afraid of the sex that pornography creates because it hurts people, I am not afraid of talking about an alternative to the cruelty and brutality of the pornography industry. I need that conversation. I can't do this on my own. I'm not smart enough and I'm not strong enough. I know the direction I want to move, but I stumble on the way. I have made mistakes that have hurt others and hurt myself. I can correct some of those mistakes on my own, but none of us can do this completely on our own.

So, can we start talking about how to move our sexual imaginations toward respect, toward empathy, toward connections based on equality not domination? Can we give up enough of our fear of the unknown to try to imagine together what that might look like?

This culture tends to talk about sex in terms of heat: Who's hot, what kind of sex is hot. What if we shifted to a language of light? Sex not as something that produces heat, but something that shines light. Can we talk about moving toward the light? The light that is inside me and inside you. The same light that is inside Dynamite.

I want to live in a world in which Dynamite can tell us her name, not the pornographers' name. I want to live in a world in which we hear about her hopes and dreams and desires, not the pornographers.' I want to live in that world not just for her sake but for my own, because it is that world in which I can find my own authentic hopes and dreams and desires.

We have given the pornographers far too much power to construct our sexual imaginations. It is our world, not theirs. It is our world to take back. This is not just about taking back the night, but taking back the whole day, taking back the culture's imagination, taking back the way we see men and women and sex. If we do not, I fear that the light inside us will dim. Our hopes and dreams will be increasingly shaped by the pornographers. And our hopes for a desire based on equality, maybe even the dream of equality, may not survive. I am afraid of that.

We all need to work to make sure that does not happen. For Dynamite's sake. For your own. For all of us.

A version of this essay was delivered as a talk to the Sexual Assault Network of Delaware annual conference, Woodside, DE, April 5, 2005.

Notes

1. For a summary, see Gail Dines, Robert Jensen and Ann Russo, *Pornography: The Production and Consumption of Inequality* (New York: Routledge, 1998).

2. This appeal to men is fully developed in Robert Jensen, *Getting Off: Pornography and the End of Masculinity* (Boston: South End Press, 2007).

3. Robert Jensen, "You are what you eat: The pervasive porn industry and what it says about you and your desires," *Clamor*, September/October 2002, pp. 54-59.

4. Melissa Farley and Howard Barkan, "Prostitution, Violence, and Post-Traumatic Stress Disorder," *Women & Health*, 27:3 (1998): 37-49. Available online at http://prostitutionresearch.com/c-prostitution-research.html.

5. Melissa Farley, et al, "Prostitution and Trafficking in 9 Countries: Update on Violence and Posttraumatic Stress Disorder," *Journal of Trauma Practice*, 2:3/4 (2003): 33-74. Available online at http://prostitutionresearch.com/c-prostitution-research.html.

6. For a cogent discussion of this argument in the context of prostitution, see M. Madden Dempsey, "Rethinking Wolfenden: Prostitute-Use, Criminal Law, and Remote Harm," *Criminal Law Review* (2005): 444-455.

7. Robert Jensen, "A cruel edge: The painful truth about today's pornography and what men can do about it," *MS Magazine*, Spring 2004, pp. 54-58.

8. Drake Bennett, "X-ed out: What happened to the anti-porn feminists?" *Boston Globe*, March 6, 2005, p. D-1. http://www.boston.com/news/globe/ideas/articles/2005/03/06/x_ed_out?pg=full

WOMEN, VIOLENCE AND HUMAN RIGHTS

The chapters in this section explore a multiplicity of issues relating to women's human rights and will focus particularly on discrimination and violence against women within the contemporary social world. —*Jeffery Klaehn, editor*

It is absolutely imperative that more attention be accorded all forms of discrimination against women within the context of human rights scholarship. Many, many issues are urgently pressing: structural misogyny, enforced abortion, rape as a weapon of war, forced sterilization, poverty, social isolation, patriarchal structures, imperialism, uneven development, structural adjustment and economic liberalization policies, gender and exclusion, civil and political rights and equality of access. This 'list' is by no means exhaustive. Scholars have a particular responsibility to be critical minded in exploring human rights in relation to institutionalized social structures of inequality.

Contemporary human rights scholarship that is critical and on the cutting-edge ought to explore human rights within the context of social structure, in relation to the actions and inactions of particular states, and should also connect political and civil rights to social and economic rights. As O'Byrne notes,

> If human rights violations, such as those which subordinate and degrade women, are perpetuated in the name of culture and tradition (and in many cases conveniently overlooked by the state, which may have added its support to international treaties opposing such practices), then the principles of society are violated.[1]

The role of the state, and the interplay between capitalism, political-economy and the social, cultural and ideological realms, ought to be primary areas of focus. In order for progressive changes to truly be realized, individual states must uphold women's rights.

> The year 2005 marked the anniversaries of two landmark events in the history of women and human rights: the 26th anniversary of the 1979 Convention on the Elimination of All Forms of Discrimination Against Women (CEDAW) and the 10th anniversary of the 1995 Conference on Women held in Beijing. Since then, several other international treaties and protocols have been adopted to address and remedy gender-specific issues. A commonly held view among human rights proponents and activists remains, however, that women around the world are still being treated as second-class citizens: there is a large gap between the legal documents supporting women's rights and their implementation by individual states, and despite the increasing body of international treaties dealing with human rights for women, women's rights continue to take a second place to those of men.[2]

Notes

1. Darren O'Byrne, *Human Rights: An Introduction* (Essex: Pearson Education, 2003), p. 392.
2. Reeta Tremblay, James Kelly, Michael Lipson and Jean Francois Mayer, *Understanding Human Rights: Origins, Currents and Critiques* (Toronto: Thomson Nelson, 2008), p. 155.

Anna Miroslawa Wilk, MA Student, Sociology, Wilfrid Laurier University, Age: 24

Chapter Seven

Globalization of the Sex Industry, Violence and Commodification of Human Beings

Richard Poulin

> Finally, there came a time when everything that men had considered as in-alienable became an object of exchange, of traffic and could be alienated.
> —Karl Marx[1]

> Everything is bought and sold and, nevertheless, everything cannot be bought and sold without undermining the bases of the humanity. —André Gauron[2]

FEW analyses integrated into studies of global capitalist explore the growing development of the sex industries and their impact on women and children, one of society's worst forms of exploitation. It bears highlighting, then, that the success of neo-liberalism has kept pace with the commodification of the sex industry and its increasing legitimization. Prostitution and its corollary, the trafficking in women and children for sexual exploitation, are now viewed by a number of States as a means of economic development. This "sector" of the worldwide economy is today growing at an astonishing rate. It produces important movements of populations (key elements of "women across borders", in the first sense of the term) and generates phenomenal profits world-wide. Millions of women and children are today living in red-light districts of big cities within their own countries or in those of the nearby or distant countries. Women and children in Southern countries and, more recently, in Eastern Europe are the most affected and in fact constitute the source of one of the most profitable sectors of the world economy.

The explosion of the sex industries world-wide is largely controlled by organized crime, which plays a decisive role within the sex markets. Violence—more particularly various forms of sexual violence—is central in the production of "sexual commodities".

Preliminary

Global capitaliism today involves an unprecedented "commodification" of human beings. In the last 40 years, the rapidly growing sex trade has been massively "industrialized" worldwide.[3] This process of industrialization, in both its legal and illegal forms, generates profits amounting to billions of dollars: estimated at $1000 billion US annually.[4] It has created a market—of sexual exchanges—in which millions of women and children have been converted into sexual commodities. This "sex market" has been created due to the massive deployment of prostitution (one of the effects of the presence of military forces engaged in wars and/or territorial occupations[5], particularly within various emerging economies, the unprecedented expansion of tourism worldwide[6], the global growth and normalization of pornography[7], and the internationalization of arranged marriages and mail-order brides.[8]

The sex industries, previously considered marginal in economic terms, have come to occupy strategic and central positions in the development of international capitalism. At present, the sex industries are increasingly taking the guise of ordinary sectors of various economies world-wide. This particular aspect of globalization involves an entire range of issues crucial to understanding the world we live in. These include such processes as economic exploitation, sexual oppression, capital accumulation, international migration, and unequal development and such related conditions as racism and poverty.

The first aim of this chapter, then, is to document and analyze the development of the sex industries as well as the role of organized crime within the context of the expansion of markets world-wide. The second objective is to explore processes of commodification and examine the mechanisms by which particular human beings are alienated and in effect produced as sexual commodities.

Globalization Of The Sex Industries

The industrialization of the sex trade has involved the mass production of sexual commodities structured around a regional and international division of labor. These commodities are human beings who are prostituted. Because the international market in these commodities occurs at the local and regional levels, its economic impact is significant. Prostitution and related sex industries—bars, dancing clubs, massage parlors, pornography producers, etc.—depend upon a massive underground economy that is controlled by organized crime.[9] Businesses such as international hotel chains, airline companies, and the tourist industries benefit greatly from the sex industry. In 1998, the International Labor Organization (ILO) estimated that prostitution represented between 2 and 14% of the economic activities of Thailand, Indonesia, Malaysia, and the Philippines.[10] The prostitution industry accounts for 5% of the economic activities of the Netherlands and South Korea and between 1 and 3% of the Japanese economy.[11]

The industrialization of the sex trade and its globalization make contemporary prostitution qualitatively different from prostitution as it existed within earlier periods. Clients in the economic North now have access to "exotic" and young, very young, bodies world-wide. Children now constitute 48 % of the trafficking victims.[12]

The sex industry is diversified, sophisticated, and specialized: it can create and meet all types of demands. Another factor, which confers a qualitatively different character on the current sex trade is the fact that prostitution has become a development strategy for some countries. Under obligations of debt repayment, numerous Asian, Latin American, and African States were encouraged by international organizations such as the International Monetary Fund (IMF) and the World Bank (WB) to develop their tourism and entertainment industries. In each case, the development of these sectors gave rise to the development of the sex trade.[13] In certain cases, as in Nepal, women and children were transferred to regional or international markets (notably in India and in Hong-Kong) without the country experiencing a significant expansion of local prostitution. In other cases, as in Thailand, local, regional, and international markets developed simultaneously.[14] In each case, the "commodities" in each market moved regionally and internationally from regions with weak concentrations of capital toward regions with stronger concentrations. Foreign women are generally at the bottom of the prostitution hierarchy, are socially and culturally isolated, and operate in the worst possible conditions.

Any political economic analysis of prostitution and trafficking in women and children must take into account structural discrimination, uneven development, and hierarchical relationships between imperialist and dependent countries and between men and women. In recent years under the impact of structural adjustment and economic liberalization policies in numerous countries of the Third World, as well as in the ex-USSR, Eastern Europe and the Balkans, women and children have become "new raw resources" within the framework of national and international business development. Capitalist globalization is more and more characterized by a feminization of migration.[15] Women of ethnic minorities and other relatively powerless groups are particularly exploited. So, the internal trafficking of Thai females consists mostly of 12-16 year olds from hill tribes of the North and the Northeast.[16] In Western Canada, aboriginal women and girls are over-represented in prostitution.[17]

At the world level, customers in the North abuse women of the South and of the East as well as local women from disadvantaged and oppressed groups. From an economic point of view, these "commodities" are doubly valuable because a body is both a "good" and a "service". More precisely, we have seen a commodification not only of human bodies, but also of women and children as human beings, sold successively to procurers' networks. This has led many to see this trafficking in women and children for the purposes of prostitution as a form of new slavery that they often set against "free prostitution".[18]

The Scale Of The Sex Industries

Over the last four decades, most of the countries of the Southern Hemisphere have experienced phenomenal growth of prostitution. For more than a decade, this has also been the case for the countries of the ex-USSR, Eastern Europe and the Balkans.

The International Organization for Migration (IMO) declared in 2001 that four million persons were victims of trafficking worldwide, about 90% are trafficked for purposes of sexual exploitation.[19] The IMO is particularly active in this area. It is in fact working in the frontlines in many regions of the world. It is the organization mandated to set up protected services for people who are victims of international trafficking and alert the public in the various source countries of the risks involved. The United Nations Economic and Social Council has endorsed the same estimate in a report by its Special Rapporteur, Gabriela Rodríguez Pizarro.[20] The United Nations Office on Drugs and Crime (UNODC) estimates that 33 million people in Southeast Asia were victims of human trafficking in the 1990s—or an average of 3.3 million a year for this region of the world alone.[21] Today, various governmental and international sources put the number of victims of human trafficking worldwide annually at between 700,000 and 4 million. The most cautious and conservative estimate is that of the US State Department[22], which makes it clear that it does not count domestic internal trafficking, which is assessed at millions of people each year. We know that in Thailand, for example, there is significant domestic trafficking of women and young girls from the North to the South. It is important to be critical in examining estimate numbers and to consider possible political bias.

A 2005 report by the International Labour Organization (ILO)—an organization favorable to recognizing prostitution as "sex work"—stated that over two million persons annually are victims of trafficking for "forced" prostitution. At the conclusion of this chapter I will explain why the recognition of prostitution as "sex work" is significant. For now, consider that even when (conservatively) limiting its view of trafficking to that which is defined as "forced", the ILO survey indicated that trafficking is a large-scale phenomenon that affects millions of persons each year. In 2004, UNICEF estimated that 1.2 million children annually are victims of trafficking.[23] No one disputes this estimate. If this undisputed figure is justified—as it indeed seems to be—then the global trade in human beings for the purposes of prostitution is obviously more extensive than the trafficking in children alone. As far as the various international organizations are concerned, including those that favor the regulation of prostitution—which, one could argue, legitimizes it—trafficking in children is by definition "forced" (the concept of consent cannot under any circumstances be seen to apply).

In 2006, using a database set up under the global program on human trafficking that collects information from over 500 sources, the UNODC estimates that 92% of the victims of human trafficking are destined for prostitution, and 48% of them are children.[24] According to the ILO, women and girls made up 98% of victims of trafficking for the purposes of sexual exploitation in 2005. Also note that the UNODC estimates that human trafficking affects millions of people annually. Practically no country in the contemporary world is spared: the organization lists 127 source countries and 137 destination countries.

A recent study published by the ILO estimated profits of "forced prostitution" (at the world-level) to be $33.9 billion US. This sector of the world-wide sex industry entails the exploitation and "forced prostitution" of 1.7 million women annually and functions on an international scale. Trafficking involving "forced prostitution" results in profits of $27.8 billion US annually.[25] If we accept the estimations of this study, which are rather cautious and plausible, then the annual "profit-margin" of the global sex industry (in real terms) is at least $1000 billion US. To put these numbers into perspective, consider that world-wide pharmacy profits totaled roughly $600 billion US in 2005 and the cosmetics industry $300 billion US. In real dollar terms, then, within the context of global capitalism, the sex industry must by any standard be considered extremely significant.

In 2003, estimates of the profit-level involved in the sex industries in Japan were $83 billion US each year[26]. According to an ILO study, sexual tourism in Thailand translates into profit in excess of $30 billion US dollars.[27] In Germany, according to governmental authorities, there are approx. 400,000 prostituted persons. At approx. $50 US dollars per prostituted act, that would translate into profits of $20 million US dollars everyday. In the early 1990s, German prostituted persons had 1.2 million clients each day.[28]

Millions of women, teenagers, and children live in the red-light districts of urban metropolises in the modern world. One estimate puts the number of persons prostituted in the United States at roughly one million, in India and in Thailand, at several millions. In certain countries, such as the Ukraine, Moldavia and Romania, complete groups of women are the victims of trafficking and prostitution abroad. In Korea, one fifth of women aged 16 to 29 years old were prostituted, which translates to 1.2 to 1.5 million women.[29] At the beginning of the millennium, the number of prostituted persons was estimated to be 42 million globally.[30]

Trafficking in women and children for prostitution, legal or not, "forced" or not, results in annual profits between $60 and $94.5 billion US for traffickers. The astonishing levels of income and gross profit explain the increasing involvement of organized crime in global trafficking. High returns on very low "investments" coupled with relatively weak risks have resulted in the development of informal networks of criminal "amateurs" who have become involved in sex trafficking.[31]

Be that as it may, whatever the various estimates are, it is clear that prostitution and trafficking for the purposes of prostitution are industrial-scale activities that exploit millions of women and children, each day, each month, each year. Victims are shipped from one market to another, generally from poorer regions to countries that are less poor, or on to wealthy countries. Such is the current vista – now let us consider the importance of the numbers and the meaning and significance of the real-world context.

Over- or Understatement?

When we discuss estimates, we extrapolate from known cases. There are a number of factors that explain the lack of reliable data on the prostitution trade. In many cases, they are the same factors that explain the lack of information about the prostitution industry at the national level. For some people, these figures are exaggerated, but we consider them an understatement.

1. Trafficking for purposes of sexual exploitation is an activity that is very often clandestine and illegal. It is therefore difficult to obtain data precisely because it is clandestine.

2. A part of the trafficking is legal. This is the case in countries like Canada, Switzerland, Cyprus, Slovenia, Japan, South Korea, Thailand, Luxembourg and others that annually issue tens of thousands of "artist" visas to nude dancers and those who work in the adult entertainment industry. In 2004, Swiss embassies issued 5,953 "L" visas for

nightclub dancers, the preferred mechanism of pimps and traffickers who prostitute women. That same year, Slovenia issued 650 visas, most of them to Ukrainian women. In 2004, the Japanese government issued 71,084 visas to Filipino women. A number of Caribbean countries—St Lucia, the Bahamas, Jamaica and Surinam—issue visas to "dancers" to allow them to work "entertaining" men. This is also the case in the Netherlands Antilles, where prostitution is regulated, particularly St Marten, Curacao and Bonaire. Those concerned do not appear in the official statistics on human trafficking, because the activity is legal, and therefore not a part of the trade in human beings, which, of course, is a criminal activity!

3. The victims of trafficking for purposes of prostitution are reluctant to report themselves to the authorities in transit or destination countries, or are prevented from doing so by intimidation or fear of reprisals; they are also afraid of deportation.

4. Combating the trafficking of women and children for purposes of prostitution is not a government priority; as a result, neither is research into it. Moreover, there are some governments that encourage trafficking for prostitution. One example among others is the travel guide for Ukrainian women published by the GTZ, a specialized agency of the federal Ministry of Cooperation in Germany, which offers advice to women on how to cross borders without difficulty in order to get into the prostitution industry.[32]

5. Many countries have no laws against trafficking in people. There are accordingly no national statistics.

6. Lastly, the data are a political issue. For many organizations and for governments that regulate prostitution, when the trafficking for purposes of sexual exploitation is considered "voluntary," it is not trafficking. Therefore, such organizations systematically minimize the scale of the phenomenon.

Just as the development of local prostitution is tied up with rural migration towards cities, hundreds of thousands of young women are moving internationally towards the urban areas of Japan, Western Europe, and North America. These rural migrations towards close or distant urban areas show no sign of slowing down.[33] On the contrary, everything indicates that it is continuing and that the trafficking in women and children is widespread.

The Legalization Of Prostitution And Its Impact On Trafficking In Women And Children

In past years, several countries have regulated prostitution and legalized procurement: Australia, majority of the Austrian *Länder*, Germany, Greece, Hungary, the Netherlands, New Zealand and Switzerland. In some countries, brothels are state institutions (Turkey, Indonesia). Elsewhere, the prostitution industry is often considered as a vital sector for the development of the country (such as in the Philippines and in Thailand). The impacts on trafficking in women and children are considerable.

The example of the Netherlands is a good indicator of the expansion of the sex industries: 2,500 prostitutes in 1981, 10,000 in 1985, 20,000 in 1989[34] and 30,000 in 1997.[35] The Netherlands has become a key destination for world sexual tourism. In Amsterdam, where there are 250 brothels, 80% of the prostitutes are of foreign origin and 70% lack papers, strongly suggesting that they have been the victims of trafficking.[36] Prostitutes have to rent the shop windows in which they expose themselves; this costs them about $90 US each day. Here, they receive between 10 and 24 customers during 12 to 17 hour days. In 1960, 95% of the prostitutes of the Netherlands were Dutch; in 1999 only 20%. To say that foreigners are being prostituted is to say that they are being made objects of trafficking, which obviously strongly implies the organization of trafficking. It is the procurement organization which makes possible the supply of roughly 700 sex-clubs and brothels in the Netherlands, where prostitution has been legal since October 1st, 2000. This legalization, which was supposed to help the prostitutes, is a failure; only 4% of the prostitutes registered themselves.[37]

In Austria, 90% of prostituted persons are originally from other countries. In Greece, in 2003, the number of victims of trafficking for the purposes of prostitution was estimated to be approximately 20,000 annually, compared to 2,100 annually at the start of the previous decade. In the span of ten years—from 1990 to 2000—77,500 young foreign women fell prey to traffickers. These women, who were frequently minors, and who could be "purchased" on the markets in the Balkans for $600 US, were subjected to an average of between 30 and 100 sexual contacts a day.[38] Ten years ago, the number of prostitutes of Greek origin was estimated at 3,400; this figure remains more or less the same today, but with the explosion of the prostitution industry, the number of prostitutes of foreign origin has multiplied by ten.

As the example of the Netherlands, Greece and Austria shows, the number of "legal" prostitutes, those who are natives of the particular country in question, is gradually dropping (in relative or absolute terms) and the number of prostitutes who are victims of trafficking is increasing. The regulation (legalization) of prostitution has thus not improved the fate of prostitutes, in contrast to the claims of activists who are in favor of such a policy. But legalization does represent a goldmine for the pimps, whose activity is now legal: the first year after the legalization of the brothels, the activities of the sex industry in the Netherlands increased by 25%.[39] The Dutch government takes $1.2 billion US annually in taxes, thereby becoming one of Europe's largest pimps

Promoters of the legalization of prostitution in Australia (in Queensland, New South Wales, Victoria and the Capital territory) argued that such a step would solve problems like the control by organized crime of the sex industry, the deregulated expansion of that industry and the violence to which street prostitutes are subjected. In fact, the legislation has solved none of these problems: on the contrary, it has given rise to new ones, including child prostitution, which has increased significantly since legalization. Brothels are expanding and the number of illegal brothels exceeds the number of legal ones. Although there was a belief that legalization would make control of the sex industry possible, the illegal industry is now "out of control". Police in Victoria estimate that there are 400 illegal brothels as against 100 legal ones.[40] Trafficking in women and children from other countries has increased significantly. As the legalization of prostitution resulted in a net growth of the industry, the trafficking in women and children to "supply" legal and illegal brothels have expanded. The "sex businessmen" have difficulty recruiting women locally to supply an expanding industry, and women from trafficking are more vulnerable and more profitable. The traffickers sell such women to the owners of Victoria's brothels for $15,000 US each. They are held in servitude by this debt. Weekly profits derived from trafficking in women in Australia are estimated at $1 million US.

In Germany, legislation that took effect on January 1st 2002 abolished the concept of "immoral activity". Prostitutes who are German (or married to Germans) now have status of "independent or salaried workers with a work contract" with the "bosses" of the Eros centers and brothels. Prostitution has to some extent become classified as a "profession like any other". In addition, all businesses with 15 or more employees, including brothels, are obligated to hire apprentices—and there are financial penalties if they fail to do so. What thinking person would encourage any girl to become an apprentice in an Eros center? The IOM estimates that almost half of the women who are victims of trafficking for the purpose of prostitution in Germany have entered the country legally.[41]

Some 50,000 women from the Dominican Republic are prostituted abroad, particularly in the Netherlands, where at one time they accounted for 70% of the occupants of Amsterdam's 400 prostitutes' "windows".[42] Roughly 75 to 85% of prostitutes in the German red-light districts are foreigners. Approximately 40% of Zurich's prostitutes come from the Third World. The number of brothels has doubled since the "fiscalization" of prostitution in Switzerland.

The legalization of procurement and the regulation of prostitution has led to colossal expansion of this industry and of trafficking, which is its corollary. An "abolitionist" country like France, with a population estimated at 61 million, has half as many prostituted people as a small country like the Netherlands (16 million) and 20 times fewer than Germany, with a population of around 82.4 million. In Sweden, where legislation has been passed to prosecute clients and decriminalize activities of prostitutes, it is estimated that there are a few hundred prostitutes in the country of 9 million inhabitants. In the capital, Stockholm, the number of clients has dropped by 80%. In addition, "Sweden is the only country in Western Europe not to have been submerged by the tidal wave of girls from Eastern Europe following the fall of the Berlin wall".[43] In neighboring Finland, it is estimated that 15,000 to 17,000 persons are the victims of trafficking for the purpose of prostitution each year.

Government policies are accordingly a decisive factor in the proliferation of prostitution industries and trafficking.

As this data indicates, trafficking and prostitution have increased dramatically over the past decade in those countries that can be seen to trivialize the prostitution industry. The hallmarks of this increase are various networks originating in Eastern Europe and the Balkans, Africa, Asia and Latin America. The flow of money and recycling of money derived from prostitution is significant. Transnational crime has benefited from the discrepancy between the free circulation of goods and capital and human migration. It also benefits from its ability to corrupt customs officials, policemen, judges, politicians and public servants, who are themselves sometimes integrated into the criminal activities. It finances associations advocating the recognition and legalization of the sex industries.[44] It invades "legal" industries—nightclubs, hotels, restaurants, travel and placement agencies, transport, etc.—which are useful for all kinds of illegal trade.

The women and children of South and Southeast Asia constitute the most important group within the context of victims of trafficking in women and children. Russia and independent states from the ex-USSR constitute the second most important group, followed by Latin America and the Caribbean and Africa.[45]

Every year, nearly a quarter of a million women and children of Southeast Asia (Myanmar, Yunnan province in China, Laos and Cambodia) are bought in Thailand, a transit country, for a price varying between $6,000 and $10,000 US. In Western Europe, the current price of a European woman from the former "socialist" countries is between $15,000 and $30,000 US. Upon arrival in Japan, Thai women have a debt of $25,000 US.[46] These women have to work for years to pay off "expenses" incurred by the pimps.

Sex tourists do not limit themselves to dependent countries. Hamburg's Reeperbahn and the red-light districts of Amsterdam and Rotterdam are well known destinations. In countries that have legalized prostitution, prostitution has become an important tourist draw. NGOs from these countries are actively lobbying at the European and international levels for the recognition of prostitution as simply "sex work"—an occupation like any other.

The growth of sex tourism over the past 40 years has entailed the "prostitutionalization" of the societies involved. In Thailand, with 5.1 million sex tourists a year, 450,000 local customers buy sex every day.[47] The now massive Southeast Asian sex industry began with the Vietnam War. The U.S. government stationed servicemen not only in Vietnam, but also in Thailand and the Philippines, these last two countries serving as rear bases in the fight against the Vietminh. The resulting increase in local prostitution established the infrastructure necessary for the development of sex tourism. More importantly the military presence also provided opportunities for contact with foreigners and the social construction, through pornography, of an exotic sexual image of young Southeast Asian women. Government policies favorable to sex tourism contributed to the explosion of this industry. A decade ago there were 18,000 registered prostitutes in the service of the 43,000 US servicemen stationed in South Korea.[48] Between 1937 and 1945 the Japanese army of occupation exploited 200,000 women, mostly Korean, imprisoned in "comfort stations".[49] After the Japanese defeat, the Association for the Creation of Special Recreational Facilities, financed indirectly by the U.S. government, opened the first comfort station for U.S. soldiers. At its height this association exploited 70,000 Japanese prostitutes.[50] Today these numbers have swelled and include women from the Philippines, Russia, and other countries in sex industries around U.S. bases.[51]

The Globalization Of Procurement

According to the United Nations Development Program (UNDP), the Gross World Product reaches $1,200 billion dollars a year and constitutes 15% of world trade.[52] Migration, trafficking, prostitution, laundering of "dirty" money, corruption and drugs —crime has become a particularly interesting means for the accumulation of capital; within the context of globalization, it constitutes one of the global economy's most profitable activities, not least, because costs and risks are so nominal.[53] For example, Armenian prostitutes in the United Arab Emirates (UAE), about 500 for 20 procurers, have between 10 and 30 clients each day. They receive between $30 and $35 US per client. The procurer bought them for varying sums between $300 and $500 US. In one day or less, "he" has paid off "his" expenses. Moreover, the prostitute is in debt with him. Procurers seize passports on arrival. The majority of the women who are the objects of trade ignore the nature of the promised job. It is not uncommon to see 14 years old prostitutes. Those that rebel may be subjected to violence and rape. These brutal practices continue until their arrest by UAE authorities (due to the absence of a long stay visa). After 6 to 9 months of detention, they may be deported without a cent in their pockets.[54] The transition to a capitalist system in Armenia created an extreme social polarization, a fertile compost for the development of sex industries. The accelerated growth of nightclubs, bars of dancers, saunas, hotels, casinos—in brief, the entertainment industries—also contributed to the escalation of trade in women and girls in Armenia.

Structural adjustment has undermined mechanisms of social welfare and intensified migratory pressure. Criminal organizations have taken advantage of this. Poverty and other social disparities have resulted. Globalization has led to the growth and reproduction of various criminal activities that exploit the social and economic disintegration of entire regions. Caldwell, Galster, Kanics and Steinzor highlight this in their exploration of various Russian criminal groups involved in the trafficking of women.[55] Similarly, Bruinsma and Meershoek have studied the role of organized crime in the Netherlands in the trafficking of women from Eastern Europe towards the Netherlands.[56] Phongpaichit considers the organization of the "sex market" in Thailand in terms of criminal activities as extensive in Thailand as in Japan.[57] Savona, Adamoli and Zoffi show how Yakuzas dominate the procurement system in Japan, and the trafficking in women between Thailand and Japan.[58] The trafficking in women and children is closely linked to the economy and finance of the criminal world. Criminal organizations, which reign over the trafficking in women and children for the benefit of the procurer system that they control, use terror and dispute the state monopoly of violence. Consequently, the globalization of prostitution has been possible as a result of the globalization of procuring.[59]

Industrialization entails the production of commodities, and not only their sale in the market. Procuring reigns over prostitution, even in those countries where prostitution has been legalized. As commodities, the prostitutes are under the ownership of the procurer and the client.

"The transformation of human activity into commodities is constitutive [a characteristic] of modern societies."[60] It is one of the germane characteristics of the capitalist mode of production. Commodities that are products and means for making money are subject to the capitalist industrial processes; in this context, production is without borders.[61] Within the current neo-liberal order, nothing seems able to escape the process of commodification and within it the "monetarization of social relations".[62] One of the effects of this "monetarization" is—to take up the expression used by the political economist Karl Polanyi—the embedding of the market by the "disembeddedness" of the social. This refers to a deepening of commodification as a consequence of the systematic destruction of previous social relations in favor of new ones that legitimize private appropriation which is intrinsic to them.[63] The extension of the monetary field, "transforms into commodities that which has been not been produced as commodities".[64] This process of commodification takes place with considerable tension and violence. It turns out to be even truer in the metamorphosis of the human beings into commodities. The private appropriation of bodies, their transmutation into goods and their consumption, requires, downstream as upstream, the use of force. Constraint is essential for the commodification of human beings and their bodies. It is not without reason that "commodification of life is exploited by the mafias".[65]

From the point of view of their "owners", women and children, as commodities, have a double advantage: these human beings are at the same moment goods and services. More exactly, one of the features of the current globalization is not only the commodification of the body as sex, but also the commodification of women and children themselves: in a sense, a double commodification. In the sphere of exchange, there is not only a purchase or a kidnapping of women and children and their sale to a procurer, but also the alienation of persons: they are bought and/or sold on the market. The cost of deals depends on the age, on the prevailing customs (virgin or not), on the beauty of the girls and their origin. The second sphere, absolutely different, although conditioned by the first, is their consumption by the clients.

"The commodity [is] the elementary form of bourgeois wealth". Money "which in itself" is only a "converted form of the commodity"[66] becomes capital, in the procurer system, only when women and children are transformed into commodities, put into circulation and exploited as such. It implies that business is conquering new territory. Mass tourism and leisure industries are elements of globalization that have contributed to the development of sex markets. Criminal organizations take advantage of structural dislocations created by neo-liberal policies, economic crises or armed conflicts to establish routes and to recruit or remove persons for the benefit of the transnational sex industry. The volume of the demand is determined, among others things, by the size of the income or the capacity of payment of the clients and by the price for goods. Thus the world proliferation of prostitution has had a major impact on consumption, which has taken a mass character.

Sex markets, which are at the same time legal and illegal—both aspects being strictly connected and mutually feeding each other—*proceed in an industrial logic, a logic of mass production.* What is required is that analysis of the problem move beyond a narrow analysis of its commercial aspects. In fact, commodification does not limit itself to business activity. More exactly, the sex business (as an capitalist industry) does not only put women and children on the market, it also *makes or produces* these "commodities".

The Making Of Prostitution Commodities

It is plain that commodities cannot go to market and make exchanges of their own account. We must, therefore, have recourse to their guardians, who are also their owners. Commodities are things, and therefore without power of resistance against man. If they are wanting in docility he can use force; in other words, he can take possession of them.[67]

Prostitutes are dehumanized and reified; it is the outcome of their commodification. As a consequence, they stop belonging to themselves. They "belong" to the owner of the goods; that is, to the procurer. A very large majority of the victims of the trafficking in women are violently forced to prostitute themselves when they reach their country of destination.[68] "Once established, the power of the procurer relies on violence, sometimes on terror." [69] There are "submission camps" in the Balkans where young women are raped and made ready for prostitution.[70]

The shop windows of the Netherlands and Belgium like the rooms of the German Eros centers act as cages. Eros centers are not strictly speaking brothels, but sex supermarkets. The prostitute pays for a room at a full price—taxes included—while remaining the livestock of a procurer: "Without him registration is impossible", underlines Coquart and Huet.[71] Dirty money becomes investment, establishments and their owners (surveillance of the girls and health control) are henceforth official, and prostitution is recognized as a profession. It is now possible to recycle profits and launder dirty money without leaving the prostitution industry. In the Netherlands and Germany, prostitutes are now considered "sex professionals"; their procurers are transformed into "managers", brothel owners into "legitimate entrepreneurs" and clients into "consumers".[72]

The brothel can be called Eros center; corporation or not, it is nevertheless a brothel—in spite of its pathetic modernity—and the procurer is always a procurer. The latter gets 75 to 90% of the money pocketed by "his protégés".[73] One estimate in France, where a prostitute earns between 460 and 762 euros ($548 and $908 US), suggests that a procurer who controls a network of a dozen or so women can make up to 9,100 euros ($10,843 US) a day.[74] According to Interpol, during a year, a prostitute provides a procurer established in Europe with approximately 110,000 euros ($131,065 US) in profit.[75] In the year 2000, Russian prostitutes in Germany earned about 8,000 euros ($9,532 US) monthly, about 7,500 ($8,936 US) of which was taken by the procurer.[76] Many prostitutes in brothels rarely see the color of the money that they earn. And when they do, as they are not often permitted to leave the brothel, they must use the money to pay for the necessities of their "trade" provided at exorbitant prices by the brothel owners if not to pay fines for infractions to brothel rules. In one of the legal brothels of Nevada in the United States, a former prostitute reveals: "I was introduced for the first time into the brothels of Nevada through my ex-mackerel. You can't 'work' in a legal brothel without mackerel."[77] Some of the legal brothels in Nevada and New Mexico are fenced by surrounding walls, dogs, and keepers, in this way connoting the detention and slavery signified by the world of prostitution. In Hamburg, access to certain reserved districts is blocked by zigzag passages. In Istanbul, entry into brothel districts is kept under surveillance. In Calcutta, prostitutes offer themselves behind bars.[78] In Thailand, children are released from cages to quench sex tourists.

Industrialization not only refers to the functioning of markets but also to the manufacture of goods. Procuring reigns over prostitution, even in countries where prostitution has been legalized. As goods, the prostitutes are not free: they are under the ownership of the procurer and the customer. Various studies attest this: between 85 and 90% of prostitutes in the West are subjected to a procurer.[79]

Kidnapping, rape, and violence continue to act as midwives of this industry. They are fundamental not only for the development of markets, but also for the "manufacturing" of the "commodities", as they contribute to making them "functional" for an industry that requires a constant supply of bodies. A study of street prostitutes in England reported that 87% of the prostitutes had been victims of violence during the previous twelve months; 43% of them had suffered grave physical consequences as a result of abuse.[80] An American study in Minneapolis revealed that 78% of the prostitutes had been victims of rape at the hands of their procurers and customers, on average 49 times a year; 49% had been forcibly removed and transported from one State to another, and 27% had been mutilated.[81] Hunter estimates that the prostitutes of Portland, Oregon, were violated on average once a week.[82] Weisberg maintains that most of the young prostitutes were deceived or beaten by their procurers and their customers.[83] Some 85 % of the women interviewed by Parriott were violated.[84] The first concern of street prostitutes in Glasgow, in the United Kingdom, is client violence.[85] These women consider physical abuse as an integral and everyday aspect of prostitution. According to a study by Miller and Schwartz, 94% of the street prostitutes interviewed had experienced some type of sexual assault and 75% of them had been violated by one or by several clients.[86] A study in Chicago documents that more then 21% of the female escorts and nude dancers had been raped more than ten times.[87] According to Phillis Chester, 75% of female escorts have attempted to commit suicide.[88] Prostituted women make up 15% of suicides reported by American hospitals.[89] Women and girls involved in prostitution in Canada experience a mortality rate 40 times higher than the national average.[90]

The women and children who are the object of trafficking for sexual exploitation as well as the great majority of the prostitutes are supplied "keys in hand" to the market. "In twenty days, one can break any woman and transform her into a prostitute" claims a Bulgarian in charge of a reintegration house.[91] Their appropriation by traffickers and procurers, their metamorphosis into commodities—human beings transformed into venal things—their depersonalization and then their consumption requires the rape of their humanity. So that exchange is realized, so that commodities are sold and bought for money—which is the purpose of all these operations—*the submission of human beings is necessary*. This is what is required of commodities according to the "rules of the market". This submission is achieved through a ring of organizations which form the links in a chain of deals that assures their progress. This chain would be broken where it not for the complicity found at all levels of society.

Many researchers refuse to accept a dichotomy between the voluntary and forced, because they want to understand the social and psychological conditions of entrance into prostitution. They maintain that entrance into prostitution is the consequence of multiple factors (economic, personal, social and psychological). The manufacture of these commodities has a history, one that takes place upstream. It is the weight of this history, which allows a person to sell sex. A number of findings support this: prostitutes tend to have traumatic pasts and histories of chronic sexual abuse.[92] Research has shown that between 75 and 80% of prostitutes have been sexually abused during their childhood.[93] Judith Trinquart reports that between 80 and 95% of the prostitutes' native of France have been sexually abused during their childhood.[94] In Brazil, Gilberto Dimestein interviewed 53 girls and teenagers, 95% of which came from dysfunctional families.[95] This violence is why the teenagers run away and fall prey to the recruiters who stalk them in the train and bus stations of big cities.[96] Another study reveals that 90% of the prostitutes have been physically assaulted in their childhood; 74% were also sexually betrayed in their families and 50% by a stranger.[97] According to the Council for prostitution Alternative of Portland, of 123 survivors of prostitution interviewed, 85% had suffered from incest, 90% from physical abuse and 98% from emotional abuse.[98] It is the same figures in Canada.[99] According to Widom and Ames, a child surviving sexual abuse has a higher risk of being arrested as an adult for prostitution than a survivor of physical abuse.[100] Survivors of childhood sexual traumas are at risk of living with important dysfunctions: they often develop auto-destructive ideas and behaviors, contempt for themselves, a sense of shame, food disorders, drug abuse.[101] The rate of suicides and attempted suicide among prostitutes in the United States and France is among the highest in these societies.[102]

The average age of entry into prostitution in the United States and in Canada is 14 years old.[103] Given such conditions, it is hard to understand how some researchers can continue to treat "sex work" predominantly and simply as a freely chosen occupation or activity. To become a "commodity", regardless of whether one has a low or high class market position, the prostitute must be deprived of her humanity, be transformed into a thing, into an sexual object. One can then place her in shop windows, on pavements, in dirty brothels, in sex supermarkets, so clients can inspect the goods before they buy them. The prostitution machine does not work for the profit of the prostitutes, but for the profit of their owners: procurers and clients.

The Liberalization of the Sex Industry

In 1995 during the United Nation's Fourth World Women's Congress in Beijing the principle of "forced" prostitution was adopted. This was the first time the term "forced prostitution" was used in a UN document. This created a special category of prostitution that could be opposed without opposing the sex industry as such. Constraint/force was identified as the problem rather than the sex trade itself. The way was opened for the normalization and legalization of the industry.

In 1997 at the Hague Ministerial Conference on International Law, when the European ministers attempted to draw up guidelines harmonizing the European Union's fight against trafficking, their definition of trafficked women included only those women who were being trafficked against their will.

In 1998, the International Labor Organization (ILO) called for the economic recognition of the sex industry on the grounds that prostitutes would then benefit from workers' rights and protection and improved working conditions that it presumed would follow.[104] In June 1999, the ILO adopted an agreement on unbearable working conditions for children, the *Convention Concerning the Prohibition and Immediate Action for the Elimination of the Worst Forms of Child Labor*.[105] The agreement provides a long list of the work children do, including prostitution. This is the first time in an international text that sex work is presented as simply a job. Countries, such a France, although ratifying this Convention, have underlined that their ratification in no way recognizes prostitution as work. The United Nations' *Special Reporter on Violence against Women* was at pains in her report to the UN Human Rights Committee in April 2000 in Geneva, to distinguish trafficked women from "clandestine migrant sex professionals".[106]

All these statements tend to undermine the struggle against the growing sex industry and the system of prostitution which is at its heart, for they shift opposition from the system itself, to the use of force/constraint within the system. They aim to protect only women who have not agreed to their exploitation and *can prove this,* placing the burden of proof on already vulnerable women. In attempting to regulate this fast growing area of the economy these approaches tend to regularize it. For instance, when the European Union declares its opposition to the "illegal trafficking in persons", it implies that there is a "legal" one. Thus, as Marie-Victoire Louis has pointed out, such initiatives transform the struggle against the commodification of women and girls into its legitimization.[107]

In addition, neo-liberalism fosters a generalized "security" policy. Trafficking in persons has been approached within a framework that views it as a transnational crime, that is, as a criminal problem with a criminal law answer. It has proceeded with the active collaboration of various police and judicial authorities. Governments envisage trafficking within the context of the globalization of organized crime, the destabilization of the world economy and the threat for the national security. Respect for the victims and for their human rights is underlined, but put in background, while the necessities of repression are the highlighted priorities.

Conclusion

Over 40 years, we have seen an extremely profitable "sexualization" of many societies based on social domination. We have witnessed the industrialization of prostitution, of the trafficking in women and children, of pornography, and of sexual tourism. This once marginal market is an increasingly central aspect of current capitalist globalization. Sex multinationals have become independent economic forces (quoted on the stock exchange.[108] Sexual exploitation is more and more considered to be an entertainment industry[109], and prostitution a legitimate job.[110]

Various sex industries are prosperous; they are organized and administered by procurers' networks with the complicity of established financial and political powers. The nature of the prostitution system is exactly to have neither border, nor limit.[111] There is no prostitution without market, without commodification of human beings. In 85-90% of the cases of local prostitution in Western countries, the prostitute is a "commodity" that the procurer makes by means of force and\or skill. Procurers deploy physical, psychological and sexual constraints so that prostitutes are "functional". So that the clients can buy her day after day, and, in turn, they then become, for a moment, the owners of that sexual commodity. As with any market, commodities are made and commercialized according to the capacities of payment of the clients: from street prostitution to the luxury call girls, all dimensions of the market are covered.

The increasing size and centrality of the global sex industry helps explain why so many groups and agencies are adopting normalizing regulatory approaches in their attempts to address its harms and why beginning earlier this decade Germany and the Netherlands legalized prostitution. However, this strategy is deeply flawed. The rapidly expanding international sex market exploits above all women and children, especially members of marginal and minority groups in the Third World and in the former Communist countries. This "leisure industry" is based on the systematic violation of human rights, for it requires a market in commodified human beings and the complicity of pimps and clients who are prepared to buy and sell women and children. Indubitably, current industrialization destroys women and children, organizes them so that their sexual returns max out.

The commodification at the heart of the growing sex industry is only one among many varied instances of the commodification of all of life, which is a defining characteristic of current neo-liberalism. Patents are now issued on genetic life forms (including human genomes) and all forms of traditional knowledge.[112] Water is being privatized.[113] In the name of environmental protection and sustainable development, markets are being created for trade in CO_2 and emissions credits (the right to pollute).[114] The apparent "normalcy" of trade in human beings in this period has led to misguided regulatory approaches. Yet this very "normalcy" is what makes refusal of the sex industry as such, so essential. In this context, resisting or struggling against the commodification of women and children in the sex industry becomes a central element in the struggle against neo-liberal globalization. Anything less is complicity.

Notes

1. Marx, Karl, *Poverty of Philosophy*, [On line], Marxists.org Internet Archive, http://www.marxists.org/archive/marx/works/1847/poverty-philosophy/index.htm (1847).

2. Gauron, André, *L'empire de l'argent* (Paris: Desclée de Brouwer, 2002), 30.

3. Jeffreys, Sheila, "Globalizing sexual exploitation: Sex tourism and the traffic in women," *Leisure Studies*, 18, n° 3 (1999), 179-186.

4. Poulin, Richard, *Enfances dévastées. L'enfer de la prostitution* (Ottawa: L'Interligne, 2007), 43.

5. Strudevant, S. P. and B. Stolzfus (eds), *Let the Good Times Roll. Prostitution and the U.S. Military in Asia* (New York: The New Press, 1992) ; Poulin, Richard, "Le système de la prostitution militaire: Corée, Thaïlande et Philippines." *Bulletin d'histoire politique*, 15, n°1 (2006), 81-92.

6. Truong, T. D, Sex, *Money and Morality: Prostitution and Tourism in Southeast Asia*, (London: Zed Books, 1990).

7. Poulin, Richard, *La violence pornographique, industrie du fantasme et réalités* (Yens-sur-Morges: Cabédita, 2000).

8. Hughes, Donna M., "Rôle des agences matrimoniales dans la traite des femmes." *L'impact de l'utilisation des nouvelles technologies de communication et d'information sur la traite des êtres humains aux fins d'exploitation sexuelle* (Bruxelles: Conseil de l'Europe, 2001), 4-16.

9. Budapest Group, *The Relationship Between Organized Crime and Trafficking in Aliens* (Austria: IOM Policy Development, 1999).

10. Lim, L. L., *The Sex Sector. The Economic and Social Bases of Prostitution in Southeast Asia* (Geneva: ILO, 1998).

11. Poulin, Richard (dir.), *Prostitution, la mondialisation incarnée, Alternatives Sud*, 12, n° 3 (2005).

12. Kangaspunta, Kristiina, "Mapping the inhuman trade : preliminary finding of the data base on trafficking in human beings," *Forum on Crime and Society*, 3, n° 1-2 (2003), 81-103.

13. Hechler, David, *Child Sex Tourism*, [On line], New York: Don't buy Thai. ftp://membersaol.com/hechler/tourism.html (1995).

14. Barry, Kathleen, *The Prostitution of Sexuality* (New York: New York University Press, 1995).

15. Santos, Aida F., *Globalization, Human Rights and Sexual Exploitation*, [On line], University of Rhode Island, http:www.uri.edu/artsci/wms/hugues/mhvglo.htm (1999).

16. Barry, *The Prostitution of Sexuality*, 139.

17. Farley, M. and J. Lynne, "Prostitution in Vancouver: Pimping women and the colonization of First Nations women," in Stark, Christine and Rebecca Whisnant (eds.), *Not for Sale. Feminists Resisting Prostitution and Pornography* (North Melbourne, Spinifex, 2004), 106-130.

18. Vaz Cabral, Georgina, *La traite des êtres humains. Réalités de l'esclavage contemporain.* (Paris: La Découverte, 2006).

19. Farr, Katheryn, *Sex Trafficking. The Global Market in Women and Children* (New York: Worth Publishers, 2004).

20. Raymond, Janice, *Guide du nouveau protocole sur la traite des Nations Unies. Protocole additionnel à la convention contre la criminalite transnationale organisée, visant a prévenir, réprimer et punir la traite des personnes, en particulier des femmes et des enfants*, [On line], http://www.ldh-france.org/media/groupes/Guide%20du%20Nouveau%20Protocole%20des%20NU%20sur%20la%20traite%20des%20personnes.rtf (2001).

21. Kangaspunta, "Mapping the inhuman trade," 82.

22. U.S. State Department, *Trafficking in Persons Report* (Washington: Office to Monitor and Combat Trafficking in Persons, 2005).

23. Poulin, *Enfances dévastées*, 125.

24. Kangaspunta, "Mapping the inhuman trade," 83-87.

25. Belser, Patrick, *Forced Labour and Human Trafficking: Estimating the Profits* (Geneva: ILO, 2005).

26. Poulin, *Enfances dévastées*, 45.

27. Lim, *The Sex Sector.*

28. Ackermann L. and C. Filter, *Die Frau nach Katalog* (Freiburg: Herder Verlag, 1994).

29. Poulin, "Le système de la prostitution militaire," 88.

30. Healy, Grainne, *Presentation by Grainne Healy Chair of EWL's Observatory on Violence against Women*, [On line], EWL Seminar on Trafficking and Prostitution — side event at CSW, March 17, http://www.womenlobby.org/Document.asp?DocID=566&tod=4931 (2003).

31. Petit, Juan Miguel, *Report of the Special Rapporteur on the Sale of Children, Child Prostitution and Child Pornography* (Commission on Human Rights, Rights of the Child: E/CN.4/2006/67, 2006).

32. Poulin, *Enfances dévastées*, 27.

33. Santos, Aida F., *Globalization, Human Rights and Sexual Exploitation*, [On line], University of Rhode Island, http:www.uri.edu/artsci/wms/hugues/mhvglo.htm (1999); Chaleil, Max, *Prostitution. Le désir mystifié* (Paris: Parangon, 2002); Poulin, Richard, *La mondialisation des industries du sexe* (Ottawa: L'Interligne, 2004).

34. Coquart Élisabeth and Philippe Huet, *Le livre noir de la prostitution* (Paris: Albin Michel, 2000).

35. Poulin, *La mondialisation des industries du sexe.*

36. Louis, Marie-Victoire, "Le corps humain mis sur le marché," *Le Monde diplomatique.* (March 1997), 8.

37. Chaleil, *Prostitution*, 49.

38. Mitralias, Sonia, *La traite des femmes en Grèce, un véritable enjeu de civilisation*, [On line], Paris: Les Pénélopes, http://www.penelopes.org/xarticle.php3?id_article=4460 (2003).

39. Daley, Suzanne. 2001, "New rights for Dutch prostitutes, but no gain," *New York Times* (August 12, 2001), A1 & A4.

40. Jeffreys, Sheila, "Prostitution culture. Legalised brothel prostitution in Victoria, Australia," *Seminar on the Effects of Legalisation of Prostitution Activities* (Stockholm, 5-6 November, 2002), 22-27.

41. IOM, *Trafficking In Persons: IOM Strategy And Activities* (MC/INF/270, Eighty-sixth Session, 11 November 2003).

42. Guéricolas, Pascale, "Géographie de l'inacceptable," *Gazette des femmes*, 22, n° 1 (May-June 2000), 31.

43. Gyldén, Axel, "Le modèle suédois," *L'Express* (April 3, 2003), 10

44. Marcovich, Malka, "La traite des femmes dans le monde," in Ockrent, Christine (dir.), *Le livre noir de la condition des femmes* (Paris: XO, 2006), 449-490.

45. UUSC, *The Modern International Slave Trade* (Cambridge, MA: UUSC, 2001).

46. CATW (Coalition Against Trafficking in Women), *Factbook on Global Sexual Exploitation*, [On line], Manila: CATW, http://catwinternational.Org/fb/ (2001).

47. Barry, *The Prostitution of Sexuality*, 60.

48. *Ibid*, 139.

49. Latsetter, Jennifer, *American Military-Base Prostitution*, [On line], http://www.wm.edu/SO/monitor/spring2000/paper6.htm (2000).

50. Barry, *The Prostituion of Sexuality*, 129.

51. Moon K, *Sex Among Allies: Military Prostitution in U.S.-Korea Relations* (New York: Columbia University Press, 1997).

52. Passet, René and Jean Liberman, *Mondialisation financière et terrorisme* (Montreal: Écosociété, 2002), 60.

53. Struensee, Vanessa von, *Globalized, Wired, Sex Trafficking In Women And Children* [On line], Murdoch University Electronic Journal of Law, 7, n° 2, http://www.murdoch.edu.au/elaw/issues/v7n2/struensee72nf.html (June 2000).

54. Atomyan, Marat, *Issues of Prostitution and Trafficking in Women in Armenia*, [On line], The Millenium Generation, http://www.undp.am/archive/gender/Studies/MGGS/3.htm (2000).

55. Caldwell, G., S. Galster, J. Kanics and N. Steinzor, "Capitalizing on transition economies: the role of the marxist mafiya in trafficking in women for forced prostitution," *Transnational Organised Crime*, 3, n°4 (1997), 42-73.

56. Bruinsma, G. and G. Meershoek, "Organised Crime and Trafficking in Women from Eastern Europe in the Netherlands," *Transnational Organised Crime*, 3, n° 4 (1997), 105-118.

57. Phongpaichit, P., "Trafficking in people in Thailand," *Transnational Organised Crime*, 3, n° 4 (1997), 14-41.

58. Savona E. U., S. Adamoli and P. Zoffi, *Organised Crime across the Borders* (Helsinki: HEUNI, 1995).

59. Coquart and Huet, *Le livre noir de la prostitution*; Geadah, Yolande, *La prostitution, un métier comme un autre?* (Montreal: VLB, 2003).

60. Gauron, *L'empire de l'argent*, 30.

61. Ricardo, David, *Principes de l'économie politique et de l'impôt* (Paris: Flammarion, 1977), 26.

62. Perret, Bernard, *Les nouvelles frontières de l'argent* (Paris: Seuil, 1999), 35.

63. Polanyi, Karl, *La grande transformation* (Paris: Gallimard, 1983).

64. Gauron, *L'empire de l'argent*, 34.

65. Passet and Liberman, *Mondialisation financière et terrorisme*, 38.

66. Marx, Karl, *The Process of Production of Capital. Draft Chapter 6 of Capital Results of the Direct Production Process*, [On line], Marxists.org Internet Archive, http://www.marxists.org/archive/marx/works/1864/economic/ch01.htm (1864).

67. Marx, Karl, *Capital, volume one. The Process of Production of Capital*, [On line], Marxists.org Internet Archive, http://www.marxists.org/archive/marx/works/1867-c1/index.htm (1867).

68. Dusch, Sabine, *Le trafic d'êtres humains* (Paris: Presses Universitaires de France, 2002), 110.

69. Chaleil, *Prostitution. Le désir mystifié*, 113.

70. Loncle, François, "Prostitution sans frontières. L'Europe de l'Ouest, proxénète des femmes de l'Est," *Le Monde diplomatique* (November, 2001), 8-9.

71. Coquart and Huet, *Le livre noir de la prostitution*, 201.

72. *Ibid*, 213.

73. *Ibid*, 187.

74. Dusch, *Le trafic d'êtres humains*, 151.

75. *Ibid*, 97.

76. *Ibid*, 109.

77. Ryan, Jayme, *Dans un bordel du Nevada*, [On line], Paris: Pénélopes, http://www.penelopes.org/xarticle.php3?id_article=2298 (2002).

78. Chaleil, *Prostitution. Le désir mystifié*, 265.

79. *Ibid*; Giobbe, E., Harrigan, M., Ryan, J. and Gamache, D., *Prostitution: A Matter of Violence against Women* (Minneapolis, MN: Whisper, 1990); Hunter, S. K, "Prostitution is cruelty and abuse to women and children," *Michigan Journal of Gender and Law*, n° 1 (1994), 1-14; Silbert, M. and A. M. Pines, "Entrance in to Prostitution," *Youth and Society*, 13, n° 4 (1982), 471-500; Weisberg, Kelly, *Children of the Night. A Study of Adolescent Prostitution* (Lexington, MA: Lexington Books, 1995).

80. Miller, J., "Gender and power on the streets: Street prostitution in the era of crack cocaine," *Journal of Contemporary Ethnography*, 23, n° 4 (1995), 427-452

81. Raymond, Janice, *Health Effects of Prostitution*, [On line], Kingston: University of Rhode Island, http:www.uri.edu/artsci/wms/Hugues/mhvhealth.htm (1999).

82. Hunter, S. K., "Prostitution is cruelty and abuse to women and children," *Michigan Journal of Gender and Law*, n° 1 (1994), 1-14.

83. Weisberg, *Children of the Night*.

84. Quoted by Farley, M. and V. Kelley, "Prostitution: a critical review of the medical and social sciences littérature," *Women & Criminal Justice*, 11, n° 4 (2000), 29-64.

85. Green, S.T., Goldberg, D.J., Christie, P.R., Frischer, M.,Thomson, A., Carr, S.V. and Taylor, A, "Female streetworker-prostitutes in Glasgow: A descriptive study of their lifestyle," *AIDS Care*, 5, n° 3 (1993), 321-335.

86. Miller, J, and M. D. Schwartz, "Rape myths against street prostitutes." *Deviant Behavior*, 16, n° 1 (1995), 1-23.

87. Boulet, Elsa, *Rapport sur la prostitution à Chicago*, [On line], Paris: Pénélopes http://www. penelopes.org/ xarticle.php3?id_article=2296 (2002).

88. Chester Phillis, *Partiarchy: Notes of an Expert Witness* (Monroe: Common Courage Press, 1994).

89. Farley, Melissa, *Prostitution Facts*, [On line], Washington: Aid for Teens, http//:www.aidforteens. com/prostitutionfacts.cfm?UserID=Guest&RefID= Guest (2003).

90. Baldwin, Margaret A., "Split at the Root: Prostitution and feminist discourses of law reform," *Yale Journal of Law and Feminism*, n° 5 (1992), 58.

91. Chaleil, *Prostitution, le désir mystifié*, 498.

92. Burgess, A., C. Hartman and A. McCormack, "Abused to abuser: Antecedents of socially deviant behaviors," *American Journal of Orthopsychiatry,* n° 144 (1987) 1431-1436; Giobbe, E., Harrigan, M., Ryan, J. and Gamache, D., *Prostitution: A Matter of Violence against Women*; James, J. et J. Meyerding, "Early sexual experience and prostitution." *American Journal of Psychiatry*, n°134 (1977), 1382-1385; Silbert M. and A. M. Pines, "Occupational Hazards of Street Prostitutes," *Criminal Justice Behaviour,* n° 195 (1981), 395; Silbert, M. and A. M. Pines, "Entrance in to Prostitution"; Silbert, M. and A. M. Pines, "Early sexual exploitation as an influence in prostitution," *Social Work*, n° 8 (1983), 285-289; Simons, R. L. et L. B. Whitbeck, "Sexual abuse as a precursor to prostitution and victimization among adolescent and adult homeless women." *Journal of Family Issues*, 12, n° 3 (1991), 361-379; Widom, C. S. and J. B. Kuhns, "Childhood victimization and subsequent risk for promiscuity, prostitution, and teenage pregnancy: a prospective study," *American Journal of Public Health*, 86, n°11 (1996), 1607-1612.

93. Satterfield, S. B., "Clinical Aspects of Juvenile Prostitution," *Medical Aspects of Human Sexuality,* 15, n° 9 (1981), 126; Poulin, *Enfances dévastées*, 223-225.

94. Trinquart, Judith, *La décorporalisation dans la pratique prostitutionnelle: un obstacle majeur à l'accès aux soins* (Paris: Thèse de doctorat d'État de médecine générale, 2002).

95. Dimenstein, Gilberto, *Les petites filles de la nuit. Prostitution et esclavage au Brésil* (Paris: Fayard, 1993).

96. Poulin, *Enfances dévastées*, 70.

97. Giobbe, E., Harrigan, M., Ryan, J. and Gamache, D., *Prostitution: A Matter of Violence against Women.*

98. Hunter, "Prostitution is cruelty and abuse to women and children."

99. Dufour, Rose, *Je vous salue… Le point zéro de la prostitution* (Sainte-Foy: Multimondes, 2005); Farley and Lynne, "Prostitution in Vancouver: Pimping women and the colonization of First Nations women."

100. Widom, C. S. and M. A. Ames, "Criminal consequences of childhood sexual victimization," *Child Abuse and Neglect*, 18, n° 4 (1994), 303-318.

101. Herman, J.L., *Trauma and Recovery* (New York: Basic Books, 1992).

102. Chaleil, *Prostitution, le désir mystifié*, 105.

103. Silbert, M. and A. M. Pines, "Entrance in to Prostitution"; Giobbe, Evelina, "Juvenile prostitution: Process of recruitment," *Child Trauma I: Issues and Research* (New York: Garaland Publishing, 1992); Poulin, *Enfances dévastées*.

104. Lim, *The Sex Sector*.

105. ILO, *Convention Concerning the Prohibition and Immediate Action for the Elimination of the Worst Forms of Child Labour*, (ILO, no 182, 38 I.L.M. 1207, 1999), entered into force Nov. 19, 2000.

106. Quoted by Raymond, *Guide du nouveau protocole sur la traite des Nations Unies*.

107. Louis, Marie-Victoire, "Pour construire l'abolitionnisme du XXIesiècle," *Cahiers marxistes*, n° 21 (2000), 131.

108. Poulin, *La mondialisation des industries du sexe*.

109. Oppermann M. (ed), *Sex Tourism and Prostitution: Aspects of Leisure, Recreation, and Work* (New York: Cognizant Communication Corporation, 1998).

110. Kempadoo K. and J. Doezema, *Global Sex Workers* (New York: Routledge, 1998).

111. Louis, Marie-Victoire, "Abolir la prostitution…" *L'Humanité* (20 février 2003).

112. Shiva, V., *Biopiracy: The Plunder of Nature and Knowledge* (Boston: South End Press, 1997); *Stolen Harvest: The Hijacking of the Global Food Supply* (Cambridge, MA: South End Press, 2000).

113. Barlow, Maud, *Blue Gold: The Battle Against the Corporate Theft of the World's Water* (Toronto: Stoddart, 2002).

114. Kyoto Protocol, *United Nations Framework Convention on Climate Change*, [On line], http://unfccc.int/resource/convkp/kpeng.html.

Chapter Eight

Custom Against Women[1]

Michael Parenti

IF WE uncritically immerse ourselves in the cultural context of any society, seeing it only as it sees itself, then we are embracing the self-serving illusions it has of itself. Perceiving a society "purely on its own terms" usually means seeing it through the eyes of dominant groups that exercise a preponderant influence in shaping its beliefs and practices.

Furthermore, the dominant culture frequently rests on standards that are *not* shared by everyone within the society itself. So we come upon a key question: whose culture is it anyway? Too often what passes for the established culture of a society is the exclusive preserve of the privileged, a weapon used against more vulnerable elements.

This is seen no more clearly than in the wrongdoing perpetrated against women. A United Nations report found that prejudice and violence against women "remain firmly rooted in cultures around the world."

In many countries, including the United States, women endure discrimination in wages, occupational training, and job promotion. According to a *New York Times* report (18/6/04), in sub-Saharan Africa women cannot inherit or own land—even though they cultivate it and grow 80 percent of the continent's food.

It is no secret that women are still denied control over their own reproductive activity. Throughout the world about eighty million pregnancies a year are thought to be unwanted or ill-timed. And some twenty million unsafe illegal abortions are performed annually, resulting in the deaths of some 78,000 women yearly, with millions more sustaining serious injury.

In China and other Asian countries where daughters are seen as a liability, millions of infant females are missing, having been aborted or killed at birth or done in by neglect and underfeeding.

An estimated hundred million girls in Africa and the Middle East have been genitally mutilated by clitoridectomy (excision of the clitoris) or infibulation (excision of the clitoris, labia minor, and inner walls of the labia majora, with the vulva sewed almost completely shut, allowing an opening about the circumference of a pencil).

The purpose of such mutilation is to drastically diminish a woman's capacity for sexual pleasure, insuring that she remains her husband's compliant possession. Some girls perish in the excision process (usually performed by an older female with no medical training). Long term consequences of infibulation include obstructed menstrual flow, chronic infection, hurtful coitus, and complicated childbirth.

In much of the Middle East, women have no right to drive cars or appear in public unaccompanied by a male relative. They have no right to initiate divorce proceedings but can be divorced at the husband's will.

In Latin American and Islamic countries, men sometimes go unpunished for defending their "honor" by killing their allegedly unfaithful wives or girlfriends. In fundamentalist Islamic Iran, the law explicitly allows for the execution of adulterous women by stoning, burning, or being thrown off a cliff.

In countries such as Bangladesh and India, women are murdered so that husbands can remarry for a better dowry. An average of five women a day are burned in dowry-related disputes in India, and many more cases go unreported.

In Bihar, India, women found guilty of witchcraft are still burned to death. In modern-day Ghana, there exist prison camps for females accused of being witches. In contrast, male fetish priests in Ghana have free reign with their magic practices. These priests often procure young girls from poor families that are said to owe an ancestral debt to the priest's forebears. The girls serve as the priests' sex slaves. The ones who manage to escape are not taken back by their fearful families. To survive, they must either return to the priest shrine or go to town and become prostitutes.

Millions of young females drawn from all parts of the world are pressed into sexual slavery, in what amounts to an estimated $7 billion annual business. More than a million girls and boys, many as young as five and six, are conscripted into prostitution in Asia, and perhaps an equal number in the rest of the world.

Pedophiles from the United States and other countries fuel the Asian traffic. Enjoying anonymity and impunity abroad, these "sex tourists" are inclined to treat their acts of child rape as legal and culturally acceptable.

In Afghanistan under the Taliban, women were captives in their own homes, prohibited from seeking medical attention, working, or going to school. The U.S. occupation of Afghanistan was hailed by President Bush Jr. as a liberation of Afghani women.

In fact, most of that country remains under the control of warlords who oppose any move toward female emancipation. And the plight of rural women has become yet more desperate. Scores of young women have attempted self-immolation to escape family abuse and unwanted marriages. "During the Taliban we were living in a graveyard, but we were secure," opined one female activist. "Now women are easy marks for rapists and armed marauders."

In Iraq we find a similar pattern: the plight of women worsening because of a U.S. invasion. Saddam Hussein's secular Baath Party created a despotic regime (fully backed by Washington during its most murderous period). But the Baathists did allow Iraqi women rights that were unparalleled in the Gulf region. Women could attend university, travel unaccompanied, and work alongside men in various professions. They could choose whom to marry or refrain from getting married.

But with the growing insurgency against the U.S. occupation, females are now targeted by the ascendant Islamic extremists. Clerics have imposed new restrictions on them. Women are forced to wear the traditional head covering, and girls spend most of their days indoors confined to domestic chores.

Most Iraqi women are now deprived of public education. Often the only thing left to read is the Koran. Many women fear they will never regain the freedom they enjoyed under the previous regime. As one Iraqi feminist noted, "The condition of women has been deteriorating…This current situation, this fundamentalism, is not even traditional. It is desperate and reactionary."

For all the dramatic advances made by women in the United States, they too endure daunting victimization. Tens of thousands of them either turn to prostitution because of economic need or are forced into it by a male exploiter—and kept there by acts of violence and intimidation.

An estimated three out of four women in the USA are victims of a violent crime sometime during their lifetime. Every day, four women are murdered by men to whom they have been close. Murder is the second leading cause of death among young American women.

In the United States domestic violence is the leading cause of injury among females of reproductive age. An estimated three million women are battered each year by their husbands or male partners, often repeatedly.

Statistically, a woman's home is her most dangerous place—if she has a man in it. Battered women usually lack the financial means to escape, especially if they have children. When they try, their male assailants are likely to come after them and inflict still worse retribution. Police usually are of little help. Arrest is the least frequent response to domestic violence. In most states, domestic beatings are classified as a misdemeanor.

Women who kill their longtime male abusers in desperate acts of self-defense usually end up serving lengthy prison sentences. In recent times, women's organizations have had some success in providing havens for battered women and pressuring public authorities to move against male violence.

To conclude, those who demand respect for their culture may have a legitimate claim or they may really be seeking license to oppress the more vulnerable elements within their society.

There may be practices in any culture, including our own, that are not worthy of respect. And there are basic rights that transcend all cultures, as even governments acknowledge when they outlaw certain horrific customs and sign international accords in support of human rights.

Note

1. This is a revised excerpt from Michael Parenti's book, *The Culture Struggle* (Seven Stories, 2006); reprinted with permission of the author. Other recent books by Michael Parenti include *Superpatriotism* (City Lights), *The Assassination of Julius Caesar* (New Press), and *Contrary Notions: The Michael Parenti Reader* (City Lights). For more information visit www.michaelparenti.org.
   —Editor's note

Chapter Nine

Marc Lépine and Me:
What I Learned from the Montreal Massacre

Peter Eglin

But I am a man, a man's man, a woman's man,
a spiritual man, a scholar man.

And only a man, can stop a man, if that man
is down the dark corridor of his own heart.
        —*Ron Grimes[1]*

He was not a very politically astute man, but he was, as terrorists are, more political than the people who try to understand him socially or psychologically. —Thelma McCormack[2]

Oppression involves a failure of the imagination: the failure to imagine the full humanity of other human beings. —Margaret Atwood[3]

THIS chapter is not so much about women as it is about men, or, rather, about two men, Marc Lépine, the perpetrator of the Montreal Massacre, and me, a professor of sociology with specialties in human rights and ethnomethodology and a sometime human rights activist. How then may I justify its inclusion in a book about "women challenging boundaries?" The book is, in the first place, about "roadblocks to women's equality." Marc Lépine intended his actions to be such a roadblock. He took up arms against the champions of women's right to equality, namely feminists. He saw in the women engineering students at l'École polytechnique an exemplary case of "women challenging boundaries." At first I treated the murders as human rights violations targeting persons perceived as human rights activists (feminists). Against prevailing conceptions of the murders as the insane acts of a madman I (and my co-worker, Stephen Hester) sought to preserve their character as political acts, indeed acts of terrorism. And so, secondly, we took up the analysis of the media coverage of the massacre from the point of view of our primary sociological specialty, ethnomethodology, in order to examine such versions of his actions. In the end, however, I felt that the massacre posed a further and different challenge to one who was not just a sometime human rights activist and a student of an academic discipline but also, and relevantly, a man. The ultimate challenge posed by feminism to men is "man, regard thyself." It seemed to me, then, that if I was to take my intellectual responsibility as a man in relation to these political murders really seriously, I had to interrogate my *own* political actions and my *own* relation to this enraged terrorist. To what extent am I, like Marc Lépine, a roadblock to equality? In this way, then, this chapter in a book about women came to be about men. What this man learned from his encounter with Lépine was (1) that making out the culprit as deviant relieves one of his responsibility, (2) that demonizing the complainant leaves the problem unaddressed while encouraging extremists, (3) that there's a troubling moral-emotional economy of/to sociological analysis and (4) that reifying gender categories is good intellectual preparation for terrorism. After a somewhat more extended and biographical introduction, I present these lessons in turn before explicitly comparing Marc Lépine and me, then concluding with the burden of the learned lessons.

An Elaborated Account of Coming to Take Up the Question

When Geneviève Bergeron, Hélène Colgan, Nathalie Croteau, Barbara Daigneault, Anne-Marie Edward, Maud Haviernick, Barbara Maria Klucznik, Maryse Laganière, Maryse Leclair, Anne-Marie Lemay, Sonia Pelletier, Michèle Richard, Annie St-Arneault and Annie Turcotte were shot (and in one case stabbed) and killed by Marc Lépine on December 6, 1989 it was not as persons with names that they were murdered. They were killed because they were treated as instances of a category: feminists. In the killer's reported words, "You're women. You're going to be engineers. You're all a bunch of feminists. I hate feminists." Feminists, let us recall, are women who fight for women's liberation, for women's rights, above all for equal rights. Like the six Jesuit faculty who, together with their cook and her daughter, were murdered three weeks before by members of the El Salvador armed forces in the early hours of the morning outside their residence at the José Simeon Canas University of Central America in San Salvador on November 16, 1989, the Montreal women were killed because they were (perceived as) human rights activists. The murders, that is, were political killings. Furthermore, they were students, killed, like the Jesuit faculty, in a university setting. For one about to embark on a new course in the sociology of human rights this outrage at L'École polytechnique in Montreal, occurring three weeks after the one in San Salvador, was an unavoidable topic. Nevertheless, the question remained of how I might approach such a topic.

At first I treated it as a human rights violation targeting human rights activists. Though the massacre did not appear to me to be an instance of *state* or "wholesale" terrorism, it was clearly terrorism. And though it was carried out by an individual acting alone, it did not seem to me to fit the label "retail" terrorism either. Watching it all on TV "that night in December which will haunt our collective memory forever," Monique Bosco describes her own reaction as follows: "Nauseated, I refused to accept that another new horror, a new terrorism, now existed."[4] I was forced, not before time some might say, to consider how Marc Lépine's act of violence was connected up to a terror-and-propaganda network of a different sort than that described by Herman and Chomsky.[5] Moreover, eventually I would have to find and face up to my own place in it. It is important to recall the university context at the time.

The massacre came at the end of an academic term—literally on the last day of classes at L'École polytechnique when students were making class presentations—a term that was much taken up with public discussion of "sexism on campus." This was particularly true of my university, Wilfrid Laurier University (WLU), which had achieved national notoriety in the fall of 1989 from the revelation that it was home to an institutionalized practice called "Panty Raid."[6] The panty raids and sequels had taken place on September 27-28. The culmination of the men's raid was the hanging of the women's underwear in the cafeteria. On this occasion the underwear were smeared with fake blood and feces, and labelled with slogans demeaning to women.[7] The following night, following convention, the women students raided the men's dorms for their underwear. At that time too "Wilfrid Laurier University's student newspaper The Cord Weekly face[d] censure or expulsion from the Canadian University Press (CUP) for material it published in the fall that was criticized as sexist and degrading to women."[8] I joined in campus discussion of these matters inside and outside the classroom. The occurrence of the Montreal Massacre became part and parcel of that debate, being construed on the feminist side as part of a generalized anti-feminist backlash. More concretely, people on campus came together to mark the occasion in grief and anger. And some male faculty responded by forming a Men Opposed to Violence Against Women group on campus, which I joined.[9]

It was in this ethos of heightened sensitivity to anti-feminist actions, violence against women, sexism on campus, patriarchy generally and pro-feminist actions by some men that, six months later, I got arrested ripping up sexist ("pornographic") calendars in the corner store across from the university. An impulsive, vainglorious, ineffective and harmful action, which I quickly came to regret, it got me a number of reputations that I could have done without. I return to the significance this act has come to have for me later in the chapter.

I clipped the *Globe and Mail* religiously in the days following the massacre, grimly determined to keep watch on how the actor and his action would be described by reporter and commentator alike. Would he be written off as a madman, would his announced political motives be respected, would their anti-feminist character be preserved? At the same time, from a more technical direction arising from my sociological studies in ethnomethodology, I was intrigued by his reported speech at the scene, by the sequence of categories which comprised it, by its economy – "you're women, you're going to be engineers, you're all a bunch of feminists, I hate feminists." My colleague Stephen Hester and I had begun to take up collaborative work in what we came to call, following the foundational studies of Harvey Sacks, "membership categorization analysis" (MCA).[10] Yet I didn't know what to make of this talk. At the time, it just would not submit to analysis. Nevertheless, I came to feel that perhaps the most intellectually responsible course of action I could pursue in response to the massacre was to come to understand Marc Lépine on the basis of just what he was reported to have said at the scene, including the suicide letter recovered by police from his body and made public a year later.

After initially working up a treatment of the massacre in the context of a consideration of women's rights for the Human Rights course I started teaching in January 1990, I came to include the topic in the Sociology of Suicide course that I also taught regularly (since introducing it in 1977). There it became a vehicle for the discussion of political suicide, juxtaposed with the case of Jonestown. In each case a record had been left, a suicide letter and witnesses' reports of the killer's words in the one case, a tape-recording of Jones's preaching on the infamous "White Night" preceding and accompanying the mass suicide in the other. Marc Lépine's twin acts of murder and suicide were done, he wrote, "for political reasons." And they were announced in words at the scene that were redolent with categories. Here perhaps was a case where the two enterprises could be brought together, where ethnomethodology might inform politics, where my intellectual life could be one. And so arose the dissatisfaction and disappointment. For while the political value of defending Lépine's own account of his actions *as political*, against the prevailing view that they were pathological, was clear to me—and one I could defend, interestingly enough, on purely methodological grounds—I could find no explicitly ethnomethodological purchase on the materials. Those categories stared me in the face, but would not submit to analysis. Their meaning was plain, but *how* they managed to mean what they meant was a mystery.

And so it was that for the next six or seven years I would not get beyond the position I had arrived at within a month of the massacre itself. Then, in 1996/97 Hester

and I were invited by Paul Jalbert to contribute a chapter to an anthology he was editing on ethnomethodological approaches to media studies. (Our own edited collection of studies in MCA was about to appear.[11]) After a couple of false starts I pulled
out the file of Montreal Massacre clippings I had kept, and suggested to Steve we
have a go seeing what we could make of them. He agreed. They proved fruitful. A first
analysis of the whole corpus subsequently appeared as the requested chapter in
Jalbert's book.[12] That effort showed us that there was enough to say on our materials
to fill our own book. That volume subsequently appeared.[13] One of its chapters is
taken up with "the killer's story." After six or seven years, and under the stimulation
of a renewed "attack" in collaboration with a gifted co-analyst, I suddenly saw
through the words to the actions they were performing and the methods being used
to perform them, and Marc Lépine started to come home.

As the ethnomethodological analysis of the Montreal Massacre materials took
shape in writing, teaching and presentation, its moral, emotional and political import refused to be denied. What I did not anticipate was the reflection it would occasion about my own relationship to the killer, given that Hester and I insisted on
preserving the killer's self-description as a political actor, and I was myself active in a
number of political and human rights causes. I have formulated the results of this encounter with the Montreal Massacre as a number of moral-political lessons.

Lesson 1: Making Out the Culprit as Deviant Relieves One of His Responsibility

Under the title "Deviants and Demons" I invited students taking courses from me to
notice two gross parallels in the public discussion following the Panty Raid and the
Massacre. The first parallel was the widespread use in each case of the cultural practice of making-out-the-culprit(s)-as-deviant. That is, in the subsequent public discussion this practice consisted in dividing the Panty Raid incident into (a) the
wholesome, fun-loving, gender-balanced raid itself, and (b) the unwholesome ex-
cesses of the blood-and-shit brigade who ruined it for the rest. This was notably the
case in "Some lurid confessions of a former panty raider," an article in the local
weekly newspaper by columnist and former WLU student Rick Campbell (1989).[14]
That is, both the actions and the actors of (b) were assigned the status "deviant"—a
few bad apples in an otherwise healthy crop—and separated from the rest of the
Panty Raid participants. In this way the institution and its practitioners were saved.

Similarly, Marc Lépine was assigned the category descriptor "insane" or "madman" or "crazy guy" immediately the crime was known, indeed even by witnesses as

it was going on. Whatever the truth of this characterization one thing its use accomplishes is to remove the necessity for a rational accounting of the actions of the one so designated. It leaves simply the different question of why it was he who did them. The instant biographers had no trouble constructing an account of his life consistent with the conventional grammar for mass killers: he was seen to have had a biography of troubles arising from a disordered social background. And, in the classic functionalist mode of sociological explanation, this accounting practice saves the community, notably the part made up of men. Now that the killer is assigned to the outer darkness we (men especially) need not worry about whether and how he is tied in to us; we (men especially) need not ask what he may have to teach us.

Leah Renae Kelly (with Ward Churchill) revealed the same practice at work in revisionist "cowboys-and-Indians" movies such as *Dances with Wolves* and *Thunderheart* with their "good whites" and "bad whites:"

> The propaganda function served by the revisionist formula is to allow constituents of America's dominant settler society to avoid confronting the institutional and cultural realities which led unerringly to the historical genocide of American Indians. Moreover, in first being led to demonize men like Custer, and then helped to separate themselves from them via the signification of characters like Jack Crabbe [Dustin Hoffman's character in *Little Big Man*], Christa Lee [Candice Bergen's character in *Soldier Blue*], and Costner's Lt. Dunbar [Kevin Costner's character in *Dances with Wolves*], white audiences are made to feel simultaneously "enlightened" (for having been "big" or "open" enough to concede that something ugly had occurred) and "good about themselves" (for being so different from those they imagine the perpetrators to have been).[15]

Lesson 2: Demonizing the Complainant Leaves the Problem Unaddressed while Encouraging Extremists

The second parallel consists of the practice of demonizing-the-complainant. Those who saw in both the Panty Raid and the Montreal Massacre expressions of sexism (otherwise deemed inapplicable according to the first practice), and organized their reaction to them in feminist terms, were subjected to an anti-feminist backlash (which, in its turn, was seen by feminists as confirming their analysis). "When some female students complained about the posters, they were denounced as 'Nazis,' lesbians and radical feminists."[16] For example, "A fourth-year student who circulated a petition saying the raids degrade neither sex said she was 'disappointed' to learn of the ban. Said Dale Burt, who supervises dons at a residence for more than 140 women students: 'There are radical feminists who are trying to force down our throats what we should do and think.' "[17] On 26 October 1989, *Toronto Star* columnist and nationally known feminist Michèle Landsberg devoted her column to the Panty Raid at WLU under the title "University sanctions student panty raids."[18] She fairly lambasted the President, "men in authority" and the university generally for the pre-historic condition of attention to women's safety and women's rights on campus; she noted how "bitterly self-righteous" were the panty-raiding students themselves, who regarded their critics as being like moralistic parents trying to spoil their fun. For the rest of the fall term Landsberg was subjected to a stream of vilification in the *Cord Weekly* (and in certain other quarters of WLU campus) that achieved grotesque pro-portions. The climactic low-point came on 30 November in the last issue of the term. In a poor attempt at satire headed "Landsberg Fries" the article's author tells a make-believe story in which the feminist columnist is symbolically murdered by be-ing burned alive in her own home as a would-be rescuer discovers her identity and re-turns her to the flames. A week later the massacre happened.

Two days after that the very much alive Landsberg published her response to the massacre, "Killer's rage was all too familiar."[19] In this passionately argued *cri de coeur* she herself points out that "it's no accident that the Montreal murderer blamed 'feminists' for his troubles," that "feminist" and feminism have become demonized, not least on university campuses, and that "now that 'feminism' has been turned into a dismissive insult, all the feminist issues are marginalized. If only crazy 'feminists' complain, everyone else can keep right on ignoring rankling injustices and male bru-tality." Landsberg, Monique Bosco and others asserted that bombardment of the public by anti-feminist propaganda made feminists a publicly available target of re-crimination for "angry white *males*." Queen's University had been paired with WLU in the national press for sexism on campus in the fall of 1989, affording the following presentiment: "it is not difficult to sense a more general feeling of resentment on the part of many male students toward the special measures undertaken to help women on campus, at Queen's and elsewhere."[20] One Queen's student was led to make this prescient speculation in light of the chilly campus climate there:

> It seems inevitable that unless some decisive action occurs the tension on cam-
> pus will deteriorate into a genuine crisis, as the crisis which now manifests itself
> does not appear to merit the consideration of the Queen's authorities.[21]

Although published after the Montreal murders, it appears—from the date (Novem-ber 17) of the article to which she was responding, and the fact that the massacre it-self is not mentioned—that Hartwick's letter was almost certainly written before they occurred. Monique Bosco wrote in the aftermath, "One would think that the signs of active misogyny, reported in, among others, student newspapers all over Canada, could have been identified months and even years before."[22] Nevertheless, those who, like Landsberg, made the feminist case for viewing the massacre as an extreme instance of generalized violence against women, found themselves attacked in their turn for having hijacked the "tragic" event to their political bandwagon. One is tempted to recall Puritan practices of witch-hunting.[23]

Lesson 3: There's a Troubling Moral-Emotional Economy of/to Sociological Analysis

A further issue arose when I presented a version of our analysis of the "killer's story" to an academic audience at a small conference on gender, discourse and theory. The conference was put on by the Discourse Analysis Research Group of St. Thomas University and the University of New Brunswick in March 1998 in Fredericton.[24] I was asked to provide the good of the analysis-and-presentation in the following sense: "what could the analysis offer that would justify putting the predominantly female audience through the pain and discomfort of having to confront M.L. again in the form of his suicide letter and announcement at the scene?" For, following ethnomethodological precedent, the data were made available to the audience as handouts and overheads so they could check the analysis themselves. The question, that is, was one posed in terms of the moral-emotional economy of inquiry. Does the good of the analysis outweigh the moral-emotional costs? The presentation was, in fact, interrupted early on and I was asked to provide our conclusions so that the audience could weigh that question. Following that assessment it would be decided whether I should continue. Indeed, I refused to continue until there was agreement that I should. Discussion ensued for at least half an hour, ably managed by the conference hosts. At some point into the discussion, and with considerable consternation, I complied with the request to provide the conclusions. Some sort of resolution was reached. Nobody walked out (as far as I recall). The paper was then read to the end.

During the discussion the suicide letter was characterized as, or as like, "hate literature." It was likened, that is, to such other noxious documents as *The Protocols of the Elders of Zion* or *Mein Kampf* or, according to some forms of feminist analysis, some forms of pornography. In that sense, it invited entry into debates over free speech, censorship and the like. One salient feminist contribution to such debates has been to insist on a measure of harm being incorporated into the assessment of the legitimacy of forms of questionable speech. It was precisely such a demand that was being pressed on the occasion in question.

It is true that it had not occurred to me that reproductions of documents of Lépine's "speech" could induce alarm and fear in their female readers eight years or more after the event. And that failure of imagination is revealing. It would have been quite obvious to me that, say, passing out anti-Semitic passages from Nazi documents like *Mein Kampf* to a Jewish audience on an otherwise identical academic occasion was a course of action that would require considerable care, if indeed it could be properly done at all. Why did I not see so readily the impropriety of an equivalent act where women were concerned? The answer is, I suppose, that I walk around with blinkers on. My experience is that it is a lifetime's job trying to get them off.

At the same time it is also true that my topic and approach had been announced on posters advertising the event. There was an opportunity for persons fearful of the topic and its materials to avoid the talk. Furthermore, there is a history to the "coming-out" of these materials that I think needs to be taken into account. From the moment it was revealed, the day following the massacre, that the police had in their hands a suicide letter left by the killer, with a "hit list" of prominent Quebec feminists appended, there were calls for its release and publication. The initial calls were from journalists. Putting aside the standard question of the degree to which corporate newspapers' announced civic motives are inevitably compromised by their unannounced commercial interests in such "revelations," we may note that among them the call came from Francine Pelletier. A journalist to be sure, she was (and is) not only a noted feminist but also one whose name was on the list. Moreover, when, almost a year later she was sent a copy of the letter, her paper, *La Presse* of Montreal, published it. Furthermore, the editors and publisher of the first *The Montreal Massacre, the* feminist book on the massacre, elected to include the letter in the English edition of 1991, albeit with the following "Publisher's note:"

> After much discussion, we have decided to include the letter in this edition of the book. This was a difficult decision. It is not our intention to produce a book, apologist or otherwise, about the murderer. As much as the Montreal massacre is not an act isolated in time and place, it is also an act not isolated to one man. Indeed, for these reasons, some of the contributors to this book have chosen to represent the killer by his initials, M.L., rather than his full name. We feel that the letter, somewhat ironically (for this was certainly not the killer's intention), reinforces in our minds the courage and truthfulness with which the writers in this book speak out about violence against women.[25]

In the "Preface" to the original, French edition, the editors also write:

> Whether we like it or not, the massacre at the Polytechnique is now part of our history. A concrete addition to that grievous memory, this book offers a profound understanding of what happened—personal and political reflections which will contribute indispensable perspectives to *the public debate we hope to see take place*.[26]

Furthermore, Louise Malette partially justifies producing the English edition as a further effort to provoke that "profound reflection warranted by an event like the massacre at the Polytechnique [which] does not appear to be taking place in Quebec:"

> A year after the book was published in French, we would like to claim that it in some way contributed to raising people's consciousness or to provoking the profound reflection that stimulates widespread public debate. This, we know, is necessary if a change in mentality is to come about. Alas, we are unable to make such a claim. To be sure, the book's appearance in April 1990 was politely recognized by the critical establishment, which, despite a certain embarrassment, was content to make only a cursory perusal of its contents. And then this obviously disturbing book was quickly forgotten.[27]

I do not pretend, being a (white) man as I am, that I know what it is to be literally or metaphorically in the gun sight of a very angry male. And though I have been active with respect to a number of human rights issues, including pro-feminist ones, and though I have received a death threat for my pains (scrawled across an article posted outside my office door, probably by a disgruntled student), I cannot claim, other than by sympathetic imagination (clearly flawed), to appreciate either the fear his name can evoke in women, or the courage it takes to oppose what he is said to represent. Nevertheless, I find I must stand with the editors and publisher of *The Montreal Massacre*, with Francine Pelletier and Monique Bosco, and not avoid looking into the "face of the enemy." If for women the fear is for what he might do, for me as a man the concern is for whom I will see there. For if I do avoid that view, I risk losing sight of two essential things that are at the root of the *human* sciences, which have been taught to me again as a result of doing the Montreal Massacre study. These two matters are (1) how much I am like him, and (2) how easy it is to reproduce the conceptual grammar of the course of his action. I have collapsed these two considerations into the fourth lesson taught me by the Montreal Massacre.

Lesson 4: Reifying Gender Categories Is Good Intellectual Preparation for Terrorism

Perhaps the chief finding that was borne in upon Hester and me as we carried out the ethnomethodological analysis of our Montreal Massacre materials was the pervasiveness of irony. Throughout our analysis we had repeated occasions to notice that the same methods of reasoning, that is the same conceptual grammar of politics, were deployed by Lépine the counter-revolutionary terrorist as by the feminist and pro-feminist respondents and commentators who opposed him. In our mode of analysis these methods, or this grammar, can be represented in terms of the use of three membership categorization devices.

Firstly, both "parties" build their arguments by assembling the categories "men" and "women" into a membership categorization device we may call "gender," assigning predicates to those categories, then identifying and explaining persons' actions in terms of those categories and their predicates. This is not, of course, to imply that "feminists are terrorists," or to reiterate that favourite political turn of modernist irony captured in the would-be axiom, "revolutionaries always turn into dictators."[28] Rather the point being made is in the other direction. Lépine was acting politically with the conceptual tools feminism provided. Where he differed from feminists was in finding insupportable the social consequences he perceived as the outcome of their use, and in being prepared to use terror to achieve his aims. And their responses reiterated that grammar.

Secondly, he and, in a more qualified way, some of the respondent/commentators, employ a two-category collection we identified as "parties to revolution." It comprises "revolutionaries" and "counter-revolutionaries:" those who are not with us are against us (a turn of phrase given renewed currency by George W. Bush after 9/11, 2001). I consider this further below.

Thirdly, both parties conceptualize the political arena in terms of the "immediately asymmetric, standardized collectivity relational pair," namely government/citizens (or people).[29] Whether by adopting the strategy of mobilizing the "people" in order to force change on "government," or via the reverse strategy, or through some other combined means, like terrorism, such political actors define their options, the perceived possibilities of action, in these terms. For example, the National Action Committee on the Status of Women, in a November 1998 fund-raising letter, writes:

> We have always worked from the premise that the feminist movement must be inclusive and action oriented to successfully impact government policy and society at large.

The temptation of terror lies in just the perception that the avenues of political action are blocked by the unavailability of any feasible means of peacefully influencing "government" whether directly or via the "people." All those of us who are human rights activists, or seeking the liberation of one or another oppressed group, know the temptation of using terror or some lesser degree of force to get our way. "Wouldn't it be nice to just go in there and wipe out those bastards?" we joke uneasily about our political opponents.

To be sure, I did not think of it as a case of terrorism or indeed of the use of force when I entered Forwell's, the local variety store across from the WLU campus, on the evening of July 26, 1990 intent on "taking action against sexism." Ripping up sexist calendars was an act I considered to be more like civil disobedience. I had gone into the store a few hours earlier to get a candy or newspaper while waiting for the bus to go home after work. As I walked through the door, there facing the entrance and my tuned-up eyes was a rack of wall calendars graced with scantily clad women posing as body-builders under the slogan "Determination." Sensitized as I was by the events of the previous ten months I found this simply "too much." Incensed by yet another instance of the commercialized degradation and subordination of women —and correlatively of me, the man with the consuming eyes—I nevertheless got on the bus and went home. After dinner however, I returned to the store, having phoned the *Kitchener-Waterloo Record* newsroom to tell them what I was going to do. A reporter met me outside the store. She interviewed me but said she would not accompany me into the store, as that would make the newspaper complicit in producing a staged event. But she would wait outside.[30] I went in. For what followed let me refer to what I evidently said to Tony Burke, the new editor of WLU's student newspaper *the cord*, when he interviewed me about the affair shortly after:

> I got hold of all the female calendars—there were four of them—and I stood in front of the counter and ripped them up into four pieces and dropped them onto the floor. The assistant manager looked at me, so I smiled. He said, "are you going to pay for those" and I said no.

The following sequence of events was, in retrospect, quite predictable. In fact, my ethnomethodological colleagues may never forgive me for not having anticipated what Garfinkel's "incongruity procedures" had long before revealed.

Burke: Did anyone in the store question what you were doing?

Eglin: No, business went on as usual around me as I stood there ripping up these things—a couple of people smiled and looked at me but otherwise the normal course of events went on. For a moment I thought "what am I doing this for? No-one's taking any notice" [laughs].

By "the normal course of events" I meant that customers in the store continued to go to the cash registers a few feet from me on either side, and the sales staff continued to ring up their purchases. Normal store life went on. Back to the interview:

> There was a bunch of male equivalent calendars, about six of them, and I ripped those up too. The counter girl picked up the stuff I ripped up and put it in a bag and set it on the counter so from then on whatever I ripped up I stuffed it into the bag so it was all neat and tidy.

(I fervently hope that "counter girl" was Burke's expression and not mine.) I included the male calendars to make the point that the formal equality, rather than vindicating the exploitation in the female calendars, reproduced it for men while leaving the substantive inequality embodied in the sexploitation of women quite untouched. The same argument applies to the second stage of Panty Raid when the women students would raid the men's dorms for their underwear: the formal equality does *not* make it all right. To this point Forwell's staff were still treating the event as more or less a shopping transaction, as one belonging in the setting (until proven otherwise), if nevertheless a little odd. And so I found myself with Lépine's problem. How was I to make what I was doing accountable—that is observable, and reportable—*as political protest*? It was necessary for me to tell the salesperson *why* I was doing what I was doing in order that she could see *what* I was doing.

> I talked to the assistant for a while and said to her what do you think of this stuff. She was embarrassed a bit and she said "I don't particularly like it; I just don't look at it." So I said, "every time you come in the store you must look at it there on the rack," but she had nothing more to say.

When I finished those I went back to the magazine rack and started looking around for anything that struck my eye. I wasn't looking for the standard porn stuff like *Playboy, Hustler* and that stuff—I didn't even know that they had it, and it turns out that they don't have it—I was just looking for run-of-the-mill magazines that were sexist. I picked up a couple of *Cosmopolitans* and started ripping them up. As I was doing that she asked me if I would leave the store and I said no but if she was bothered she could call the police.

In the end, that is, I had to instruct the salesperson what the next step was, namely to call the police. In due course the police arrived; I was arrested and led out of the store. The *Record* cameraperson snapped me getting into the police car. I was on the front page the following day.[32] Job done, I thought.

What I had not thought of was the consequences, consumed as I was by the compelling need not to go on submitting to yet another grotesque assault on women's equality. (Doubtless, too, that I get particularly agitated by *sexualized* displays of women's subordination reflects some suppressed desire for just what such images appear to offer.) Yet the consequences were again predictable and, in the end, humbling. There was the desired publicity. Apart from the story in the *Record*, it made CBC-Radio news on the 27th. I was later interviewed on CBC-Radio's Radio Noon on August 16. There was the interview in the student newspaper, which led to some exchange of views in the letters column. Later I appeared as a panel member on Dini Petty's national talk show on CTV when it came to town in October to tape a programme on sexism on campus.[33] What good these things did it is very hard to say. I am more confident about estimating the harm. Charged with mischief under $1000 I was faced with three months in jail or a $500 fine. Given my domestic responsibilities I could afford neither, being a new father and much in debt. Worse, the event itself had two troubling outcomes. It was plain to me that I had not only non-plussed the salesperson who dealt with me, I had also frightened or, at least, alarmed, her. Not that my appearance or my demeanour in the store were in themselves alarming; I was friendly and not aggressive. But she must have wondered what on earth was going on, and could not then have been sure that I wouldn't be violent at some point. She was about eighteen or nineteen years of age and she was a she. The bitter irony of my intendedly pro-feminist action serving to alarm one of the very people in whose interests I imagined myself to be acting was shaming; I was ridiculous.

It was also clear that such stunts did not serve to strengthen and promote feminism but, if anything, to undermine it. That a man should come along, in all his vainglory, to ride into the fray and, as it were, win the battle for women's equality single-handedly was presumptuous nonsense. And it mocked the tireless, patient, unseen work of countless workers in women's organizations. And so, being unable to afford the lawyer that would be needed to exploit the issue in court, and mindful of the harm I had already done, I ended up apologizing to Joe Forwell, to the women staff at the store and to the women's movement, and I paid for the calendars and magazines. The charge was dismissed. The apology made headlines again.[34] For some I looked like a wimp.

Coming to see through this event my kinship with Marc Lépine has been long in gestation. I had entertained the possibility theoretically and symbolically since the first act of mourning following the massacre itself. But all I shared in common with him, I had thought, was the accident of gender (notwithstanding all that gender means for us). Despite appreciating Ron Grimes's poem, part of which is quoted at the head of this chapter, I didn't really believe it about *myself*. Nothing particular about *my* thoughts, feelings, desires, emotions and actions was actually like ML's, I told myself. There was no little guy with a big gun lurking down the corridor of *my* heart. Until coming to work on this chapter, in which I had decided to lump together "pin-up," "panty raid" and "massacre," I had not seen just how much in common I have with him.

Me and Marc Lépine

First, there is the anger. I have certainly felt the anger. None of it directed at women, I hasten to add, but since hearing Chomsky's Massey Lectures on CBC Radio in the fall of 1988 I have burned with anger at the endless economic and social injustice in the world, the boundless economy with the truth in official pronouncements, and the bottomless equanimity of the complicit onlookers. I have wanted to act drastically and decisively, to shout out the truth, to refuse and reject my own involuntary participation in war-making and economic exploitation, to give away my possessions, to live as Charles Page has been doing at the "world wage," to live in a household without a trace of gender inequality. I have wanted to stop life as usual. Unlike Marc Lépine I have not felt myself to be oppressed, to have had my life ruined, but on the contrary to be only blessed and unfairly privileged (despite a fair amount of admittedly self-induced hardship). And if there is some group that angers me the way feminists angered him it would be the owners of wealth. Murder, though, is simply out of the question.

Second, there is the political method. It is disturbing to see the formal similarity between my exploit in the local corner store and his in the neighbouring university. Putting aside the scale of the violence involved, consider that, like him, I anonymized and depersonalized the persons in the scene, rendering them as no more than props for my performance. Like him, while speaking *to* the persons present I spoke *for* an overhearing audience, the newspaper-reading public. I acted out of fiercely held principle, yet I hurt would-be beneficiaries (women) and my cause (women's equality); he acted out of principle (and also, clearly, from overwhelming and apparently long-nurtured personal resentment) and, apart from murdering his "enemies," ended up killing a would-be beneficiary (himself) and damaging his cause (anti-feminism)—the following year more women students than ever enrolled in engineering at L'École polytechnique. My act itself, of ripping up "speech," of silencing "speech," courted comparison with the book-burning antics of the fanatics of the religious and political far right, the very constituencies I imagined myself to be diametrically opposed to, the kind of place where Marc Lépine might have found a home. And like him, I acted alone.

So, in *these* senses, I am not so different from Marc Lépine, or he from me. If I am saying here that Lépine is a recognizable political actor and, in *this* sense, like me, indeed as "good" as those of us who are feminist or pro-feminist and who take the gender question seriously (for he certainly takes it seriously), then what I am also saying is that I must be sure not to follow him, and be as "bad" as him. This conclusion follows not simply from political considerations but from the humanistic foundations of both democratic politics and the human sciences.

By "following him" I mean adopting his practices of political conceptualization. I owe this point to Steve Hester who was the principal author of the following passage from our *The Montreal Massacre*:

> By naming his intended victims as feminists, Lépine "anonymises" them; he speaks to them not as individual persons, with names, biographies, families, plans and projects of their own; rather, he speaks categorially to them as *representatives* of feminism; he depersonalizes his victims and in so doing he politicizes them. His action, whilst concrete, is then also abstract since he kills not unique individual human beings but exemplars of categories in a political membership categorization device which comprises two membership categories: feminist "revolutionaries" and anti-feminist "counter-revolutionaries." Similarly, his task is to reveal, for his victims and for the general public or polity which constitutes his wider overhearing and political audience, that he is not acting as Marc Lépine *per se* but as a political actor, as a representative of a political stance. By invoking this device, Lépine categorizes both himself and his victims and in so doing he provides instructions for making his action rationally accountable as political.[35]

In order to draw out further the specifically dangerous aspects of Lépine's reasoning with these resources, let me note the following additional "grammatical" considerations. Firstly, "feminist" is a term of self-avowal, not other-description. More precisely, it is true that others may doubt or question whether the term is correctly self-applied. Others, that is, have rights of ratification of a member's self-description as feminist. They may dispute it, claiming that one or more of the publicly available, conventionally certifiable grounds for its application does or do not obtain in a particular case. But others may not confer the title on a member without the member's agreement. That is, they may not do so properly or legitimately. State-capitalist reactionaries were fond of labelling anyone who minimally opposed the unbridled sway of their rule as "communist" (nowadays "terrorist"), the better to justify killing them —this, with complete indifference to whether their opponents were indeed self-avowed communists. But this was precisely Lépine's method. He ascribed "feminist" to his targeted opponents on the basis of a category search to be sure, but one that did not include the self-descriptions of the members themselves. As we know, many of his victims would not have called themselves feminists.

Secondly, there is the practice of treating those to whom a category may be properly applied as what Jayyusi calls a "morally organized group." Hester and I have written in *The Montreal Massacre* about the delicate matter of treating the categories "men" and "women" categorially or summatively.[36] "Man" and "woman" are also what we have called "personal" membership categories, whereas terms such as "the bank," "the army," "the police" and so on have been called "collectivity categories." The aggregate terms "men" and "women" may be used, in a sense, to name collectivities, but only in the nominalist practices of professional sociologists are these "groups." That is, unlike, say, "the liberal party" or "the girl guides," "men" and "women" are not groups in the sense of "morally organized" entities. They do not have constitutions, rules of proper practice, membership criteria and dues, scheduled meetings, ceremonial occasions, gathering places and the like (gender-specific institutions like certain clubs notwithstanding). Not all of sociology and anthropology's quasi-ethnographic, metaphorical representation of the categories "men" and "women" *as if* they were "statuses" with attached institutionalized "roles" and "relationships" *like* those of morally organized groups can establish that identity. Or rather, to turn the argument around, this functionalist language of gender *constitutes* a collection of methods for *constructing* identities for these categories.

But then, this is just what some feminist politics may be described as. In "Hundreds in Toronto mourn killing of 14 women," noted Canadian reporter Stevie Cameron opens the article as follows:

> Weeping and holding one another for comfort, hundreds of women and men—most of them students, professors, politicians and community activists—met yesterday before a statue of a crucified woman on the University of Toronto campus to mourn the 14 women who were murdered in Montreal on Wednesday night.[37]

Notice first that the actions "weeping" and "holding one another for comfort" are here predicated of the categories "women" and "men." Consider second, however, that such actions are conventionally tied to the categories making up the class of "intimate" standardized relational pairs (parent-child, husband-wife, lover-lover, friend-friend...); they are proper actions of incumbents of these categories in tragic personal or family circumstances, in which members may search for help from one another. In news coverage the victims of the massacre were repeatedly described as daughters (or wife, or girlfriend, or friend) and the reactions of parents (husband, boyfriend, friend) sought and described. Consider third, that such actions are also extendable to the whole population on occasions of major public tragedies (such as this one); that is, they may properly be done by persons who otherwise would be described as "strangers." In these circumstances they are ascribable to such categories as "everyone," "people," "this person," "this man," "that woman," "Montrealers," and so on.

Returning to the passage from Cameron's article, notice again that the actions in question are here appropriated and ascribed to the categories "women" and "men." That is, these predicates that are properly bound to the "intimate" subset of standardized relational pairs are attached here to membership categories not conventionally members of this collection of categories at all, namely "women" and "men." The construction invites the reader, as it were, to see the "tragedy" as a matter relevant to the "relationship" between woman and woman, man and man and, presumably, woman and man. That is, whatever relationships there may have otherwise been among the people there assembled (were not some of them friends, classmates, spouses, lovers...?), or however permissible it may have been on account of this public tragedy for *anybody* to have been seen *weeping* or for *people* to have been *holding one another for comfort*, the reporter describes these actions as ones being done by "women" and "men."

This is not to say, of course, that these people were not women and men, for they surely were. Nor is it to say that describing them as "women" and "men" was not relevant and appropriate, for it surely was. (Notice, particularly, that the terms fit, that is are "co-selected," with the use of the category "women" to describe the victims.) What it is to say is that the use of these descriptors represents or embodies a category *election* on the reporter's part. She could have referred to those assembled as simply "people," together with the qualifying occupational categories ("students, professors, politicians and community activists"). But she elects to foreground their gender by the use of "women" and "men." That election conveys, I would argue, a politics. As Sacks argued for "hotrodder" (as a preferred self-description among a group of young people to the other-description "teenager"), revolutionary social change is (at least) a matter of changing the categories of everyday life: "there's an order of revolution which is an attempt to change how it is that persons see reality."[38] The irony is that in so doing Stevie Cameron, the feminist reporter, takes her cue from Marc Lépine, the anti-feminist terrorist, who treats a category ("women") as a group. And conversely, Lépine himself may be said to be following the (more dangerous) conceptual practices of some feminist politics. Moreover, these practices themselves may be said to be rooted in long-standing lay and professional sociological methods of rendering persons as gendered creatures.[39]

Conclusion: The Burden of the Lessons

Anonymizing and depersonalizing people, rendering them as instances of a political category for the purposes of acting towards them—these are the practices of dehumanization that rationalize inhuman acts. But not following Lépine in his use of these practices includes not treating *him* in this way. I cannot render him asocial by refusing him his identity by not giving him his name, or by refusing to hear his words. I cannot reduce him to being the mere determinate (or indeterminate) outcome of a pathological social and psychological process, by refusing to recognize his all-too-plainly stated motives, the planning of his course of action, and both his will and ability to carry it out. I cannot deny him reason by rendering him mad, if his actions can be shown to follow from his motives, as indeed they can. I cannot deny him his humanity by not recognizing his rage. To render (morally-based) rage as (somatically-based) madness heightens horror but it eliminates the meaning of action. That includes the real and frightening threat he may be said to represent.

I cannot do these things, not in the first instance from subscribing to a humane politics, but because I am a human scientist. As such I am enjoined, as a methodological requirement, to find my subjects human if I can. Thanks to my WLU colleague Ron Grimes, who put me on to this source, I found a reminder of this foundation in J.Z. Smith's essay, "The Devil in Mr. Jones."[40] It was illuminating to read in the opening of Smith's work on Jonestown about the radical, not to say revolutionary, character of the notion of "the humanities" in nineteenth-century "curriculum development." Smith was writing about the emergence of "religious studies" from theology in terms of a movement from divinity to humanity as a guiding principle of university scholarship. The humanities, in this sense, are part of the human rights movement. He brings this understanding to an analysis of the tape-recording of Jones's last speech or sermon on the infamous "White Night" before the mass suicide. What he reveals is not the ramblings of a fatigued, drugged-up, megalomaniacal sex fiend (as contemporary press reports painted Jones), but the more-or-less coherent, religiously motivated and founded, preparing of his followers for "revolutionary suicide."

To be sure, I am not intending to provide an apologia for Lépine, nor, heaven forbid, to rehabilitate him politically. On the contrary I have sought to learn from him by identifying where he went wrong, so that I could avoid reproducing the grammar of his politics. Apart from not letting anger become rage and get the better of you, it means, I think, refusing to follow him in his reductive and constructive ways (not to mention murder). As Chomsky says of the demand for hate laws as an answer to the public pronouncements of Holocaust revisionists:

> It is a poor service to the memory of the victims to adopt a central doctrine of their murderers.[41]

Notes

1. Ronald L. Grimes, "No Safe Place," in *Marrying and Burying: Rites of Passage in a Man's Life* (Boulder, CO: Westview, 1995), 242.

2. Thelma McCormack, "Questions in the Aftermath: Engineering Feminism," *This Magazine*, 24, no. 1 (June 1990), 32.

3. Margaret Atwood, "A Disneyland of the Soul," in *The Writer and Human Rights*, ed. Toronto Arts Group for Human Rights (Toronto: Lester and Orpen Dennys, 1983), 132.

4. Monique Bosco, "The Will to Know," in *The Montreal Massacre*, ed. Louise Malette and Marie Chalouh (Charlottetown, PEI: Gynergy Books, 1991), 171.

5. Edward S. Herman, *The Real Terror Network: Terrorism in Fact and Propaganda* (Montreal, QUE: Black Rose, 1982); Edward S. Herman and Gerry O'Sullivan, *The "Terrorism" Industry: The Experts and Institutions That Shape Our View of Terror* (New York: Pantheon, 1989); Noam Chomsky, *Pirates and Emperors, Old and New: International Terrorism in the Real World* (Toronto, ON: Between the Lines, 2002 (1987)); Peter Eglin, "Propaganda and its Affordances: El Salvador in the Globe and Mail and the Question of Intellectual Responsibility," in *Filtering the News: Essays on Herman and Chomsky's Propaganda Model*, ed. Jeff Klaehn (Montreal, QUE: Black Rose, 2005), 95-119; idem, "Partnership in an Evil Action: Canadian Universities, Indonesia, East Timor and the Question of Intellectual Responsibility Again," in *Bound by Power: Intended Consequences*, ed. Jeff Klaehn (Montreal, QUE: Black Rose, 2006), 217-258.

6. For other than local news coverage see, for example, Sean Fine, "University Officials Assailed Over Tradition of Panty Raids," *Globe and Mail*, 20 October, 1989; Tracey Tyler and Matt Maychak, "Students Defend Panty Raids as 'Harmless Ritual,'" *Toronto Star*, 26 October, 1989, A8; Editorial, "Black Eye for Laurier," *Toronto Star*, 26 October, 1989, A32; Tracey Tyler, "Why Campus Pranks Turning Nasty," *Toronto Star*, 5 November, 1989, A3; Orland French, "Sex Wars Still Rage on Cam-

pus," *Globe and Mail*, Saturday, 11 November, 1989, Focus sec., D1; Susan Donaldson and Will Kymlicka (Analysis), "No Thaw in Chilly Campus Climate," *Globe and Mail*, 17 November, 1989, A8.

7. Grimes, *Marrying and Burying*, 236.

8. Greg Crone, "WLU Paper Faces Censure," *Kitchener-Waterloo Record*, 29 December 1989, B1.

9. "Men's Group Supports the Women's Centre [collective letter]," *the cord* (WLU), 29 November 1989, 11.

10. Peter Eglin and Stephen Hester, "Category, Predicate and Task: The Pragmatics of Practical Action [Review article on Lena Jayyusi, *Categorization and the Moral Order*]," *Semiotica* 88 (1992): 243-268.

11. Stephen Hester and Peter Eglin, ed., *Culture in Action: Studies in Membership Categorization Analysis* (Washington, D.C.: International Institute for Ethnomethodology and Conversation Analysis, and University Press of America, 1997).

12. Peter Eglin and Stephen Hester, "Moral Order and the Montreal Massacre: A Story of Membership Categorization Analysis," in *Media Studies: Ethnomethodological Approaches*, ed. Paul Jalbert (Lanham, Maryland: University Press of America, and International Institute for Ethnomethodology and Conversation Analysis, 1999), 195-230. (Reprinted in Michael Lynch and Wes Sharrock, ed., *Harold Garfinkel*, vol. III, Sage Masters of Modern Social Thought [London: Sage, 2003], 175-210.)

13. Peter Eglin and Stephen Hester, *The Montreal Massacre: A Story of Membership Categorization Analysis* (Waterloo, ON: Wilfrid Laurier University Press, 2003).

14. Rick Campbell, "Some Lurid Confessions of a Former Panty Raider," *Waterloo Chronicle*, 1 November 1989, 7.

15. Leah Renae Kelly (with Ward Churchill), "*Smoke Signals* in Context: An Historical Overview," in *In My Own Voice: Explorations in the Sociopolitical Context of Art and Cinema* (Winnipeg, MAN: Arbeiter Ring, 2001), 126. (Originally published by Ward Churchill in *Z Magazine*, 11, no. 11 [November 1998].)

16. Frances Kelly, "Panty Raids Banned at Wilfrid Laurier," *Sunday Toronto Star*, 29 October 1989.

17. Canadian Press, "Panty Raiders Caught Short," *Sunday Toronto Sun*, 29 October 1989.

18. Michèle Landsberg, "University Sanctions Student Panty Raids," *Toronto Star*, 26 October 1989.

19. Michèle Landsberg, "Killer's Rage Was All Too Familiar," *Toronto Star*, 8 December 1989, A1.

20. Susan Donaldson and Will Kymlicka, "No Thaw in Chilly Campus Climate," *Globe and Mail*, 17 November 1989, A8.

21. Jeny Hartwick, "Image of Neanderthal U [letter]," *Globe and Mail*, 12 December 1989, A6.

22. Bosco, "The Will To Know," 174.

23. Kai T. Erikson, *Wayward Puritans: A Study in the Sociology of Deviance* (New York: John Wiley, 1966); Stephen Hester and Peter Eglin, *A Sociology of Crime* (London and New York: Routledge, 1992), 263-264.

24. A strictly ethnomethodological treatment of the matter discussed below in the text can be found in Chapter 8 of Eglin and Hester, *The Montreal Massacre*.

25. Louise Malette and Marie Chalouh, ed., *The Montreal Massacre*, trans. Marlene Wildeman (Charlottetown, PEI: Gynergy Books, 1991), 9-10. (Originally published in French in 1990.)

26. Ibid., 15, emphasis added.

27. Louise Malette, "Preface to the English Edition," in Malette and Chalouh, *The Montreal Massacre*, 13.

28. Edward Said, "A Note on Modernism," in *Culture and Imperialism* (New York: Vintage, 1994), 186-190.

29. Lena Jayyusi, *Categorization and the Moral Order* (Boston, MA: Routledge and Kegan Paul, 1984), 126; see also Jeff Coulter, "Remarks on the Conceptualization of Social Structure," *Philosophy of the Social Sciences* 12 (1982): 33-46.

30. William K. Carroll and R. S. Ratner, "Media Strategies and Political Projects: A Comparative Study of Social Movements," *Canadian Journal of Sociology* 24, no. 1 (1999): 12.

31. "Frankly Speaking," *the cord* (WLU), 6 September 1990, 7, 10.

32. Susan Chung, "'Sexist' Calendars Ripped Up," *Kitchener-Waterloo Record*, 27 July 1990, B1.

33. Katherine Dowling, "Dini Petty's Show on Sexism Useless," *the cord* (WLU), 25 October 1990, 3.

34. Rose Simone, "Prof Sorry He Ripped Up Calendars," *Kitchener-Waterloo Record*, 15 August 1990; "Charge Withdrawn Against Professor," *Kitchener-Waterloo Record*, 16 August 1990, B1.

35. Eglin and Hester, *The Montreal Massacre*, 55.

36. Harvey Sacks, "Everyone Has to Lie," in *Sociocultural Dimensions of Language Use*, ed. M. Sanches and B. Blount (New York: Academic Press, 1975), 57-79.

37. Stevie Cameron, "Hundreds in Toronto Mourn Killing of 14 Women," *Globe and Mail*, 8 December 1989, A13.

38. Harvey Sacks, *Lectures on Conversation*, vol. 1 (Oxford: Blackwell, 1992), 398; idem, "Hotrodder: A Revolutionary Category," in *Everyday Language: Studies in Ethnomethodology*, ed. George Psathas (New York: Irvington, 1979), 9.

39. For extended discussion of the general issue at stake here see David Francis, Stephen Hester and Peter Elgin, "Ethnomethodology, Conversation Analysis and Gender," (forthcoming); Peter Eglin, David Francis and Stephen Hester, "On Men and Women: Knowledge Protected Against Induction and the Productive Use of Categories," forthcoming.

40. J.Z. Smith, "The Devil in Mr. Jones," in *Imagining Religion: From Babylon to Jonestown* (Chicago, IL: University of Chicago Press, 1982), 102-120.

41. Chomsky, in *Manufacturing Consent: Noam Chomsky and the Media*, ed. Mark Achbar (Montreal: Black Rose, 1994), 191.

Chapter Ten

Women's Experiences of Separation/Divorce Sexual Assault in Rural Ohio[1]

Walter S. DeKeseredy, Danielle Fagen, Mandy Hall and Martin D. Schwartz

FEW social scientific areas of inquiry have moved as far and fast as the study of male-to-female physical, sexual, and psychological abuse. Only 35 years ago, a comprehensive bibliography of North American sources on wife beating would fit on an index card.[2] Today, hundreds of journal articles, scores of books, and several important international and interdisciplinary journals such as *Violence Against Women* specifically address a variety of forms of woman abuse. We now have rich data on and many theories of woman abuse in a variety of relationships and social settings, making it clear that living in conditions of patriarchal tyranny is a dangerous attack on a woman's psychological as well as physical health. However, some abused women have received much more attention than do others. For example, the empirical and theoretical work done so far in North America focuses mainly on the abuse of women in dating and marriage/cohabitation.[3] Clearly, the women harmed in these ongoing relationships "do not represent the entire spectrum of abused women."[4]

Breaking up with a violent man is one of the most dangerous events in a woman's life[5] but relatively little attention has been paid to the victimization of women who want to leave, are in the process of leaving, or who have left their marital/cohabiting partners. Further, the limited work that has been done on this topic has focused on physical violence.[6] Abuse, of course, is multidimensional in nature and a few studies show that women are also at high risk of being sexually assaulted during and after separation/divorce.[7] Still, almost all of the research on this problem, regardless of whether it is qualitative or quantitative, was done in urban U.S. areas, such as Boston and San Francisco.

The main purpose of this chapter, then, is to help fill a research gap by presenting the results of an exploratory qualitative study of separation/divorce sexual assault in rural Ohio. Certainly, this is the first North American study of its kind and this project sensitizes us to some brutal roadblocks to equality that many rural women face. Moreover, the data provided by 43 women who participated in the study challenge the notion that rural communities offer women more safety than do urban areas. Here, following Websdale[8] and Wuest and Merritt-Gray,[9] rather than simply restrict a definition of rural to population size or living in the countryside, rural communities are referred to as those "where people know each other's business, come into regular contact with each other, and share a larger core of values than is true of people in urban areas." One of the key risk factors identified in this study is patriarchal male peer support, which is defined here as "attachments to male peers and the resources they provide which encourage and legitimate woman abuse."[10] What makes this finding particularly unique is that, except for Websdale's (1998) Kentucky study, no empirical attempt has been made to discern the existence, nature, and content of pro-abuse male social networks in rural U.S. communities. Most male peer support research is done on college campuses and not one study has documented whether male peer support contributes to sexual assault during or after the termination of any type of intimate relationship.[11]

Consider, too, that most male peer support studies rely on quantitative methods. These techniques provide valuable information; however, qualitative methods, such as those used in this study, elicit rich data on male peer group support discourses and practices that are unlikely to be uncovered in cross-sectional survey research.[12] Therefore, another major goal of this paper is to move male peer support research beyond the limited realm of middle-class students' dating experiences.[13]

Definition of Separation/Divorce

Can only couples that live apart be considered separated/divorced? Many surveys of martial rape,[14] as well as surveys of nonsexual types of woman abuse, seem to define separation/divorce this way. This approach is highly problematic because it neglects assaults after women's decisions and/or attempts to leave while they are locked in relationships.[15] Many men have a "fanatical determination" to not let their spouses/live-in partners go and will use violence "to keep them in their place."[16] Another point to consider is that many women defy men's patriarchal control by emotionally separating from them.[17] Emotional separation, a major predictor of a permanent end to a relationship, is defined as a women's denial or restriction of sexual relations and other intimate exchanges.[18] Emotionally exiting a relationship can be just as dangerous as physically or legally exiting one because it, too, increases the likelihood of male violence and sexual abuse.[19]

In sum, then, separation/divorce is not simply a function of proximity. Moreover, a woman does not have to be legally tied to a man to experience the pain and suffering caused by sexual or physical assault.[20] For example, Brownridge and Halli's review of fourteen studies: eight done in the U.S., five in Canada, and one in New Zealand, reveals "quite dramatic" differences in violence rates obtained from married persons and cohabiters.[21] In fact, they found that typically, the rate of violence for the latter exceeds that of the former by two times, but the difference can be greater than four times. Cohabiting women are also more likely to experience more severe types of violence than their married counterparts. Further, Canadian national representative sample survey data show that many women are sexually abused by their common-law partners, and male cohabitors are more likely to sexually abuse their partners than those in casual or serious dating relationships.[22] As Campbell points out, "a marriage license probably does not change the dynamics of sexual abuse within an ongoing intimate relationship."[23]

It is fair to assume that male cohabitors may be at higher risk of being sexually abusive than married men and this risk probably increases when their partners try to leave or do leave them. Finkelhor and Yllo tested this hypothesis and found that twenty-three percent of the women in their sample who experienced forced sex left their cohabiting partners, while three percent of married women were victimized this way.[24] Note, too, that twenty-five percent of the women who reported forced sex were legally separated/divorced.

Based on the above arguments and data presented elsewhere,[25] here, we use the term separation/divorce to mean physically, legally, or emotionally exiting a marital/cohabiting relationship. Further, our project focused on women-initiated separations/divorces because, as Sev'er reminds us, "they are the decisions that challenge male hegemony the most."[26] We also use a broad definition of sexual assault because it, like the physical and psychological abuse of women, takes many shapes and forms.

Definition of Sexual Assault

There are a number of problems with the use of narrow definitions of sexual assault, which have been covered elsewhere.[27] Unlike many, if not most, studies of sexual assault, a broad definition was used here that is not restricted to acts of forced penetration. Many women experience a wide range of sexually abusive behaviours, such as assaults when they were drunk or high, or when they were unable to give consent.[28] Moreover, many married and cohabiting women experience other kinds of threats that can result in painful unwanted sex and "blackmail rapes" (e.g., refusal to pay child support). Just because there was no threat or actual use of force does not mean that women's experiences were not frightening or highly injurious.

Most definitions also do not include unwanted sex "out of a sense of obligation,"[29] sexual relations stemming from ex-partners threats of fighting for sole custody of children, and other acts that do not involve the use of threats of force. Unfortunately, excluding the abusive behaviours identified here exacerbates the problem of underreporting and ultimately underestimates the extent of sexual assault.[30] Thus, guided by Koss, Gidycz and Wisniewski's conceptual and empirical work,[31] below is how we classified the types of sexual assault described by our interviewees.

- *Sexual Contact* includes sex play (fondling, kissing, or petting) arising from menacing verbal pressure, misuse of authority, threats of harm, or actual physical force.
- *Sexual Coercion* includes unwanted sexual intercourse arising from the use of menacing verbal pressure or the misuse of authority.
- *Attempted rape* includes attempted unwanted sexual intercourse arising from the use of or threats of force, or the use of drugs or alcohol.
- *Rape* includes unwanted sexual intercourse arising from the use of or threats of force and other unwanted sex acts (anal or oral intercourse or penetration by objects other than the penis) arising from the use of or threat of force, or the use of drugs or alcohol.

Rurality, Violence, and Male Peer Support for Sexual Assault

The first problem in any study of rural communities is to attempt to grasp the notion of what "rural" could mean. "Like concepts such as 'truth,' 'beauty,' or 'justice,' everyone knows the term rural, but no one can define the term very precisely."[32] Even some of the most basic problems are still somewhat at issue. Traditional literature makes much of a rural/urban difference in Western society, even if rural culture has not been studied much. Some have argued that this dichotomy is no longer useful, or only partially useful, since the standardization of education, communication and transportation has removed any unique part of rural culture.[33] Those who still believe in a rural culture presume that a major difference is that there is more homogeneity in rural areas, leading to a more collective control on deviant behaviour.[34]

This concept of homogeneity, however, has been sharply challenged in recent years by those who argue that there are different types of rural communities, and important variations between these communities. For example, Jobes, Barclay, Weinand and Donnermeyer found six different kinds of rural communities, ranging up to the highly disorganized small community with high crime rates.[35] Nisbett argued that violence rates in rural America depend on cultural factors, and found that the herding regions of the American South followed a culture of honour that was associated with high rates of interpersonal violence, especially between acquaintances.[36] Certainly criminologists who accept official statistics as valid have argued that there is less overall crime in rural areas, and that the greatest rural/urban difference is in violent crime. The difference is particularly striking in robbery rates.[37]

Most studies depend on official statistics to support theories about the extent of rural crime. Unfortunately, under the best of circumstances official statistics are notoriously poor at gathering information on marital rape and domestic violence.[38] Rural communities have characteristics that make it less likely that women will report such crimes, including the acceptance of stereotypical gender roles,[39] geographic and social isolation, such as from social services,[40] the absence of public transportation,[41] and a lack of economic opportunities. This lack of support and opportunity may not affect the ability of rural communities to reduce most types of crime, but it would actually act to increase interpersonal violence within the family.[42] Websdale argues similarly that rural areas are characterized by social forces that have overall and generally kept violent crime to levels below those experienced in urban areas.[43] However, his work is based on the argument that the reason is rural patriarchal relations, including the existence of a powerful "ol' boys network." Websdale suggests that while there is a system of social practices that generally serve to dominate and oppress women, it operates differently in rural areas. "(T)he domination of women by men across cultures is a consistent international trend and if there is one unifying theme, one seemingly universal thread of patriarchy that inhabits most cultures, it is that of male violence."[44]

Thus, Gagne reported in her study of Appalachian women that many of them were not only victimized, but also further convinced by their complete lack of support that they (at least temporarily) had no alternative but to put up with oppressive conditions.[45] For example, women know that the local police can be friends with their abuser and may refuse to arrest on the grounds of friendship.[46] Others, following in Websdale's path, argue that it is not these specific actions that combine to make conditions oppressive for these women, but that the very nature of rurality is based on male standards, making women generally invisible when decisions are made.[47] A variety of studies "have demonstrated how male dominance and supremacy are displayed through symbolic leisure activities as well as more severe manifestations of control (sometimes violent)."[48] Interpersonal violence for these men may be a form of proving both to themselves and others their essential masculinity and heterosexuality, at least as they define it.[49] Further, there is a greater distrust of government in rural areas, which means that even when crimes such as marital rape occur the victim may be less likely to want the police involved than would her urban counterpart.[50] If rural areas are characterized by less crime generally, but the crime that is seen is more likely to be against acquaintances and violent, and rural patriarchy serves to encourage and exacerbate men's feelings of control and power over women, then we would expect to find a high degree of physical and sexual assault against intimate partners in rural areas.

As noted above, we use male peer support to refer to the multidimensional attachments men form to male peers who themselves sexually assault women and/or provide resources that perpetuate and legitimate such assaults.[51] There are a variety of sociological and social psychological processes by which peers influence men to sexually victimize women,[52] but the key point here is that such all-male groups encourage, justify and support the abuse of women by their members. For example, such men provide informational support, which refers to the guidance and advice that influences men to sexually abuse their partners. Male peer support theory sees such support as a motivational factor, allowing men to develop pro-abuse attitudes and behaviours as a result of the encouragement and support of other males, if not of the broader culture at large.[53]

This form of peer pressure that legitimizes the sexual objectification of women and the sexual exploitation of them can be found in all types of cultures throughout the world. For example, Wilson found that inner-city African-American men found themselves under considerable peer pressure:

> ...to be sexually active. They said that the members of their peer networks brag about their encounters and that they feel obligated to reveal their own sexual exploits. Little consideration is given to the implications or consequences of sexual matters for the longer-term relationship.[54]

Far from Wilson's research site, Campbell found that male pub drinking practices in rural New Zealand reinforced dominant understandings of legitimate masculine behaviour.[55] In this rural area, male pub behaviour included men from across the community, making pubs "the key sites for maintaining the legitimacy of hegemonic masculinity in the wider community."[56]

Again, most of the work on male peer support theory has been quantitative in nature and conducted on college campuses.[57] A few researchers have both used qualitative methods and left the college campus to study the relationship between male peer support and various types of woman abuse in urban areas of concentrated disadvantage.[58] Sinclair found in a qualitative study that male peer support helped to explain woman abuse behaviour among socially displaced youth in an eastern Ontario city.[59] Further, DeKeseredy and Schwartz offer a male peer support theory of woman abuse in public housing, but did not gather any data specifically on this topic.[60] The topic of interest in this chapter – sexual assault of women who are breaking up or trying to break up intimate relationships – is one that has been outside the purview of all of the prior studies, as has for the most part been the study of male peer support for sexually aggressive men in rural areas.

Methods

Immediately after receiving approval to conduct this study from Ohio University's Institutional Review Board, the research team began this project by developing a "preparatory component of qualitative investigation."[61] This involved several meetings, electronic mail exchanges, and in-depth telephone conversations with leading researchers in the field,[62] local shelter staff, sexual assault survivor advocates, police officers, mental health workers, and others with a vested interest in curbing the pain and suffering uncovered by this research. Service providers were given copies of the research proposal and screening questions, and were helpful in shaping the final versions of each. They sensitized the research team to such issues as the influence of broader Ohio state politics, and put us into contact with service providers and criminal justice officials throughout Ohio, such as those affiliated with the Ohio Domestic Violence Network (ODVN) and the Ohio Coalition Against Sexual Assault (OCASA). Practitioners also referred six of the forty-three women who participated in this study. As Schechter points out, activists and practitioners are experts on woman abuse and "can help researchers formulate sophisticated and intellectually rich questions."[63]

Prior data on the relationship between separation/divorce and non-lethal forms of woman abuse (e.g., beatings) have been primarily derived from surveys. To develop a richer understanding of these issues it is necessary to listen to women's voices because it "may be the only way to describe a complex reality for which we have few names."[64] The effects of the geography, economy and culture of rural communities like those in Ohio and how they affect the residents has been discussed. However, these same problems present themselves in any attempt to gain access in a telephone or self-report survey.[65] Like women living in other poor rural communities, a sizeable portion of those residing in the counties where this study was conducted cannot afford telephones or cars.[66] To make matters worse, many rural women have abusive current or former partners who "feed off of" women's isolation and poverty to magnify their isolation. And, they often use tactics such as disabling care or forbidding women to leave the house.[67]

Box 1: Newspaper Advertisement

Call For Interested Women Of Athens, Hocking, And Vinton Counties For Participation In An Ohio University Research Project

Have you ever had unwanted sexual experiences while trying to leave your husband or male live-in partner?

Or, have you ever had unwanted sexual experiences after you left your husband or male live-in partner?

We would greatly appreciate your participation in a confidential interview. Your name will not be given to anyone.

We will pay you $25.00 for your time and transportation costs. Also, we will talk to you at a time and location of your choosing.

If you would like to be interviewed, please call Mae at (xxx) xxx-xxxx or Carolyn at (xxx) xxx-xxxx.

Techniques like those employed by Bowker in Milwaukee generated our sample.[68] For example, the advertisement presented in Box 1 was placed once a week during two different six-week periods in a free newspaper available throughout Athens County, Ohio. Also, posters about the study were pinned up in public places, such as courthouses, and were given to social service providers who came into contact with abused women. In addition:

- Two local newspapers gave considerable coverage to the project.
- Ohio University sent out a press release to newspapers and other Ohio-based media.
- Three local radio stations and Ohio University's television station carried public service announcements about the study.
- The PI and the director of the local shelter appeared on a local television news show to discuss this project and broader issues related to it.
- The Ohio Domestic Violence Network and other agencies told interested parties (e.g., rural shelter workers) about the study and helped to recruit participants.

- Local shelter staff, a police department social worker, employees of the county sheriff's department, Planned Parenthood, Women's Center staff at a local two-year college, and employees of the local Sexual Assault Survivor Advocate Program informed possible respondents about the study.

- Ohio University sociologist Judith Grant told women who participated in her addiction study about our research.

- Index-like cards with the information provided in the recruiting poster were routinely placed on top of newspaper boxes inside stores and on sidewalks in Athens.

Two female research assistants carried cellular phones twenty-four hours a day to receive calls from women interested in participating in the study. Callers were told the purpose of the study and were then asked a series of screening questions to determine their eligibility to be interviewed. The main criteria were being eighteen years of age or older and having ever had any type of unwanted sexual experience when they wanted to end, were trying to end, or after they had ended a relationship with a husband or live-in male partner. If they met the selection criteria, the women were then invited to a semi-structured face-to-face interview at a time and place of their choosing, and they were paid $25.00 for their time and up to $7.75 for travel expenses. Six Interviews were conducted over the phone, five were held off-campus, and the rest were done in an Ohio University office. It should also be noted in passing that most of the participants who came to the campus to be interviewed did not disclose how they got there. However, we assume that friends or relatives drove them. Further, all of the participants did not disclose how they had access to telephones. It is reasonable to assume that they felt that revealing such information would jeopardize their safety.

Female research assistants who also tape-recorded and transcribed them did all of the interviews. Most of the interviews were ninety minutes in length and a total of forty-three women participated in this study. Posters placed in public places attracted most of our respondents (n=27). Eight women called the number after exposure to ads or stories about the study in the media and the same number were referred to us by individuals or organizations (n=8). Most of the respondents (n=30) lived in Athens County, three lived in Hocking County, one lived in Vinton County, and nine lived in other rural parts of the state. The mean age of the sample was thirty-five and the mean income for 2002 was $13,588. Sixty-five percent (n=28) had some type of post-secondary education and close to half of the participants were unemployed. Of the twenty-five who had been married, all were divorced or legally separated, but only five remarried. Most of respondents also had children.

Findings

Earlier we listed the definitions of the four types of sexual assault used in this study. The number of respondents who ever experienced one or more of these behaviours is presented in Table 1. Only a few of the forty-three respondents experienced just one of the above forms of separation/divorce sexual assault, and virtually all experienced rape or attempted rape. As stated previously, "blackmail rapes" during the course of separation/divorce are not uncommon. For example, Tina wanted to leave her partner but was afraid of losing her children. Asked why her partner sexually assaulted, she replied:

> Um, to punish me for leaving him. To punish me for getting pregnant, um, to punish me for embarrassing him and um, to control me…. And then something would happen and he would know it was getting close to the end of our relationship once again and he would start it. And the whole time I would be crying, but I couldn't cry loud enough because if his parents heard us he swore he would take our children away. I know he did this when he thought I was getting ready to leave and he knew that I couldn't live without my children.

Women who are the victims of intimate interpersonal violence are rarely victimized only by sexual assault. Rather, they typically suffer from a variety of male behaviours that include physical violence, psychological abuse, economic blackmail or abuse such as denying the woman money even if she earns a wage, harm to animals or possessions to which she has an attachment, or stalking behaviour. Most (80%) of the women here were victimized by two or more of these forms of abuse. The rates at which they report this abuse is listed in Table 2, where each different type of abuse is counted once, but a single person can be counted in more than one category.

Table 1: Separation/Divorce Sexual Assault Prevalence Rates (N = 43)

TYPE OF SEXUAL ASSAULT	N	%
Sexual Contact	19	44
Sexual Coercion	32	74
Attempted Rape	8	18
Rape	35	81

Table 2: Nonsexual Abuse Prevalence Rates (N = 43)

TYPE OF NONSEXUAL ABUSE	N	%
Physical Violence	36	84
Psychological Abuse	38	88
Economic Abuse	30	70
Abuse of Pets	5	12
Stalking	16	37
Destruction of Prized Possessions	22	51

Joan was one interviewee who was harmed by various types of abuse during the process of exiting her relationship:

> Well, what happened was that he got drunk and wanted sex from me and I told him no. I said, "Stay away from me. I can't stand you when you're drinking. Get away from me. He started grabbling my butt, and playing with my legs, and trying to grab my boobs. And everything, anything to get what he wanted. And I told him, I kicked him in the leg and I told him, "Get away from me." And then got into a fight over it and the he started throwing stuff at my face and I went to the phone and I said, "I'm gonna call your probation officer." I says, "If you don't leave me alone and you've been drinking, you're acting like an ass. Leave me the hell alone." And he wouldn't. He unplugged the phone. I plugged it in, I plugged it, you know. It was back and forth. He unplugged, I plugged it in. He unplugged it, I plugged it in…. [W]hen he was trying to prevent me from getting the phone, he stepped on my foot, which fractured the top of my foot. I was on crutches for two weeks.

Thus, Table 2 shows that most victims of separation/divorce sexual assault are also hurt by other highly injurious acts. Sometimes they are not the only ones injured by ex-partners. For example, nineteen percent of our respondents stated that their partners abused their children and one woman believes that her ex-partner raped her as a means of killing her unborn child. Below is what Trina's ex-husband did to her daughter:

He came back October of the same year for a so-called emergency visitation, and he was able to take my daughter away from me for eight hours even though the DNA had never been proven. And, when my daughter finally came back, she had severe diaper rash, smelled like cigarettes and alcohol, and had bruises right, right on her thighs and on her wrists.

When is the most likely time for separation/divorce sexual assault to occur? As other studies discovered, it may be when a woman expresses a desire to leave a relationship.[69] Seventy-four (N = 32) of our respondents stated that they were sexually assaulted at that time. Forty-nine percent (N = 21) were sexually abused while they were trying to leave or while they were leaving and thirty-three percent (N = 14) were victimized after they left. Obviously many of these women were victimized at two or more of these times.

Although it is difficult to make hard comparisons from small numbers, there is no question that in this sample the formerly married women reported a higher rate of sexual assault at each stage than the cohabiting women. For example, compared to cohabiting women (33%, n=6), married women (47%, n=12) were more likely to report being abused while still in the relationship, before expressing a desire to exit, trying to exit, or exiting their relationships. At the next stage, when the women reported that they wanted to leave their abusive relationship, twenty of the twenty-five married women (80%) stated that they were sexually assaulted, while twelve of the eighteen (67%) cohabiting women stated that their assaults occurred at this point in time.

Male Peer Support

One of our interests in this study was whether there was any link between male peer support and the abuse of women. Here sixty-seven percent (n=29) of the women reported on a variety of ways in which the partner's male peers perpetuated and legitimated separation/divorce sexual assault. Three methods in particular stand out: frequently drinking with male friends, informational support, and attachment to abusive peers. Informational support refers to the guidance and advice that influences men to sexually, physically, and psychologically abuse their female partners and attachment to abusive peers is defined as having male friends who also abuse women. These factors are identical to those found to be highly significant in predicting which men on college campuses will admit to being sexual predators.[70]

The first factor is *frequent drinking with friends*. Such drinking has often been associated with the development of a particular kind of masculinity that objectifies women and endorses male behaviour that can be physically and sexually violent.[71] While seventy-seven percent (N=33) of the women said that their former partners frequently drank alcohol, sixty-three (n=27) said their partners spent large amounts of time with their male friends and most of the time spent together involved drinking alcohol. Further, as is the case with college men who sexually abuse women, "nights out drinking with the boys" were seen by many respondents as contexts that often supported patriarchal conversations about women and how to control them.[72] As Susan told us after we probed for more information about the evenings her partner spent drinking with male friends:

> Um, they're basically like him. They sit around, talk about women and gossip. They're the biggest gossips there ever was. But they sit around and brag how many times they get it and how they keep their women in line and you know just like crap, you know.

The social settings described by Susan and other respondents are also examples of the second factor of *informational support*, although these were not restricted to group drinking events. For example, one respondent's abusive partner spent much time with his cousin, a man who "hated women" and often called them "fuckin bitches" and "whore sluts." Note, too, that although most of the participants did not explicitly label their partners' peers as patriarchal, most of them are. As Lynn told us, "And they just think women are their property and they can lay 'em anytime they want to. That's just their whole attitude about it." Further, forty-seven percent (n=20) of the sample stated that they knew that their partners' friends also physically or sexually abused women. In fact, Betty told us that *all* of her ex-partners' friends hit women or sexually assault them, and several women told us that they directly observed their partners' friends abusing female intimates. Jackie is one such participant and she told us: "I watched a friend of his who shoved a friend of mine up against a wall...and try to, you know, have his way with her."

A few perpetrators also enlisted the help of their friends to sexually abuse some of the women we interviewed. Such male peer support frequently involved forcing women to have sex with friends. Consider what happened to Marie:

> Well, him and his friend got me so wasted. They took turns with me and I remembered most of it, but, um, there was also drugs involved where not as much on my behalf as theirs. I was just drunk. And I did remember most of it and the next morning I woke up feeling so dirty and so degraded and then it ended up getting around that I was the slut...And in my eyes that was rape

due to the fact that I was so drunk. And I definitely didn't deserve that. And I was hurting. I was hurting the next day.

This incident is similar to what Sanday uncovered in her study of fraternity gang rape.[73] In groups, some men do not rely on force to have sex with women, but rather use alcohol or drugs to "work a yes" out of them. In other words, some perpetrators, either alone or in a group, purposely get women so drunk that they cannot resist their advances, which is a form of felony forcible rape in Ohio and most other states. Although the incident described below by Carrie did not involve male peer support, it is another glaring example of using alcohol as a means of "working a yes out":

I agreed to meet with him to discuss visitation and child support for our daughter and I wanted to go to a public place after everything he had done because it wasn't just sexual, it was mental, physical. And I showed up there. I had a couple friends who were sitting throughout keeping an eye on me. Ordered the drink, got up to use the bathroom, drank my drink and that was pretty much the last thing I remembered until the next morning when I woke up with a killer headache and my daughter crying in her crib.... He was in bed next to me.... I had strangulation marks around my neck. I had marks around my wrists and an open wound on my face and he had obviously had sex.

A few women who were forced to have group sex were also beaten after going through brutal degradation ceremonies. As Janet reveals,

He ended up bringing someone into the relationship, which I didn't want, but he told me that if I didn't do it he would leave me. And I ended up staying with him. He was more into group sex and, and uh trying to be the big man. He wanted sex as a group thing or with his buddies or made me have sex with a friend of his. See one time he made me have sex with a friend of his for him to watch, and then he got mad and hit me afterwards. I mean he tied me up so I could watch him have sex with a 13-year-old girl. And then he ended up going to prison for it. So, I mean it was nasty.

Lorraine recalled this incident that occurred during the end of her relationship:

He wanted me to have sex with a few people. Okay, like I was telling you earlier, and I didn't want to.... And, uh, I finally did. And then I got beat for it because I did. I tried not to, but then when we did, I got beat.

Illustrations of Patriarchy

Seventy-nine percent of the sample told us that their partners strongly believed that men should be in charge and control of domestic household settings, and many women said that the men who abused them used tactics such as those described by one interviewee to maintain control: "He, uh, wanted to be in control. He was in control for us, or you know I felt it." Another woman said that her estranged partner behaved in a similar fashion:

> He didn't allow me to socialize at all. My place was at home with the children and that's where I was most of the time. The only thing I went out for was if they had a parent-teacher conference at school. I went for that. But no, I had no outside contact.

This is how another respondent's partner treated her until she managed to leave him:

> His favourite thing was, "If you are not going to be at work, you're going to be here cooking and cleaning, doing laundry. And if I ever catch you sitting on your ass, I am going to beat the fuck out of you, you know."

Note, too, most respondents stated that they were raped during or after separation/divorce because their partners wanted to show them "who was in charge." Tanya is just one of many women we interviewed who had a partner that was determined not to let her go:

> He did it because I was his and he felt he could. And it was his way of letting me know that, ah, first of all, of letting me know that I was his. And secondly, letting me know that um, that I wasn't safe anywhere. And I, when we were together, when he had forced me to go back together with him, ah, he, ah...raped me as another form of, of possession. And I think also as a reminder of what could happen. And ultimately, at one point, I believed that he raped me as part of his means of killing my unborn child.

The fact that close to eighty percent of the men who abused their partners adhered to the ideology of familial and/or societal patriarchy may also partially explain why so many perpetrators had peers who were sexist or abusive. For example, DeKeseredy and Schwartz uncovered a strong statistical relationship between Canadian college men's patriarchal attitudes and beliefs and their affiliations with male peers who perpetuate and legitimate physical, sexual, and psychological abuse in dating relationships.[74] More specifically, these researchers found that Canadian college men who report abusing their girlfriends and dating partners are more likely than those who do not report abusive behaviour to endorse an ideology of familial patriarchy. They also found that these men are even more likely to be abusive if male peers support their sexist ideology and injurious behaviours.

Below is one major example of how male peers supported an interviewee's husband's "right" to maintain his patriarchal control with abuse. This incident happened shortly after her husband found out that she wanted to leave him:

> I remember my husband making me have sex with him one time when people were in the next room and none of them guys would come in and help me. And they knew he was hitting me, but they figured that he was my husband. If it were a stranger it would have been different.

Did male peers teach interviewees' partners to engage in separation/divorce sexual assault, or do abusive men simply seek the friendship and support of violent peers? These are important empirical questions that can only be answered empirically. Hopefully, future research on rural separation/divorce sexual assault will be specifically designed to uncover richer data on the complex relationship between patriarchy and male peer support.

Pornography

A few studies found that the contribution of pornography to woman abuse in dating is related to male peer support.[75] For example, some men learn to sexually objectify women through their exposure to pornographic media,[76] and they often learn these lessons in groups, such as pornographic film showings at fraternity houses.[77] Similarly, some rural Ohio survivors of separation/divorce sexual assault said that their partners consumed pornography with their male friends while drinking excessive amounts of alcohol. Agnes is one interviewee who experienced this problem:

> They were drinking and carrying on and they had, um, they had a bunch of porno stuff in the garage and I had walked in and I had started to tear it up. And I was, I was, I thought it was gross. I was mad at it. I was mad at him for being around it. And he just started charging after me and I started running to my car as fast as I could. And he got into the car and he threw me down in the seat and he just kept punching me, punching me.

Regardless of whether they consumed it in groups, 65% of the sample's estranged partners viewed pornography and were reported to be involved in sexually abusive events experienced by thirty-percent of our interviewees. But, does pornography cause separation/divorce sexual assault and other forms of woman abuse? Certainly this question cannot be answered from the data generated by this study. Rather, it requires a long-term and expensive longitudinal research design. Indeed, there are some important competing arguments. For example, it may well be that for men who are physically and sexually abusing women, pornography is just one more weapon in their arsenal. Thus, a man who knows that his partner would be scared or angry might not try to expose her to the lessons he learned from a pornographic movie, while his abusive friend might try to force his estranged partner to act out such scenes over her objections.[78]

In a somewhat related argument, it might very well be that the same factors that cause a man to abuse women also cause him to purchase pornography. In other words, the abuse came first, followed by an interest in pornography. In these scenarios, eliminating pornography might not have an effect on the amount of woman abuse, since the men are generally abusive anyway. However, this study and those that focused on other groups of women demonstrate that pornography certainly is a component of the problem of woman abuse.[79]

Conclusions

The data gathered by this exploratory study yield several conclusions. First, separation/divorce sexual assault occurs in some rural parts of Ohio as it probably does in other parts of North America. Further, like many survivors of marital rape and other forms of woman abuse, most of the women we interviewed experienced multiple forms of abuse, including physical violence. This finding is consistent with previous studies that reveal the prevalence of "battering rapes" among women who are both physically and sexually assaulted by their partners.[80] Consider, too, that many participants were emotionally pressured to have sex against their will. This is not surprising, given 79% of the women stated that the men who abused them strongly believed that they "should be in charge." As Bergen and Bukovec remind us, "Men who believe that they have a right, or entitlement to sex within their intimate partnerships, often rely on emotional pressure or coercion to force their partners to comply."[81]

The qualitative data presented here also provide further evidence that the sexual abuse of women is behaviour that is fostered by male peer support. Thus, although the bulk of previous studies on pro-abuse male peer support have been done on college campuses, this study provides additional evidence showing that men in a variety of locations are affected by patriarchal male peer group discourses and practices. As Bowker points out, any male support for the development of a sexist subculture of violence is not restricted to one specific time, place, or sociodemographic group.[82]

Of course, most men do not sexually abuse women during or after separation/divorce. However, the exploratory data we uncovered strongly suggest that separation/divorce sexual assault is a problem in rural Ohio, and further advance the study of the abuse of women who want to leave, are in the process of leaving, or who have left their partners. This study discovered that male peer support may play a major role in intimate sexual assault, but that other factors that must investigated in the future include the heavy use of alcohol, some uses of pornography, and the adherence by some men to an ideology of male dominance and control.

There has been some concern that some of the literature on various types of woman abuse in intimate relationships appears to view male peer support as a "universal risk factor" in that all men receive this support regardless of their place on the economic, political or social ladder of society.[83] However, what was found here is that pro-abuse male peer support in rural Ohio communities seems to operate in a similar fashion to that found on college campuses[84] and among single youth in poor urban neighbourhoods and centers of concentrated disadvantage.[85] Certainly, in this study we only examined women's points of view on this issue, but in previous studies men have not differed in their answers on these issues significantly from asking women about men.[86]

Although this study enhances a sociological understanding of a crime that has received little empirical and theoretical attention, further research is clearly necessary. For example, regardless of whether separation/divorce sexual assault studies are conducted in rural or urban settings, data gathered from men are needed to more accurately determine the factors that motivate them to abuse women. Representative sample surveys of rural populations are also necessary to determine the incidence and prevalence of separation/divorce sexual assault. Such research is undoubtedly difficult to do, given the methodological obstacles discussed previously. Moreover, theoretical work is needed to advance a better understanding of sexual assault during various stages of exiting marital/cohabiting relationships.[87] So far, one integrated theory of separation/divorce sexual assault has been developed, but it has not been tested and it is not specifically designed to explain the victimization of women in rural communities.[88]

For women like those who participated in our study, above all, what is needed are policies specifically aimed at curbing separation/divorce sexual assault. Effective control and prevention strategies are in short supply in rural Ohio as they are other rural parts of the U.S.[89] Further, very few women we interviewed knew where they could turn for help. Worse, there is some reason to believe that the kind of services that might be available in rural areas (e.g., restraining orders, mandatory arrest and prosecution for battering, shelter houses) could trigger a backlash from these men that might make it more dangerous for these women to leave their relationships than to stay in them.[90]

Until these problems are addressed we will continue to hear accounts similar to this one:

> I was his property that he wanted to own me. And I was his. That's how he looked at it. I was his property and that's all that I felt I was to him, way just a lay, you know. But that's all he wanted me for was to satisfy himself…He would deprive me. It was more of a mental torture, emotionally, mental torture than physical except in the sex it was physical. "You're mine and I'm gonna have you whether you want it or not. I want you." He was in control. And that's what it's all about with men like that. They have to be in control.

Notes

1. A revised version of this chapter was presented at the 2004 annual meeting of the American Society of Criminology, Nashville. The research reported here was supported by National Institute of Justice grant 2002-WG-BX-0004 and financial assistance provided by the College of Arts and Sciences and the Office of the Vice President for Research at Ohio University. Arguments and findings included in this paper are those of the authors and do not represent the official position of the U.S. Department of Justice or Ohio University. The authors would like to thank Bernard Auchter, Karen Bachar, the California Coalition Against Sexual Assault, Megan Cameron, Katharine Darke, Judith Grant, Carolyn Joseph, Jeffery Klaehn, Mary Koss, My Sister's Place, the Ohio Domestic Violence Network, Claire Renzetti, McKenzie Rogness, Leora Rosen, and all the service providers who worked with us for their input. Please send all correspondence to Walter S. DeKeseredy. All of the names of women who participated in the study and who are quoted here have been changed to maintain confidentiality.

2. Martin D. Schwartz and Walter S. DeKeseredy, "Liberal feminism on violence against women," *Social Justice* 15, (1988): 213-221.

3. Ruth E. Fleury, Cris M. Sullivan, and Deborah I. Bybee, "When ending the relationship does not end the violence: Women's experiences of violence by former partners," *Violence Against Women* 6, (2000): 1363-1383.

4. Aysan Sev'er, *Fleeing the House of Horrors: Women Who Have Left Abusive Partners* (Toronto: University of Toronto Press, 2002), 12.

5. Jacquelyn C. Campbell, Daniel Webster, Jane Koziol-McLain, Carolyn Block, Doris Campbell, D and Mary Ann Curry, "Risk factors for femicide in abusive relationships," *American Journal of Public Health* 93, (2003): 1089-1097.

6. For in-depth reviews of the literature on male-to-female physical assaults during and after separation/divorce see Walter S. DeKeseredy, McKenzie Rogness, and Martin D. Schwartz, "Separation/divorce sexual assault: The current state of social scientific knowledge," *Aggression and Violent Behavior* 9, (2004): 675-691 and Jennifer L. Hardesty, "Separation assault in the context of post-divorce parenting: An integrative review of the literature," *Violence Against Women* 8, (2002): 597-621.

7. See Raquel Kennedy Bergen, *Wife Rape: Understanding the Response of Survivors and Service Providers* (Thousand Oaks, California: Sage, 1996); Walter S. DeKeseredy and Carolyn Joseph, "Separation/divorce sexual assault in rural Ohio: Preliminary results of an exploratory study," *Violence Against Women* 12, (2006): 301-311; Walter S. DeKeseredy, Martin D. Schwartz, Danielle Fagen, and Mandy Hall, "Separation/divorce sexual assault: The contribution of male peer support," *Feminist Criminology* 1, (2006): 1-23; David Finkelhor and Kersti Yllo, *License to Rape: Sexual Abuse of Wives* (New York: Holt, Rinehart and Winston, 1985); Demie Kurz, *For Richer, For Poorer: Mothers Confront Divorce* (New York: Routledge, 1995) and Diana E.H. Russell, *Rape in Marriage* (New York: Macmillan Press, 1990).

8. As quoted in Neil Websdale, "An ethnographic assessment of policing of domestic violence in rural eastern Kentucky," *Social Justice* 22, (1995): 102.

9. Judith Wuest and Marilyn Merritt-Gray, "Not going back: Sustaining the separation process of leaving abusive relationships," *Violence Against Women* 5, (1999): 110-133.

10. Walter S. DeKeseredy, "Male peer support and woman abuse: The current state of knowledge," *Sociological Focus* 23, (1990): 130.

11. For in-depth reviews of the extant social scientific literature on male peer support and woman abuse see Walter S. DeKeseredy and Martin D. Schwartz, *Woman Abuse on Campus: Results from the Canadian National Survey* (Thousand Oaks, California: Sage, 1998) and Martin D. Schwartz and Walter S. DeKeseredy, *Sexual Assault on the College Campus: The Role of Male Peer Support* (Thousand Oaks, California: Sage, 1997).

12. DeKeseredy and Schwartz, *Women Abuse on Campus*.

13. A few researchers, however, have qualitatively studied the relationship between male peer support and various types of woman abuse in urban areas of concentrated disadvantage. See Elijah Anderson, *Code of the Street: Decency, Violence, and the Moral Life of the Inner City* (New York: Norton, 1999); Philippe Bourgois, *In Search of Respect: Selling Crack in El Barrio* (New York: Cambridge University Press, 1995); William Julius Wilson, *When Work Disappears: The World of the New Urban Poor* (New York: Knopf, 1996). For a qualitative Canadian study of male peer support among socially displaced youth in an eastern Ontario city see Roberta Lynn Sinclair, "Male peer support and male-to-female dating abuse committed by socially displaced male youth: An exploratory study," PhD diss., Ottawa: Carleton University, 2002. Further, in Walter S. DeKeseredy and Martin D. Schwartz, "Theorizing public housing woman abuse as a function of economic exclusion and male peer support," *Women's Health and Urban Life* 1, (2002): 26-45, a male peer support theory of woman abuse in public housing is offered, but data was not gathered specifically on this topic.

14. See Finkelhor and Yllo, *License to Rape* and Patricia Godeke Tjaden and Nancy Thonnes, *Extent, Nature and Consequences of Intimate Partner Violence: Findings from the National Violence Against Women Survey* (Washington, D.C.: U.S. Department of Justice, 2000).

15. Martha R. Mahoney, "Legal issues of battered women: Redefining the issue of separation," *Michigan Law Review* 90, (1991): 1-94 and James Ptacek, *Battered Women in the Courtroom: The Power of Judicial Responses* (Boston: Northeastern University Press, 1999).

16. Russell, *Rape in Marriage*.

17. DeKeseredy et al., "Separation/divorce sexual assault: The current state."

18. Desmond Ellis and Walter S. DeKeseredy, "Rethinking estrangement, interventions, and intimate femicide," *Violence Against Women* 3, (1997): 590-609.

19. See DeKeseredy et al., "Separation/divorce sexual assault: The contribution;" Ellis & DeKeseredy, "Rethinking estrangement;" Karen Kayser, *When Love Dies: The Power of Marital Disaffection* (Boston: Beacon, 1993); Catherine Kirkwood, *Leaving Abusive Partners* (Newbury Park, California: Sage, 1993); Howard Markman and Clifford Notarious, *We Can Work it Out: Making Sense of Marital Conflict* (Boulder, Colorado: Rockwell, 1994) and Russell, *Rape in Marriage*.

20. Bergen, *Wife Rape*.

21. Douglas A. Brownridge and Shivalingappa S. Halli, *Explaining Violence Against Women in Canada* (Lanham, Maryland: Lexington Books, 2001).

22. DeKeseredy and Schwartz, *Woman Abuse on Campus*.

23. Jacquelyn C. Campbell, "Women's response to sexual abuse in intimate relationships," *Health Care for Women International* 10, (1989): 336.

24. See Finkelhor and Yllo, *License to Rape*.

25. For example, see DeKeseredy et al., "Separation/divorce sexual assault: The current state."

26. Aysan Sev'er, "Recent or imminent separation and intimate violence against women: A conceptual overview and some Canadian examples," *Violence Against Women* 3, (1997): 567.

27. Walter S. DeKeseredy, "Current controversies on defining nonlethal violence against women in intimate heterosexual relationships: Empirical implications," *Violence Against Women* 6, (2000): 728-746.

28. See Karen J. Bachar and Mary P. Koss, "From prevalence to prevention: Closing the gap between what we know about rape and what we do," in Claire M. Renzetti, Jeffrey L. Edleson, & Raquel Kennedy Bergen eds., *Sourcebook on Violence Against Women* (Thousand Oaks, California: Sage, 2001), 117-142 and Martin D. Schwartz and Molly S. Leggett, "Bad dates or emotional trauma? The aftermath of campus sexual assault," *Violence Against Women* 5, (1999): 251-271.

29. Bergen, *Wife Rape*.

30. DeKeseredy et al., "Separation/divorce sexual assault: The current state."

31. Mary P. Koss, Christine A. Gidycz and Nadine Wisniewski, "The scope of rape: Incidence and prevalence of sexual aggression and victimization in a national sample of higher education students," *Journal of Consulting and Clinical Psychology* 55, (1987): 166.

32. Ralph A. Weisheit, David N. Falcone and L. Edward Wells, *Crime and Policing in Rural and Small-Town America* (Prospect Heights, Illinois: Waveland Press, 1996), 6.

33. See Claude S. Fischer, "The spread of violent crime from city to countryside, 1955-1975," *Rural Sociology* 45, (1980): 416-434 and Thomas A. Petee and Gregory S. Kowalski, "Modeling rural violent crime rates: A test of social disorganization theory," *Sociological Focus* 26, (1993): 87-89.

34. Neil Websdale, *Rural Woman Battering and the Justice System: An Ethnography* (Thousand Oaks, California: Sage, 1998).

35. Patrick C. Jobes, Elaine Barclay, Herb Weinand and Joseph F. Donnermeyer, "A structural analysis of social disorganization and crime in rural communities in Australia," *The Australian and New Zealand Journal of Criminology* 37, (2004): 114-140.

36. Richard E. Nisbett, "Violence and U.S. regional culture," *American Psychologist* 48, (1993): 441-449.

37. See Ralph A. Weisheit, David N. Falcone and L. Edward Wells, *Rural Crime and Rural Policing* (Washington, D.C.: National Institute of Justice Research in Action Report, 1994).

38. DeKeseredy et al., "Separation/divorce sexual assault: The current state" and Martin D. Schwartz, "Methodological issues in the use of survey data for measuring and characterizing violence against women," *Violence Against Women* 6, (2000): 815-838.

39. Jo Little, "'Riding the rural love train': Heterosexuality and the rural community," *Sociologia Ruralis* 43, (2003): 401-417.

40. Mary Ann Dutton, Aileen Worrell, Darci Terrell, Sharon Denaro and Robin Thompson, *National Evaluation of the Rural Domestic Violence and Child Victimization Enforcement Grant Program: Final Report, Volume 1* (Washington, D.C.: National Institute of Justice, 2002); Satya P. Krishnan, Judith C. Hilbert and Dawn VanLeeuwen, "Domestic violence and help-seeking behaviors among rural women: Results from a shelter-based study," *Family Community Health* 24, (2001): 28-38 and T.K. Logan, Robert Walker and Carl G. Leukefeld, "Rural, urban influenced, and urban differences among domestic violence arrestees," *Journal of Interpersonal Violence* 16, (2001): 266-283.

41. Susan H. Lewis, *Unspoken Crimes: Sexual Assault in Rural America* (Enola, Pennsylvania: National Sexual Violence Resource Center, 2003).

42. D. Wayne Osgood and Jeff M. Chambers, "Social disorganization outside the metropolis: An analysis of rural youth violence," *Criminology* 38, (2000): 81-115.

43. Websdale, *Rural Woman Battering*.

44. Ibid., 48.

45. Patricia L. Gagne, "Appalachian women: Violence and social control," *Journal of Contemporary Ethnography* 20, (1992): 387-415.

46. See Daniel J. Bell, "Family violence in small cities," *Police Studies* 12, (1989): 25-31. Also, L. Coorey, "Policing of violence in rural areas," in Tom Cullen, Peter Dunn and Geoffrey Lawrence eds., *Rural Health and Welfare in Australia* (Wagga Wagga, New South Wales, Australia: Centre for Rural Welfare Research, Charles Sturt University, 1990), 80-101.

47. Margaret Alston, "Women's representation in an Australian rural context," *Sociologia Ruralis* 43, (2003): 474-487.

48. Jo Little and Ruth Panelli, "Gender research in rural geography," *Gender, Place and Culture* 10, (2003): 283.

49. Walter S. DeKeseredy and Martin D. Schwartz, "Masculinities and interpersonal violence," in R.W. Connell, Michael S. Kimmel and Jeff Hearn eds., *The Handbook of Studies on Men and Masculinities* (Thousand Oaks, California: Sage, 2005), 353-366.

50. Weisheit et al., *Rural Crime and Rural Policing.*

51. DeKeseredy, "Male peer support and woman abuse."

52. Martin D. Schwartz and Walter S. DeKeseredy, *Sexual Assault on the College Campus: The Role of Male Peer Support* (Thousand Oaks, California: Sage, 1997).

53. Martin D. Schwartz, Walter S. DeKeseredy, David Tait and Shahid Alvi, "Male peer support and a feminist routine activities theory: Understanding sexual assault on the college campus," *Justice Quarterly* 18, (2001): 623-649.

54. Wilson, *When Work Disappears*, 99.

55. Hugh Campbell, "The glass phallus: Pub(lic) masculinity and drinking in rural New Zealand," *Rural Sociology* 65, (2000): 562-581.

56. Ibid, 579.

57. Walter S. DeKeseredy and Martin D. Schwartz, "Male peer support and woman abuse in postsecondary school courtship: Suggestions for new directions in sociological research," in Raquel Kennedy Bergen ed., *Issues in Intimate Violence* (Thousand Oaks, California: Sage, 1998), 83-96.

58. See Anderson, *Code of the Street*; Bourgois, *In Search of Respect* and Wilson, *When Work Disappears*.

59. Sinclair, "Male peer support."

60. DeKeseredy and Schwartz, "Theorizing public housing."

61. Brian D. MacLean, "A program of local crime-survey research for Canada," in Brian D. MacLean ed., *Crime and Society: Readings in Critical Criminology* (Toronto: Copp Clark, 1996), 73-105.

62. Raquel Kennedy Bergen, Mary Koss, Karen Bachar, and Claire Renzetti devoted a substantial amount of time and effort to helping us develop this study.

63. Susan Schechter, "Building bridges between activists, professionals, and researchers," in Kersti Yllo and Michele Louise Bograd eds., *Feminist Perspectives on Wife Abuse* (Beverly Hills, California: Sage, 1988), 311. Further, the Principal Investigator (PI) and his staff routinely shared their findings with all of the practitioners who helped them and the PI served on the Board of Directors of an Athens, Ohio shelter. He also became an active member of the Athens County Coaltion Against Sexual Assault during the data-gathering phase of this project and is a member of the ODVN's Board of Directors.

64. Mahoney, "Legal issues of battered women," 41.

65. Weisheit et al., *Rural Crime and Rural Policing.*

66. Krishnan et al., "Domestic violence" and Lewis, *Unspoken Crimes*.

67. Websdale, *Rural Woman Battering.*

68. Lee H. Bowker, *Beating Wife-Beating* (Lexington, Massachusetts: Lexington Books, 1983).

69. For example, see Sev'er, "Recent or imminent separation."

70. See Schwartz et al., "Male peer support" and DeKeseredy & Schwartz, "Male peer support and woman abuse."

71. See Campbell, "The glass phallus" and DeKeseredy & Schwartz, "Masculinities and interpersonal violence."

72. See Schwartz and DeKeseredy, *Sexual Assault* and Schwartz et al., "Male peer support" for more detailed information on the relationship between all-male sexist conversations, alcohol consumption, and sexual assault on the college campus.

73. Peggy Reeves Sanday, *Fraternity Gang Rape* (New York: New York University Press, 1990).

74. DeKeseredy and Schwartz, *Woman Abuse on Campus*.

75. Ibid. Also see Martin D. Schwartz and Walter S. DeKeseredy, "Pornography and the abuse of Canadian women in dating relationships," *Humanity & Society* 22, (1998) 137-154.

76. Robert Jensen, "Pornographic lives," *Violence Against Women* 1, (1995): 32-54.

77. Sanday, *Fraternity Gang Rape*.

78. Schwartz & DeKeseredy, "Pornography."

79. See Raquel Kennedy Bergen and K.A. Bogle, "Exploring the connection between pornography and sexual violence," *Violence and Victims* 15, (2000): 227-234; DeKeseredy & Schwartz, *Woman Abuse on Campus* and P.A. Harmon and James V. P. Check, *The Role of Pornography in Woman Abuse* (Toronto: York University's LaMarsh Research Center on Violence and Conflict Resolution, 1989).

80. See Bergen, *Wife Rape*; Raquel Kennedy Bergen and Paul Bukovec, "Men and intimate partner rape: Characteristics of men who sexually abuse their partners," *Journal of Interpersonal Violence* 21, no.10 (2006); Finkelhor and Yllo, *License to Rape*; and Russell, *Rape in Marriage*.

81. Bergen and Bukovec, "Men and intimate partner rape," 8.

82. Bowker, *Beating Wife-Beating*.

83. Ibid.

84. Schwartz & DeKeseredy, *Sexual Assault on the College Campus*.

85. Sinclair, "Male peer support."

86. Schwartz et al., "Male peer support."

87. T.K. Logan and Robert Walker, "Separation as a risk factor for victims of intimate partner violence: Beyond lethality and injury," *Journal of Interpersonal Violence* 19, (2004): 1478-1486.

88. See DeKeseredy et al., "Separation/divorce sexual assault: The current state."

89. DeKeseredy & Joseph, "Separation/divorce sexual assault" and T.K. Logan, Erin Stevenson, Lucy Evans and Carl Leukefeld, "Rural and urban women's perceptions to barriers to health, mental health, and criminal justice services: Implications for victim services," *Violence and Victims* 19, (2004): 37-62.

90. Laura Dugan, Daniel S. Nagin and Richard Rosenfeld, "Do domestic violence services save lives?" *National Institute of Justice Journal* no. 250, (2003): 20-25.

POLITICS, KNOWLEDGE AND AGE

The chapters in this section explore issues concerning politics, knowledge and age—numerous important topics and issues are discussed, including why aging and women's activism matter, women in higher education and challenges faced by women within contemporary universities, and the experiences of girls and what it means to do girlhood research. —*Jeffery Klaehn*

I spent twenty-three years of my life growing up in Mississauga, a neighboring community of Toronto. I never had to reflect on my identity as a Sikh woman until I began my graduate studies at Wilfrid Laurier University, in the master's of sociology program. It was the first time in my life I was confronted and reminded of who I was—the 'other.' Through this process I had begun to question who I was, where I came from and most importantly what aspects are entailed in living in a Sikh home. One of the common differences I began to recognize was the perception my community had on aging and knowledge. There is this interconnection between aging and knowledge, which is often blurred in the Western society. We need to understand that knowledge expands beyond ideas of intellectuals and from institutions such as universities, but is in our very own homes—and that is the life experiences that our elders have. The knowledge that our grandparents and respected elders possess has often been taken for granted.

Elders within the Sikh communities are highly praised and looked upon with possessing wisdom. Much of the older population was not given the advantage of attaining a post secondary education and thus have been taught morals and life values from their own elders when living in India. As a result, elders are highly respected within the communities and their homes. Their life experiences and stories are passed on from generation to generation.

As the Sikh population ages, more than often they live with one of their children after they retire. They are rarely ever sent to live in nursing homes because they are not viewed as 'burdens' by their families. Rather, they are celebrated, taken care of, and appreciated, for their knowledge and also for their hard work. Eurocentric and Western communities, however, have a different perspective in terms of ageing and knowledge. Elders are not highly praised nor are they viewed as sources of wisdom. From my own experiences and interactions among the dominant group, I have noticed that many individuals would rather move away from their parents or rather send them to nursing homes when they are too sick—when they eventually become 'burdens.' Nursing homes have been an easy way out for those families who refuse to take on responsibility, and this trend in turn has been exploited by private for-profit enterprises.

My own grandmother, Kirpal Kalsi, had brought up six children on her own, in a country that was foreign to her. With no education and English as a second language, she was able to raise a family. Abandoning her in a nursing home today would be disrespectful. Although, my grandmother at age 76 is very ill and unhealthy, it is a privilege to have her living with my family. Her presence and wisdom makes my family complete.

Neetin Kalsi, MA Student, Sociology, Wilfrid Laurier University, Age: 23

Chapter Eleven

The Raging Grannies: Meddlesome Crones Protest with Wit and Flair

Carole Roy

AGING is a gendered experience and the increasingly aging society is a "female society."[1] While aging is usually portrayed as a negative experience and old women often stereotyped as medical cases or social burdens, rather than the contributors that they are, aging is an experience with more dimensions than stereotypes reveal. Aging brings challenges and, at times, hardships but it also offers gifts. In this chapter I look at a group of older women activists, the Raging Grannies, who started in Canada, cross borders, and are now found across the United States and as far as Japan, Greece, and Israel. The Raging Grannies are women who not only cross national borders but also the metaphorical border of age and its attendant stereotypes. They use songs and humour to straddle the border between performance and activism. The Raging Grannies are a dynamic example of a group of older women refusing the confines of age and gender, and in this light, are important messengers from a land we will all travel through, that of aging and old age. The material used in this chapter comes from a research project that led to a doctoral thesis on the Raging Grannies as adult educators. For that project, 46 interviews were carried out with 36 Raging Grannies from twelve groups from Victoria to Halifax. Archives from four groups were examined in detail as well as a wide range of media reports. At the time (early 2000) there was no comprehensive work on the Raging Grannies, only short articles, even though they had been active since 1987. This lack of in-depth examination of this unique group of activists highlighted the absence of older women as dynamic figures in society and in political protests in the feminist literature and the literature on adult education. One goal of this research project was to record this example of vibrant activism, help dispel stereotypes of older women and myths about aging, and offer recognition to a group of spirited activists that continue to struggle along with other groups for justice, peace, and ecological protection. It is also to offer recognition for the power of imagination, creativity and humour as educational bridges that allow us to move beyond anger and despair into hope and action. Documenting resistance hopefully will provide a bridge to those in the future curious about the past and help prevent the stereotype of women as passive members of their society. Resistance, then, offers us a bridge across borders but also across time. Before examining the Raging Grannies' use of songs and humour in protests, I start by examining two aspects relevant to this topic: the need to record women's activism and the need to include older women activists.

> …among the most subversive and powerful activities women can engage in are activities of constructing women's visible and forceful traditions, of making real our positive existence, of celebrating our lives and of resisting disappearance in the process.[2]

Why Record Women's Activism

Women fought against slavery and offered shelter to hunted runaways, demanded economic justice for the starving or working poor, raised their voices when rights were trampled, their fists when their children were murdered. Women's collective acts of resistance have played, and continue to play, a vital but often unacknowledged role in humanising social, political, and economic policies. To death, danger, and oppression women have frequently responded in life-affirming ways, contributions often concealed in invisibility and silence. Invisibility and the absence of women as a force to be reckoned with are conditions necessary for the preservation of patriarchy.[3] There is a subtly denigrating myth that women have done little worthy of inclusion in the historical record.[4] "Lying is done with words, and also with silence"[5]; kings and popes populate history books but of women, little is said. This invisibility matters: in the absence of stories of resistance and opposition, we internalise patriarchy's ideology and transmit its rules to the next generation.[6] The semblance of superiority of patriarchal thought comes not from any superiority in content, form or achievement over all other thought but is "built on the systematic silencing of other voices."[7] Those silenced voices have been women's voices. Yet, in the "dangerous nooks and crannies of women's lives"[8] we find a creativity that seeks all possible crevices for its expression. We need to reclaim women's examples of activism to offer recognition for creative or courageous efforts but also to empower, stimulate imagination, break isolation, incite to action, and inspire with practical models.[9] This heritage of courage is a necessary inheritance in a world desperate for new modes of behaviour, new notions of political action that require both defiance of oppression and respect for life. Although feminists have started reclaiming women's accomplishments from the past,[10] Dale Spender cautions us:

> [W]hile we are prepared to put much energy into reclaiming women from the distant past, our record is not so good when it comes to preserving our more recent heritage. In fact, we have sometimes been careless about the way we have discarded that very heritage.[11]

One of the invisible faces of this contemporary heritage of resistance is the activism of some older women. They and their daring, vibrant activism are practically invisible in the literature, just as women and their contributions were forty years ago. Older women, sadly, have been invisible not only to society in general but, until recently, they were largely ignored by feminists as well. Being a meddlesome crone is a vocation some older women have chosen. "Meddlesome" invokes someone who recognises that abuse of power sometimes hides behind the personal/public divide and thus refuses to mind her own business. It suggests wilful interference from someone who is not in a position of power but will not shut up because of the lack of official authority. It also suggests that the world is her business. The word "crone" refers to an archetype that at some point in the past denoted women of wisdom. It has been devalued, like all things female, but there are now feminists reclaiming the word as a positive term, a thread of connection to the distant past. These older activists make the world their business and use their experience and wisdom to confront abuse of power, greed, and thoughtlessness. Although a literature search yielded almost nothing on older women and activism, many older women are dynamic activists individually or as members of groups. A short list of such examples in Canada since the 1980s would include: the Haida grandmothers' civil disobedience action to protect South Moresby, British Columbia (BC), and have it declare a United Nations Heritage Site; the grandmothers of the MotherPeace (1986) and the GrandMotherPeace (1988) civil disobedience actions in Nanoose Bay, BC, to protest the visits of U.S. nuclear-armed or nuclear-powered submarines and warships in Canadian waters; the Raging Grannies who started in 1987 in Victoria, BC, in response to the nuclear threat and have spread beyond borders; the three grandmothers jailed for their participation in the Clayoquot Sound Anti-Logging Protest (1993) on Vancouver Island, BC; the older women of the Age of Beauty project (2004) who raised money for flood relief in Peterborough, Ontario; and numerous individuals who have been involved in issues related to forestry, land conservancy, fishing, community gardens, water and energy conservation, to name a few.

Why Age Matters

> The old woman finds herself captured by stereotypes which drain her initia-
> tive and shatter her self-respect. The mythical prototypes of the Wicked Old
> Witch with unnatural powers, the Old Bad Mother with neurotic power
> needs, and the Little Old Lady, ludicrously powerless, cloud the individuality
> of every woman past sixty. Since childhood all of us have been bombarded by
> systematic distortions of female aging in fairy tales, legends, books, movies,
> plays and TV. Age prejudice encourages substitution of these manufactured
> realities for the real human being with real personal powers whom we en-
> counter. Ageism rationalizes the discarding of old women.[12]

In our society of images and print, the elderly are often misrepresented or invisible.
"Our culture gives us many images from grandmothers in Norman Rockwell magazine covers to bag ladies on street corners to adolescent mentalities in aged bodies
on TV sitcoms,"[13] all stereotypes of rigid roles, poverty, or social conventions. Recog-
nising that what we see, and do not see, affect our perspective, Kelchner suggests
that the absence or misrepresentation of elderly people in media, especially older
women, lead us to believe that "their existence is insignificant and inconsequential
to our lives."[14] However more serious than the blindness of media and professional
gerontologists to ageism has been the failure of feminists to recognise the theoretical and experiential importance of old age and its impact on all women. The women's
movement "has resonated with its silence on…the status of old women."[15] The concerns of second wave feminists "reflected…young women's concerns: reproductive
issues; female sexuality; child care; violence against women; equal opportunity in education and jobs; balancing careers and intimate relationships."[16] In the early 1980s,
Emily M. Nett claimed that gerontological research took place within the "male paradigms of the academic disciplines, especially of sociology and psychology"[17] and
Arlene T. McLaren called for more research on the "contributions of elderly women
to society,"[18] suggesting that while elderly women in Canada…tend to subsist below
the poverty line set by the Economic Council of Canada (National Council on Welfare,
1979) and are "underemployed, underpaid, underfinanced, underhoused, undervalued, and underloved" (Jacobs 1976), these portrayals greatly underestimate the contributions elderly women make to society.[19]

> Marilyn Bell had this to say about the absence of material on older women:

> [I]n the academic realm, few writers of textbooks address elder women at all.
> A quick review of text materials in women's studies…will immediately show

the reader that little is included regarding elder women; a few paragraphs on the empty nest syndrome, menopause, depression in middle age, or the lack of older women in the movement seems to suffice. A similar situation can be found in gerontology texts...A few paragraphs on widowhood appear, perhaps mention of menopause or depression. The research underlying the theories of ageing has often not even included women.[20]

Denise Belisle Gonault, who published an annotated bibliography on women and aging in Canada, remarked that "the striking conclusion of this research is how very few clearly feminist works on older women there are."[21] The overall majority of works listed focused on medical and social problems older women encountered and individual coping mechanisms to deal with aging.[22] Little was said about older people's political participation, let alone women's activism. In 1996, fourteen years after McClaren's call for older women's contributions to be recognised, Meredith Minkler demanded once again that we look at older women's strengths as well as their problems.[23] As recently as 1999, older adults, especially women, were still characterised by "dependency, disease, disability, and depression."[24] The medicalisation of older women is remarkable: other than their needs for medical treatment or advice, older women are almost invisible. Women's invisibility seems to increase with age: patriarchal societies loose interest in women beyond reproductive age and this also seems to be the case with many feminists. J. Dianne Garner suggests the invisibility of old women protects us from having "to confront our patriarchal myths about what makes life valuable or dying painful."[25]

> In some societies age gives status, so that only those towards the end of their lives are regarded as having enough experience and wisdom to deal with the most important issues and crises in their societies. We, however, have successfully deprived age of authority and of interest...in Britain, as elsewhere, older women are regarded at best as amiable old ladies, at worst as a group of weak and defenceless pensioners. The label is unjust, unkind and unsuitable.[26]

Aging appears as a biological phenomenon but some feminist gerontologists suggest it is also the product of a social construct. Like the recognised "iron triangle" of class, gender, and race, age also serves as a significant organising principle for individual identities as well as social life in general.[27] There is an illusion that age and aging are ahistorical, prediscursive-natural.[28] Gullette argues that contemporary age ideology is a narrative of natural decline, something that can happen only because "age is still at the stage where gender and race used to be: hidden by its supposed foundation in the 'body.' "[29] That master narrative, like those of race and gender, deeply affects our own personal experience.[30] But unlike class, gender, or race, oppression by age gradually invades "defences carefully constructed against it. Age passing becomes a state of mind, a measure of self-worth."[31] Culture in a broad sense, including discourses, feelings, practices, institutions, material conditions, is saturated with concepts of age and aging.[32] In North America, there is a cult of youth and youthfulness, which is assumed to be the "normal" human condition; as long as "old age is equated with illness and dependency...it defies the cultural ideals of youth, activity and independence...of the "normal" human condition."[33] To grow old in a society whose dominant values are speed, productivity, efficiency, increase of material wealth through work and competition, means to be devalued. An ambivalent attitude toward non-work means that we do not have ways of thinking that give it status and legitimacy.[34] We lack a concept like "gender" or "race" to identify the system that keeps a regime of age knowledge circulating.[35] In spite of the diversity of circumstances, personalities, and experiences, "old age is frequently assumed to be homogeneous and uniformly negative life stage."[36] While aging is real and is affected by many factors, including class, gender, race, sexual orientation, ageism "rearranges power relationships, just like any other kind of discrimination or prejudice. When one ages, one may gain or lose. With ageism, one is shaped into something that is *always* less than what one really is."[37] Gullette suggests that an alternative is to construct "life as a process of losing our false fears, our overly pessimistic anticipation,"[38] not losing one's nerve to handle the future.

We need to reclaim the meaning of "old" as "sagacity, kindliness, wisdom, generosity, even graciousness and beauty."[39] Some have started calling themselves Crones, at times Hags, reclaiming the devalued

> archetype of female age...The Crone, under one name or another, was part of the mythology of people from eastern Asia to Ireland, from Scandinavia to Northern Africa. In Christian Europe, she suffered the most complete obliteration; the persecution of her earthly representatives was carried to the greatest extremes in the burning times. Walker builds a strong case that the ageism and social rejection which limits old women today is one of the most persistent legacies of that erasure...archetypes of the Virgin and the Mother were consolidated into the Christian figure of Mary, but the feared archetype of female age, the Crone, was eradicated...Thus the "wise, wilful, wolfish Crone" was female power and danger in its most potent form. In patriarchy, she had to be erased.[40]

The Crone stage of life for women was a time of freedom from conventions. According to Sheila Wilkinson,

> It is only the hag that rides free…that is why she is feared, ostracised, tortured and murdered. Or worse, she is deformed into a stereotype—the more easily to recognise and discount her. But the old woman, the crone, is that aspect of womanhood that is no longer controlled; she is the self that flies free.[41]

The Crone survived imposed limitations but now refuses to be confined to any borders as she has an overview and crosses freely over lines drawn by a patriarchal system intent on labels and divisions.[42] Lately, a chorus of voices from feminists and feminist gerontologists has been rising, ready to respond to Nett's call and "search for the images of women as elders" in a diversity of fields, "to investigate the multitudes of meanings for this stage in our human life…to discover more about strengths, our creativity, and the continuity of our Selves over our lifetimes."[43] Reclaiming women's, and older women's, positive images and contributions is necessary in order to gain a sense of continuity. We must keep in mind that contemporary society does not make it easy for old women's voices to be heard.[44] There is a need "to uncover and report upon the lives of older women, concentrating upon a more complete account of their thoughts, feelings and activities."[45] We should be "less concerned with charting decline and predicting outcomes, and more with outlining possibilities."[46] Although not acknowledged much in the literature, experience shows that female old age provides an opportunity for radical change and self-expression, although there is still little recognition of older women as powerful, respected, or influential. As Barbara Walker wrote:

> [T]he real threat posed by older women in a patriarchal society may be the "evil eye" of sharp judgement honed by disillusioning experience, which pierces male myths and scrutinizes male motives in the hard, unflattering light of critical appraisal. It may be that the witch's evil eye was only an eye from which the scales had fallen.[47]

"Old women have rarely been portrayed as the resourceful, productive, vital, angry and joyful women many of us are."[48] Older women must understand who they are and refuse to be socialise in a way that negates their potential: after all, the mind of postmenopausal woman is uncharted.[49] In fact, feminist research has recently shown that post-menopausal women "are often endowed with new energy and vitality" in spite of a society that "perceives them as declining and almost obsolete."[50] The Crone "needs to be integrated into the feminist model of female identity. We need to reinvent the image of powerful, rebellious old women."[51] Sheila Wilkinson reports that in *Trojan Women,* Gwendolyn MacEwan

> shows that an unquestioning loyalty to a bankrupt culture, especially one that is built around the paradigm of stereotypic gender roles, is deadly. But MacEwan also shows that it is the figure of the crone who is the freeing agent; the old woman (who knows all the past and who is willing to call the present into account) is able to accomplish this because she moves beyond patriarch rules. And because she is more free than most of us it is old woman who is righting our stories.[52]

To reclaim the Crone then is to enter a process of liberation: the Crone is about strength, vision, vulnerability, and insights. To reclaim the Crone is a chance to pull the veil of lies and look at reality in stark honesty. Strength and insights gathered from surviving the long journey in patriarchal land are necessary resources to confront aging for women living under a patriarchal system.

Raging Grannies: Rebels in Disguise

In spite of this absence in the literature, older women are involved politically. A Canadian example that has successfully crossed national borders is the Raging Grannies. Warren Magnusson, professor of political sciences at the University of Victoria, called the Raging Grannies a "brilliant example of a group acting out their protests" and using their credibility as grandmothers to "undercut the legitimacy of military violence, corporate greed, and governmental insensitivity."[53] The Raging Grannies began in 1987 in Victoria, BC, and quickly touched a nerve with older women: dynamic and active groups of Raging Grannies have since been established across Canada and beyond. The Raging Granny persona allows individual creativity yet also provides the opportunity for a collective identity:

> *We've put on our hat*
> *Our apron and our shawl*
> *Cause we'll never grow*
> *Too old to dream*
> *Of justice for one and all.[54]*

Consistently using humour, they created a new cultural figure which has become a unique Canadian institution of protest, challenging authorities and stereotypes of older women, and engaging in public education. Their popularity reveals the desire of older women to claim their space on the political scene. They have no central organization and each "gaggle" is free to do as they please. They maintain an electronic list for members and a newsletter published three times a year as some members do not have computers or access to internet. They hold an "Un-convention" every second year to exchange views and songs, learn about media, lobbying techniques, discuss civil disobedience and issues gaggles are working on. It is remarkable how consistent their views are from one end of the continent to the other even though they have never met and come from a diversity of backgrounds: religious or non-religious, union or business; some were political activists , others volunteers with charitable organizations; a few are lesbians, some are single, others divorced, many are married or widowed; a few were born in rich families, others in working class or middle class families; and some are immigrants or political refugees. Some Raging Grannies sing in French, others in Spanish, Greek, Hebrew, Japanese, but the majority speak English. Their ages span five decades as the youngest are in their late forties while others are in their nineties, including Muriel Duckworth from Halifax who is the oldest Granny at one hundred years of age! While many have been socially and/or politically engaged since early adulthood, or earlier, some discover their vocation of meddlesome crones when their grandchildren are born. In spite of the diversity of their backgrounds, they hold in common a commitment to peace and justice. They confront local or global issues with wit, daring, and a dose of zest and flashiness.

Started after the accident at Chernobyl and in reaction to the fear and despair they felt from the visits of U.S. nuclear warships and submarines in the Victoria harbour, the range of issues they tackle quickly expanded to include women's and environmental issues, trade and economic justice issues, peace, anti-war, and non-violence, human rights and anti-racism, and various local issues they identify as concerns. They write satirical songs to share their analysis of current issues, like this song against logging in British Columbia titled "Take Me Out to the Clearcut,"

> We'll picnic on a few stumps
> I want you to know I'm a tree farming nut
> Who thinks like a chainsaw that's stuck in a rut!
> Mac Bloedel gets a Hip Hooray!
> They make black picnic grounds pay
> So it's ONE gets you TWO, dear investors, thank you:
>   . . .
> The timber's been tidied away.

It' s been sold down the stream
In a businessman's dream
It's swell to stand here in a landscape so clean!
It's off to lumbering elsewhere,

. . .

It's the buzz of the mill that produces the thrill
Worth a million trees, So take me out to the clearcut,
Who needs tall cedars, I say?
The air is depleted, and so is the earth

. . .

Let's all get into the greenhouse,

. . .

If God wanted trees, he'd not make it so ea...sy
To whack them away!
   Tune: Take Me Out To The Ballgame

They tend to wear frilly aprons, colourful shawls, running shoes (sometimes pink), and flamboyant hats decorated with birds, flowers, dusting feathers, pins of all sort, and whatever else they can find that will stay on the hats. But you may also find them sporting hard hats and bikinis, overalls and reverse baseball caps like teenage boys when they rap, or long gloves, patent leather purses and pearls to symbolize matronly dignity. They are flexible, adaptable and will use a vast array of disguises and imaginative props to get attention.

Raging Grannies are well versed in the challenges of being older women and know they must be seen to be heard. Many, like Granny Angela Silver, report becoming invisible:

Older women are considered invisible. You fade into the woodwork. You're not a producing vital woman, the important woman who is working and earning and has a voice. When you retired you're supposed to go to some retirement community and play golf or bingo or whatever. (Pers. comm., March 27, 2002)

However Grannies don't deny the impact aging has on them. According to Granny Eva Munro, "We've got enough problems looking after our eyes and ears and knees and feet. I have five doctors' appointments this week. I think I've seen them all!" (Pers. comm., March 13, 2002) In the song, "Oh Dear What Can The Matter Be?" they make fun of themselves and introduce gender to the aging experience:

We've been attacked by the forces of gravity,
Fat has appeared where we once had concavity,

Nobody said life was fair.
Older men become more adorable,
Even though their figure's deplorable
Their physique is always insurable,
With or without their grey hair.
Older women are thought unattractive,
They're shunned as if they were radioactive,

    . . .

Well, these grey mares,
We ain't what we used to be,
We've given up on respectability,
Don't give a fig for acceptability,
We're far too busy to care.
   Tune: Oh Dear What Can The Matter Be?

Others, like Granny Alma Norman, claim age as an enabler:

> When you're our age, we have a lot more freedom. Nobody can hold our job
> as a club over us and say, "You'll loose our job. I see you in that demonstration
> and you're out. You're not getting a promotion." Or our husbands, if we're
> still married, are also probably at that point in their lives so that kind of black-
> mail is less powerful. (Pers. comm., October 22, 2001)

Granny Eva Munro agrees: "Younger women are very busy usually. They're trying to
achieve work and jobs and stuff like that, so they don't have the energy or the time.
We have more time and energy, we don't have the restraints that they do." She adds,
"as older women, we really don't care what people think of us," revealing how freedom from others' opinions is empowering (pers. comm., March 13, 2002). For Granny
Rose Deshaw, age is empowering in another way: "You don't know how much longer
you've got and you want to be sure to get the important parts out because you're
looking at the end of your life" (pers. comm., March 21, 2002). A Raging Granny, according to Granny Mary Rose, doesn't tend to think of herself as someone "who sits
in a rocking chair and watches the world go by" (pers. comm., May 10, 2002) but
rather as someone who acts out her vocation, as Granny Barbara Seifred puts it:

> It's my real work. We used to do peace demonstrations and peace marches
> and things on the street. Lots of people would stand there and argue with you
> or they'd back off if they didn't want to know anything about it. But with the
> Grannies, because we look so funny, they kind of lean in instead of leaning

out. There's a connection, they want to know a little more about what these crazy women are up to. So then they stop and listen and they open up. They don't generally argue with us too too much. The other thing that keeps us going, there is a certain amount of that that replenishes us and recharges our batteries because when you really think of the problems that we're confronting, they're very depressing. But we do keep recharging and we can go on. (Pers. comm., March 28, 2002)

What is remarkable with the Raging Grannies is the seemingly inextinguishable well of creative ideas for satirical songs and dynamic humorous actions. For Valentine's Day they offered a huge broken heart, an Un-valentine, to their elected representative for his lack of action on nuclear issues, carrying along an old ratty umbrella full of holes as a symbol of the absurdity of sheltering under the nuclear umbrella. Grannies have brought vacuums, mops and buckets to clean up the base in Victoria where U.S. nuclear warships and submarines often stopped for sailors' rest and recreation. They held a tea party on the deck of a U.S. warship until being unceremoniously escorted out on the orders of the Captain who did not find it humorous to have his open house crashed by this group of tea drinkers! They launched their Grannies' Navy and learned to paddle kayaks and canoes, or drive zodiacs, to serenade sailors stuck on U.S. warships anchored in the harbour, small crafts offering the appropriate contrast to the floating behemoths. They carried their "briefs, "a clothes line of women's underwear, in a laundry basket to symbolize women's work of cleaning up after messes, to a commission studying the lifting of a moratorium on uranium mining in British Columbia. The Fredericton Raging Grannies showed up at the local city hall armed with spoons and an apron that read "Closets are for Brooms" to protest the homophobic city council's refusal to issue a permit for a Gay Pride parade; this action generated letters to the editor and public opinion forced the mayor and council to reverse their decision. Grannies also love to share their understanding of economics and wrote the following song during a time when governments kept the corporate world happy with downsizing and cuts to programs:

> *Our Favourite Things*
> *Rightsizing, downsizing, rationalizing*
> *Insourcing, outsourcing, pri-vatizing*
> *Dis-entanglement, cutting the strings*
> *These are a few of our favourite things*
> *Off loading, downloading, re-engineering*

Divest, restructure, promote volunteering
Tax cuts to fund our friends Florida flings

  . . .

Housing's not part of this government's mandate
Vulnerable people just need a band aid
We won't give handouts, they need a hand up
Let's start by grabbing that fellow's tin cup
Improve education by inventing crises
Can't tell the difference 'tween values and prices
Close down more hospitals, costs are too high
Isn't it cheaper to let people die?
      Tune: Our Favourite Things

Of course Raging Grannies are not always welcome but that is part of the fun. They keep abreast of the activities of various governments, always on the lookout for an opportunity to contribute their skills, experience and wisdom. When the Canadian Department of Defence (DOD) could not find very important papers requested by the commission looking into what has been called the Somalia Affair (where Canadian soldiers engaged in violence and brutality toward Somalian civilians), Ottawa Raging Grannies were only too happy to show up at the DOD office armed with magnifying glasses and endlessly pawing through briefcases and waste baskets in their efforts to search for the missing papers! They keep tabs on official visitors' schedules, as the former Canadian Minister of Trade Pat Carney found out during the talks that led to the Free Trade deal between Canada and the U.S. During her visit to Victoria, Grannies subversively used their grey hair and lined up like a receiving line at the door of the elegant hotel where the Minister was having lunch. As she walked by, smiling and shaking the Grannies' hands they launched, off key, into a ditty:

Free Trade Trot
Oh Oh Oh Free Trade
Of you we're not afraid
Our fears have been allayed
This deal was heaven made.
Who needs a culture or an identity
When we have Dynasty on our TV (Kazoo)
Oh Oh Oh Free Trade—
The deal we've waited for

Our bucks will buy us more
Consumer goods galore
We may not know where
Our next jobs' coming from
But we'll have Calvin Klein on all our
Bum, bum, bum, bum, bums.
  Tune: *Playmates Come And Play With Me*

Acidly, the Minister told the Grannies that their singing was a whole lot better than their logic! In a word, Raging Grannies like to have fun!

One action has been especially noteworthy. In the fall 1990 during the escalation of threats that led to the first Gulf War, Victoria Raging Grannies dressed in "military uniforms" and went to the local Armed Forces Recruitment Centre to sign up for a tour of duty in Iraq and save their grandchildren

> Unable by law to ask the Grannies their age, the baffled recruiters ploughed through the necessary paper work straight-faced; one Granny was even invited back for a math test! Back we were a week later with knitting needles and wool. We sat down for an hour, chatting and knitting scarves and comforts for the troops![55]

While it was repeated by Raging Grannies in Toronto and Montreal, it came to media attention once again in the summer of 2005 when the Tucson Raging Grannies were inspired to enlist to go to Iraq at their local U.S. Army Recruitment Centre. They were arrested and media reported the news across North America and Europe with the news. While charges were later dropped, a group of 18 Raging Grannies and other grandmothers took part in an action on October 17, 2005, which they called "We insist we enlist," at the Times Square U.S. Army Recruitment Centre in New York City. They were arrested but this time charges were not dropped so these women aged 60 to 91, armed with walkers and various canes, spent a week at the Manhattan Criminal Court before the "not guilty" verdict was pronounced. In fact, the Granny Peace Brigade, as they came to be known, was victim of wrongful arrest. "We insist we enlist" actions have since been repeated by Raging Grannies in towns and cities across the U.S. and on Valentine's Day 2006 at least fifteen groups joined in to highlight their opposition to the war in Iraq. Ottawa Raging Grannies wrote the following song earlier, which is very appropriate in light of actions at Army Recruitment centers:

Criminal Grans
We're criminals exposing stuff that's going wrong

Belting out our biting messages in songs
We poke and pry and then expose
What you'd prefer folks didn't know
We're an old and wrinkled Danger.
We're pesky Raging Grans.
We're mouthy older women
We pesky Raging Grans
We've got our eyes upon you, we're checking out your plans
We're done it twice and will once more
Expose your sneaky tricks before
They end in Too Much Damage
We're watchful Raging Grans.
Try and put the lid on, try and shut us up!
Pepper spray won't do it—nothing makes us stop
We've been around and we don't scare
We're here, we're there—we're EVERYWHERE
Don't even think to Gag us
Here come the Raging Grans!
    Tune: Lili Marlene

An action by the Peninsula Raging Grannies in San Francisco also generated attention. On Mothers' Day, May 8, 2005, Raging Grannies and other peace activists held a peaceful demonstration against the war in Iraq at the State Capitol in Sacramento and asked Governor Arnold Schwarzenegger, commander in chief of the California National Guard, "to bring the Guard home from Iraq."[56] But matters did not stop there. The San Jose Mercury News wrote

> Schwarzenegger's office called on the same National Guard to monitor the protest as part of its new intelligence unit's "Information Synchronization, Knowledge Management and Intelligence Fusion" program. It has "broad authority" to monitor terrorists' threats, which becomes distorted and violates the Article 1, Sect. 1 rights of those who clearly are not terrorists.[57]

When the spying on domestic protesters was revealed in the media, the Peninsula Raging Grannies, instead of reacting with fear, accepted to meet the Acting Adjutant General of the National Guard at their headquarters, in spite of wondering how the National Guard could prove they had not spied on them. Although under scrutiny by authorities, the Grannies held to their principles and did not run away but faced the

Guard with homemade cookies and spirit. The investigation that resulted from media reports generated from this event later led to the successful dismantling of this illegal program of the Guard by Senator Dunn and other elected officials who had been unaware of such program until then. Since the 19th century it is illegal in the U.S. for military organisations to spy on citizens as it contravenes the fundamental right to dissent. In typical Raging Grannies spirit, Gail Sredanovic remarked,

> Aside from the disturbing civil liberties aspects of the Pentagon spying on local peace groups, it makes me scared to think that the folks in charge of protecting us from possible terrorist attacks can't tell the difference between a terrorist threat and a peaceful citizen gathering. Are they really that stupid?[58]

Humour

From the beginning the Raging Grannies grasp the educational potential of humour. According to Granny Alma Norman, it is easier to get under the skin of authorities with ridicule and satire than with logical questions, which often leads to pointless defensive arguments and long explanations of why something is the way it is. Granny Muriel Duckworth, the oldest Raging Granny at one hundred years old and who has been a peace activist and feminist educator for over sixty years, suggests that humor is good pedagogy. As nurses and other health practitioners know, humour can provide relief in times of stress. Humor is transformative, helps people face anxiety, and is also a communal experience: TV or radio comedy shows have sound tracks of laughter as people like to laugh with others. Laughing reveals common understanding, even among strangers.[59] Satire is often an act of protest which can allow citizens to express dissent against a state's efforts to exert control or frighten them so they do not criticize or express dissenting opinions.[60] Humor is rebellious as laughing remains an act of freedom that cannot be coerced, says Jo Anna Isaak in her book, *Feminism and Contemporary Art*. Humour demands tolerance of ambiguity and paradox as it requires bringing together frames of reference that are not usually associated. Their name, Raging Grannies, reflects that ability as we rarely associated rage with grandmothers. To produce humour requires excellent analytical skills to understand issues, conceptual flexibility to reframe information, and creativity to find new connections.[61]

Many Grannies believe humour is needed in difficult times and for groups on the margins as it is "a survival mechanism that helps to handle such exceedingly tragic material" (Granny Fran Thoburn, pers. comm., May 13, 2002). "Most humour comes out of pain," says Granny Rose DeShaw who thinks it also helps prevent burn-outs (pers. comm., March 21, 2002). Humour helps to get a different perspective says Granny Ava Louwe:

> Laughter by its very nature changes your perspective on things. It takes you to a higher plane. When you're in a certain frame of mind and something strikes you as funny it automatically opens you up and elevates you, and you get a new perspective. (Pers. comm., March 23, 2002)

Regina Barreca, who writes on humour, agrees:

> Humor doesn't dismiss a subject but, rather, often opens that subject up for discussion...Humor can be a shortcut, an eye-opener...to get to the truth of the matter. The best humor allows...for joy, compassion, and a new way of looking at a very old world. Seeing humor as a way of making our feelings and responses available to others without terrifying our listeners can free us to take ourselves less gloomily, although not less seriously...When we can frame a difficult matter with humor, we can often reach someone who would otherwise withdraw.[62]

Humour is empowering and helps prevent a sense of paralysis when confronting difficult and tragic information as Granny Rose says: "If you thought about some of the things that are going on you'd be weeping all the time, and if you don't relieve it you just can't go on. So you have to break up the tension and laughter does it" (pers. comm., May 10, 2002). Granny Pearl Rice, who lived in England during World War II, suggests that a joke helped people cope with the stress and difficulties as a laugh lightened things up (pers. comm., June 10, 2002). Humour allows people to connect by breaking down barriers and isolation as people laugh together. It also helps broaden our perspective. Barreca writes that women

> are more likely than men to make fun of those in high and seemingly invulnerable positions...as women look at those in power, or at those institutions we were taught to revere, and laugh. In this way women's comedy is more "dangerous" than men's because it challenges authority by refusing to take it seriously...[and] calls into question the largest issues, questions the way the world is put together.[63]

Humour is creative and requires sophisticated analysis and imaginative metaphors to reveal new connections between facts not usually related. Yet Kate Clinton, like the Raging Grannies, sees the seriousness of humour and describes it as

> lichen secreting tiny amounts of acid, year after year, eating into the rock, making places for water to gather, to freeze and crack the rocks a bit, making

soil, making way for grasses to grow…It is the lichen which begins the splitting apart of the rocks, the changing of the shoreline, the shape of the earth. Feminist humor is serious, and it is about changing the world.[64]

Yet Nancy Walker warns us that women's humour, domestic and political, has "been largely omitted from the official canon," and gone out of print.[65] According to Granny Lorna Drew, the Raging Grannies are the clowns, the wise fools who tell the truth with humour but run the risk of being vulnerable but which also "invites people to put down their defenses as well" (pers. comm., March 11, 2002). This song, "Wrinkle Wrinkle Aging Star" pokes fun at themselves:

> *Wrinkle wrinkle aging star*
> *Who cares how old you are?*
> *Your hair is grey, your dentures click*
> *Your bosom sags, your ankle's thick*
> *Your joints all creak, your arthritis plagues*
> *. . .*
> *. . . to hell with being beige*
> *We won't stay cooped up in a cage*
> *Our eyes are dim but our tongues are sharp*
> *We go out on a limb, our wits are sharp*
> > *Tune: Twinkle Twinkle Little Star*

Barrecca agrees and suggests humour is a show of strength and vulnerability at the same time, requiring the author to take the step and trust the response of listeners. She adds, "pointing to the absurdity of a situation, turning embarrassment or unease into something to be shared instead of repressed is risky, but it is also often exactly what is needed."[66] As the Raging Grannies challenge authorities and stereotypes, they transform despair and anger into action and teach us that wit, fun, and solidarity make vulnerability and despair tolerable and allow us to sustain hope and resistance. Gatherings of "Hags…have embarrassed and harassed the powerful into responding to their demands…have refused to be silenced by a thrown bone, or discouraged by the lack of female support or impressed by belated congratulations."[67] This is reminiscent of the Raging Grannies who create embarrassments and disturbances for authorities. The irreverence and subversivity of the Grannies is in part due to the fact that they identified older women with an "un-motherly" public rage:

> *We're your moms and grannies, and you know that we're tough*
> *When we understand that we are right.*

We've been robbed, and double-talked, and lied to enough,
And we're raging, mad enough to fight.
'Though we may disturb the peace,
Shouting out against the frauds,
Some folks say we're rather sweet . . .
Others say we're loud-mouthed broads.
But if you can hear the lies big business promotes
In the mouths of politicians, then
You will realize that there's a foot on your throats,
And you'll see that Granny's right again.
Hear the wisdom love imparts
Through Port Townsend's streets and halls.
Some folks say we break their hearts . . .
Others say we break their balls.
But if you consider well the charges we make,
Maybe then you might get angry, too.
When you are convinced that it's your country at stake,
Then you might decide there's work to do.
After we've harangued you for . . .an hour . . or . . two,
Then you might decide to act up, too.
        Tune: Maybe Then I Might Fall Back on You

Conclusions

[T]he Crone does not participate in the politics of reform; her bag is transforming the thought processes that interfere with the civil rights of spontaneous persons with creative gifts. She is distinguished by her ability to dream dreams and conjures up visions for the survival of the Web, weaving into the fabric a lively wit that refuses to take seriously the small mind, loaded with the self-righteous hyperbole, or conversely, the professional academic drowning in self-analysis. Her instinct for survival is at gut level, she has solved the problems of want by wanting little, possessions have little value to the true Crone. She lives to live, to speculate and to risk, she will not be found in the nest of privileged security or at the table of greed or envy, she has pared her life down to the minimum. She will speak for peace but not expect it, speak for love, but not bet on it, speak for harmony among women knowing how far off is the reality, but she will speak, for she is a spinner of possibilities, a teller of truths too long avoided.[68]

We must seek patterns of hopefulness and new meanings of aging without look-ing with rose-coloured optimism. The Raging Grannies allow us to expand the nar-row range of images associated with aging and encourage feminists to include older women and aging in their analysis to develop an adequate understanding of women's lives and capabilities. Otherwise old women are "stereotyped as Other—old fash-ioned, ugly, apolitical, powerless among women, invisible—just as the patriarchs hoped when they eradicated the Crone."[69]

> *It's time we gave witness,*
> *attention, attention must be paid,*
> *or we'll march hand in hand,*
> *together strong as a battering ram,*
> *create situations until others*
> *understand we're not designed*
> *to rust. Some day they'll be us.*[70]

As Marilyn Waring said, "It is not books that politicize people and often not ideas ei-ther. It tends to be experience,"[71] especially experience of those on the margins. Rage and anger transformed Raging Grannies from private individuals to public actors with a voice, and provided them with an antidote to fear, anger and despair. As is ob-vious with the Raging Grannies, older women have much to contribute to society, in-cluding their bold dreams for the future and their active hope for a better world.

> *A Granny's Life for Me*
> *...*
> *A fancy hat and a walking cane*
> *The courage to speak when the world's in pain*
> *...*
> *The wisdom that comes when we're growing old*
> *More interests and friends than our arms can hold*
> *...*
> *Aging's not really rum*
> *Personal freedom at last has come*
> *We've finally learned how to make things hum...*
> > *Tune: Fox and Cat from "Pinocchio."*

Notes

1. Peace quoted in Linda M. Rhodes, "Women aging: Address before the United Nations NGO Committee on Aging at the Secretariat, New York, January 17, 1982," *Resources for Feminist Research/ Documentation pour la Recherche Feministe* 11, no. 2 (1982): 207.

2. Dale Spender, *Women of Ideas (And What Men Have Done to Them): From Aphra Behn to Adrienne Rich* (London: Routledge, 1982/1983), 696.

3. Ibid., 5, 13.

4. B. S. Anderson and J. P. Zinsser, A History of Their Own: Women in Europe from Prehistory to the Present Volume 1. New York: Harper & Row, 1988), xiii.

5. Adrienne Rich, *On Lies, Secrets, and Silence: Selected Prose 1966-1978* (New York: W. W. Norton & Company, 1979), 186.

6. Gerda Lerner, *Why History Matters: Life and Thought* (New York: Oxford University Press, 1997), 207-208.

7. Gerda Lerner, *The Creation of Feminist Consciousness: From the Middle-Ages to Eighteen-Seventy* (New York: Oxford University Press, 1993), 281.

8. Davis quoted in Ardis Cameron, *Radicals of the Worst Sort: Laboring Women in Lawrence, Mass, 1860-1912* (Chicago: University of Illinois Press, 1993), 11.

9. Pam McAllister, *You Can't Kill the Spirit: Stories of Women and Non-Violent Action* (Philadelphia, PA: New Society Publishers, 1988), 10.

10. Sheila Rowbotham, *Women, Resistance and Revolution: A History of Women and Revolution in the Modern World* (New York: Pantheon Books, 1972), 16.

11. Quoted in S. Reinharz, *Feminist Methods in Social Research* (New York: Oxford University Press, 1992), 215.

12. Baba Copper, *Over the Hill: Reflections on Ageism Between Women* (Freedom, California: The Crossing Press, 1988), 14-15.

13. Marilyn J. Bell (ed.), "Introduction." *Women as Elders: The Feminist Politics of Aging* (New York: Harrington Park Press, 1986), 1.

14. Elizabeth S. Kelchner, "Ageism's impact and effect on society: Not just a concern for the old," *Journal of Gerontological Social Work* 32, no. 4 (1999): 93.

15. Janet Ford and Ruth Sinclair, *Sixty Years On: Women Talk About Old Age* (London: The Women's Press, 1987), 160.

16. Evelyn R. Rosenthal, "Women and varieties of ageism," *Journal of Women and Aging* 2, no. 1 (1990): 1.

17. Emily M. Nett, "Introduction," Resources for Feminist Research/Documentation pour la Recherche Feministe 11, no. 2 (1982): 203.

18. Arlene T. McLaren, "The myth of dependency," *Resources for Feminist Research/ Documentation pour la Recherche Feministe* 11, no. 2 (1982): 214.

19. Ibid., 213.

20. Bell, "Introduction," 1.

21. Denise Belisle Gonault, *Women and Aging in Canada: Multidisciplinary Annotated Bibliography 1975-1989* (Université d'Ottawa/Carleton University, 1990), v.

22. Ibid., vi.

23. Meredith Minkler, "Critical perspectives on ageing: New challenges for gerontology," *Ageing and Society* 16, no. 4 (1996): 472.

24. R. J. Scheidt, D. R. Humpherys, and J. B. Yorgason, "Successful aging: What's not to like," *Journal of Applied Gerontology: The Official Journal of the Southern Gerontological Society* 18, no. 3 (1999): 278.

25. J. Dianne Garner ed., "Feminism and feminist gerontology," *Fundamentals of Feminist Gerontology* (New York: The Haworth Press, 1999), 3.

26. Ford and Sinclair, *Sixty Years On*, 1.

27. Tracy X. Karner, "Introduction: Identity issues in research on aging," *Research on Aging* 20, no. 1(1998):6.

28. M. Hepworth, "In defiance of an ageing culture," Review of Margaret Morganroth Gullette, *Declining to Decline: Cultural Combat and the Politics of the Midlife, Aging and Society* 19, no. 1(1999): 141.

29. Margaret Morganroth Gullette, *Declining to Decline: Cultural Combat and the Politics of the Midlife* (Charlottesville and London: University of Virginia Press, 1997), 202.

30. Ibid.

31. Copper, *Over the Hill*, 18-19.

32. Gullette, *Declining to Decline,* 3.

33. Hennessy quoted in Laura Hurd, "We're not old!" Older women's negotiation of aging and oldness," *Journal of Aging Studies* 13, no. 4 (1999): 420.

34. Ford and Sinclair, *Sixty Years On,* 2.

35. Gullette, *Declining to Decline,* 212.

36. Hurd, "We're not old!," 420.

37. Copper, *Over the Hill,* 3.

38. Gullette, *Declining to Decline,* xix.

39. Lou Cottin, *Elders in Rebellion: A Guide to Senior Activism* (Garden City, New York: Anchor Press / Doubleday, 1979), 1.

40. Copper, *Over the Hill,* 58.

41. S. Wilkinson, "Old woman, 'bearer of keys to unknown doorways,'" *Canadian Woman Studies* 12, no. 2 (1992): 103.

42. Gert Beadle, "The nature of crones," in Marilyn J. Bell ed., *Women as Elders: The Feminist Politics of Aging* (New York: Harrington Park Press, 1986), xiii.

43. Emily M. Nett, "A call for feminist correctives to research on elders," *Resources for Feminist Research/Documentation pour la Recherche Feministe* 11, no. 2(1982): 226.

44. Bernard and Meade quoted in Minkler, "Critical perspectives on ageing," 472.

45. Ford and Sinclair, *Sixty Years On,* 5.

46. Bond and Coleman quoted in Minkler, "Critical perspectives on ageing," 481.

47. Quoted in Copper, *Over the Hill*, 62.

48. Wilkinson, "Old woman," 103.

49. Walker quoted in Copper, *Over the Hill*, 60.

50. Cohen quoted in Wilkinson, "Old woman," 103.

51. Copper, *Over the Hill*, 59.

52. MacEwan quoted in Copper, *Over the Hill*, 59.

53. Warren Magnusson, *The Search for Political Space: Globalization, social movements, and the urban political experience* (Toronto: University of Toronto Press, 1996), 93-94.

54. Edmonton Raging Grannies quoted in Laurie Graham, "Grannies rage on," *The Gateway* (University of Alberta) (December 1, 1998), 2.

55. "Raging Grannies ready for war, head for recruitment centre today," *Times Colonist* (Victoria) November 2, 1990): A1.

56. Carol Norris, "Schwarzenegger, People's governor or flouter of First Amendment rights?" *San Francisco Chronicle* (July 13, 2005):np.

57. Ibid.

58. Quoted in Matthew Rothschild, "California National Guard Story Grows Stranger," *The Progressive* (July 7, 2005). http://www.progressive.org

59. Jo Anna Isacc, *Feminism and contemporary art: The revolutionary power of women's laughter* (London: Routledge, 1996),

60. Gregor Benton, 1988). "The origins of the political joke," in Chris Powell and George E. C. Paton (eds.), *Humour in society: Resistance and control* (New York: St. Martin's Press, 1988), 33.

61. Carole Roy, *The Raging Grannies: Wild Hats, Cheeky Songs, and Witty Actions for a Better World*. (Montreal: Black Rose Books, 2004.)

62. Regina Barreca, ed., *The Penguin Book of Women's Humor* (New York: Penguin Books, 1996), 10.

63. Ibid., 13, 14, 179.

64. Clinton quoted in Barreca, *The Penguin Book of Women's Humor*, 182-183.

65. Walker quoted in Barreca, *The Penguin Book of Women's Humor*, 185.

66. Barreca, *The Penguin Book of Women's Humor*, 10.

67. Beadle, "The nature of crones," xiv.

68. Ibid., xiii.

69. Copper, *Over the Hill*, 60.

70. Elsen Lubetsky quoted in Jo C. Searles, "Inventing freedom: The positive poetic "mutterings" of older women," *Journal of Women & Aging* 2, no. 2 (1990): 157.

71. Waring quoted in Miriam Wyman ed., *Sweeping the Earth: Women Taking Action for a Healthy Planet*. (Charlottetown, PEI: Gynergy Books, 1999), 201.

Chapter Twelve

Crossing Borders of the Mind: Women in Higher Education

Jocey Quinn

A girl with braids
sits in this corner seat, invisible,
Pleased with her solitude. And across from her
an invisible boy, dreaming. She knows
she cannot imagine his dreams. Quite swiftly
we move through our lives, swiftly, steadily, the train
rocks and bounces onwards through sleeping fields,
our unknown stillness
holding level as water sealed in glass.
—from 'Evening Train' by Denise Levertov

I'm thinking about the 'educated person.' I realise that the idea that knowledge comes from everywhere and the idea that the person is not fixed and complete are intertwined...On the bus sun shines through the trees and things feel good now. —Jocey Quinn, research diary

Borders Of The Mind

THE QUESTION of borders and border crossings—and roadblocks, of various kinds—has long preoccupied feminist scholars. Borders have been seen as both marginal places and spaces where ideas become cross-fertilised. Images of travel, of knowing and of subjectivity suffuse feminist texts of all kinds, from poetry to research diaries, as the above quotes testify. We are always at the border of some transformation, but this may be a secret journey. At one time women were perceived as eternally displaced and condemned to live on the borders of public life and public institutions such as universities-if they were allowed to enter at all. Ambitions and ideas above stations were best kept hidden. Women were pushed to the borders in terms of public knowledge, where the terms were set by men and masculinist thinking.

In some respects, this situation has changed dramatically, with women now be-coming the majority of undergraduates in many countries. It can longer be stated unproblematically that universities are men's worlds, even though their claim to be feminised is belied by the fact that most positions of power and authority are still held by men. What remains is the abiding question of women's relation to knowl-edge. Has what counts as knowledge been feminised in line with this mass participa-tion of women, or is the search for knowledge still a secret one for women?

Crossing Borders Into Higher Education

Universities have always been seen as special places and indeed women have fought long and heard to gain entry to them. We cannot be complacent about this hard won right. Recent reports from Iraq have shown women students and scholars as perse-cuted, abused and even killed by religious fundamentalists for their temerity in try-ing to continue as active university participants. As recently as 2002, British educationalist James Tooley advocated that women were being over-educated and the only outcome for such unnatural beings was a life of misery.[1] This garnered mass media attention and approbation. It seems that women's right to university educa-tion is far from unchallenged and this applies in different ways across different na-tional contexts and cultures. The response of many to the entrance of women into HE has been resistance and backlash and most of all a fear that they are 'taking over.'[2]

Universities as Imagined Spaces

Yet history demonstrates that women are prepared to fight for the right to cross that border into Higher Education, and their heroic struggles for education form part of their struggle to survive in the most difficult of circumstances. Postcolonial resis-tance and the education of women are fundamentally intertwined across the devel-oping world, although much of that learning may take place outside and beyond formal classrooms.[3] Why should women feel so strongly about university opportuni-ties? I have been researching with women academics and students in the UK and in-ternationally over the last seven years. This has included research which focused on whether feminist ideas and the mass participation of women students have trans-formed the mainstream curriculum and culture of universities[4] and research which explored the perceptions of women academics about their positioning in their uni-versity and discipline.[5] Throughout this work, I have been struck by the emotional in-vestment women feel for university life. Despite the common agreement in the West that universities are market-led institutions and students are consumers, theirs is ultimately not the language of producers and products. Universities may be the pathways to careers and professional development, but I found that women predominantly saw them as imaginary spaces of exploration and liberation.

Multiple Boundaries

Despite the power of the imagined, we cannot forget that boundaries exist. We cannot assume that:

> Space is indifferent, that it acts as a fluid medium in which mobile subjects dwell...space is not like this. For example there is the matter of boundaries. Boundaries are important...as ways of fixing and displaying the subject by making it impossible to move.[6]

There are limits and constraints on which women can enter these spaces and what happens to them when they get there. In the United Kingdom, for example, the mass participation of women is largely a middle class phenomenon, and proportions of working class students who enter HE have actually dropped since the 1960s.[7] Once there, their relation to knowledge is marginal. My research indicated that working class women were able to use their standpoint on the border to critique and identify the limits and biases of the curriculum. However there was little evidence that their lecturers made use of this knowledge, or that the students were given pedagogical space to express these ideas.

Although black women have been in the vanguard of feminist thinking, I found their position in the curriculum verged on the invisible: they were either the epitome of noble martyrdom, or the focus of erotic voyeurism. The only knowledge black women are deemed to have is about *being* black and all black women are the same. Adah, for example, who was the daughter of an African diplomat was expected to teach her fellow white students about impoverished black women writers within the United States: '*They keep asking me all the time- how do they survive? Why do they think I know*'(Adah). In *Pedagogies of Crossing,* M. Jacqui Alexander[8] demonstrates how even university diversity policies themselves are manifestations of 'a corporate context that requires an instrumental diversity so as to better position white bodies only as knowledge producers.' Just as borders mean something very different to the asylum seeker and the cosmopolitan jet-setter, so Higher Education polices its borders much more heavily against the incursions of certain groups of women.

Paradoxical Space: Power and Constraint

Globally, many women active in the women's movement were also involved in Higher Education and there has been much synergy between feminist ideas in and outside of the Academy, particularly in the development of Women's Studies. Many women faced struggles to reconcile their activism with being successful academics[9] and there remains much anxiety about succumbing to the seductions of academic life.[10] For women who see themselves as engaged in '*praxis, not just theory*' the omens do not seem good: '*I try to take my students to women's groups, get them interested in feminist ideas, but its more and more difficult*'(Ida, Lecturer, Hong Kong). One of the aspects which interested me in my research study of feminist impacts on the mainstream curriculum was to see how issues in which I had been actively engaged as a campaigning feminist in the past, such as pornography and violence against women, now became topics on the university curriculum and taught by feminist lecturers. I was concerned, even angry, that they were treated a-historically and without much judicious use of feminist insights. For example, in one American Studies curriculum that I observed, lurid representations of rape of prostitutes in film were presented and understood as simple social commentary, and classroom debates on pornography could not take students beyond the perception that it was fundamentally 'harmless':

> ...if feminist pedagogy is partly a political project...then leaving students untroubled by pornography is surely a problematic outcome. How can women students be powerful if even feminist pedagogy fails to challenge the dominant culture of female objectification? Is this classroom full of women taking over anything more than the right to oppress themselves?[11]

I had to conclude that in some respects universities have incorporated feminism and feminists. However, it is also true that universities provide unique opportunities for thinking outside of the parameters of the everyday, indeed may be the only places where the unthinkable can be thought:

> Some women's issues are never going to be taken up by government...On the one hand we have all those things going on in the university, a lot of research and we're very advanced in the knowledge field, but on the other hand in the political arena we're quite behind (Vera, Researcher, Chile).

Whilst the image of learning community dominates much rhetoric of the university, I have found it more useful to draw on Iris Marion Young and her vision of the unoppressive city. The 'unoppressive city' is a place which harbours the 'being together of strangers.' It can be a place where 'strangers encounter each other...often remaining strangers and yet acknowledging their contiguity in living and the contributions each makes to the others.'[12] Rather than the incorporation of the learning community where all values must be shared and differences hidden, Young's vision permits a university where there is 'openness to unassimilated otherness.'

In analysing the accounts that women students made of being in the university, in my focus group, interview and diary data I found them taking pleasure in the different performances of others, making symbolic links between each other and with other 'strong' women they aspired to be like. The making strange of new ideas and new people, the crossing of borders of the mind was more important than huddling together in safe communities forged through exclusions.

Whose Knowledge?

This openness to new and different forms of knowledge amongst women may imply a concomitant transformation of the curriculum. Was this the case? Given the presence of so many feminists in Higher Education and the flowering of feminist scholarship over the last 30 years, plus the sheer volume of female undergraduate bodies, I have searched in my research for a corresponding shift in notions of what constitutes knowledge. Feminists working in the 70s and 80s aimed to alter the terms of the 'male-stream curriculum' and radically change the masculine paradigms working there. I wanted to know how successful they had been. My study focused on interdisciplinary subjects, where change and transformation might be expected and which brought together disciplines across science, the humanities and social sciences, in this case Environmental Studies and American Studies, taught in two institutions which had prioritised widening participation to diverse students.[13]

Although there had been change from those decades where women despaired of ever putting feminist ideas on university agendas, the changes in what constituted valid knowledge did not match the transformations in the gendering of the student body. If women were now the majority, it by no means meant that women were positioned as the archetypal learners. I charted four different positions: feminist space in the curriculum: ghetto or refuge?; still hidden from history; women evading science and power; science and anti-feminism.

In the first of these which described the American Studies curriculum in what I call Expanding University, feminists had been able to infiltrate the curriculum to the extent that at least two modules were specifically allocated to feminist ideas. However, when it came to overturning the masculine paradigms and precepts of the curriculum as a whole, women were still living in the borderland:

> Within my American Studies module Metropolis there is not much mention of women. I think this was the only week that they have specifically addressed the very masculinised way that predominates when looking at the city. Although this week we were told about books written by women which are trying to redress this view we were not told anything other than the name and title. However, as I am taking two modules on feminism it is quite nice that women's issue are not focused on (Jenny, diary).

A feminist view is available but it has not disrupted the dominant paradigm. Meanwhile feminism exists in discrete locations and those that enter them feel saturated with 'women's issues' and want to escape them elsewhere. I concluded that although there were spaces here for feminist thought, ultimately this curriculum may represent little more than the incorporation and defusing of feminism.

The second model, still hidden from history, applied to the American Studies curriculum in what I call Pleasant College. This curriculum displayed far less innovation and interdisciplinarity and the traditional disciplines of Politics and History appeared to be dominant. With the traditional curriculum came the assigning of traditional roles to women. For example Politics was construed as only mainstream, presidential and male and not as activist, local, or feminist. Women were openly construed by one lecturer as 'a minority interest' whose concerns lay only in the personal realm and 'beyond the scope of business or economics'(Politics lecture, field notes).

In History, events were public ones and therefore the absence of women was perceived as natural and unavoidable.

> Tracey: 'In History and Politics there weren't any women so of course they aren't mentioned.'
>
> JQ: 'Well they may not have been in power but they were there.'
>
> Joanne: 'There were women involved but they didn't have the confidence to write, so of course they wouldn't appear. There are no women in History because men wrote all the books' (focus group discussion).

There seemed to be no way in which students or lecturers felt they could bridge this gap and so women were maintained, not just on the border but exiled to another country where no-one bothered to go.

The third model: women evading science, applied to the Environmental Science curriculum in Pleasant college. Women in this curriculum belonged in the developing world, where they were usually portrayed as victims. Women as scientists and as powerful producers of knowledge were largely absent:

Katy: 'A lot of modules are about the Third World, but when you're talking about the U.S. or Europe you're talking about men'

JQ: 'So you're saying there's not much about women scientists and the work that they have done?'

Katy:'No and just to be downright awkward I did my poster project on women scientists.'

JQ: ' How did that go down?'

Kat: 'They all went Who?!' (laughs)

JQ: ' And who was it?'

Katy: 'Barbara McClintock' (Katy, interview)

The invisibility of the woman scientist became a self-fulfilling prophecy on this course, as much of the students' energy went into evading science rather than embracing it. Here there were a large number of mature women, who had not studied science for a long time and felt insecure and unsupported in their early attempts at lab work. They were able to shape their degree so they subsequently successfully evaded the strongly scientific modules in favour of those which focused on environmental policy. In doing so they gave up their rights to the power/knowledge afforded to science and accepted a feminised alternative.

The last model, power, science and anti-feminism applied to the Environmental Studies curriculum in Expanding university. In some respects this was the most disturbing scenario, as it demonstrated masculinity marshalling its forces to repel and reject both women and feminist ideas. Here the dominant masculinist values of science as rational, detached and objective were repeatedly evoked and re-inforced. The claim to knowledge of others, such as feminists, was ridiculed and held as insupportable. One student involved in my focus group was literally laughed out of her tutor's office when she expressed an interest in ecofeminism:

> Lisa: 'When I said I wanted to do ecofeminism for my final year project he practically laughed me out of the room he said 'what!' and he wouldn't look me in the eyes…and he was practically, maybe he didn't mean it, but he was like disregarding anything you'd come up with (in my research project) before he'd ever read anything you'd done and the other tutor was saying 'you've got to sort out the institution, you've got to be really careful where you work, otherwise the institution's going to laugh at you and say what a pile of old manure or compost or something,' and I was like 'For God's sake no!' (focus group).

Science here is a male master-knowledge which seems afraid of feminism as well as being contemptuous of it. There is little evidence that its paradigms have shifted to mark the entry of so many women into Higher Education.

Conclusions

Teresa de Lauretis uses the image of the 'space off' to describe how the 'female subject of feminism' positions herself to resist hegemonic identities:

> It is the elsewhere of discourse here and now, the blind spots, or the space-off of its representations. I think of it as spaces in the margins of hegemonic discourses, social spaces carved in the interstices of institutions and in the chinks and cracks of the power-knowledge apparati.[14]

Despite the absolute transformation of Higher Education to become a place where women are dominant numerically, my research shows women still living in the space off of institutions when it comes to taking control of power and knowledge. However, the space off is a fecund place to be, a locus of possibility. Women use universities as imaginary spaces of exploration and liberation, opportunities for border crossings of the mind, despite the multiple boundaries of gender, race, class, age, disability and sexuality. The 'paradoxical space' of the university is a site of both power and constraint for women. In the face of the mass participation of women and the growth of feminist ideas, the construction of knowledge and who owns it remains profoundly contested.

Notes

1. James Tooley, *The Miseducation of Women*, (London, Continuum, 2002).

2. Jocey Quinn, *Powerful Subjects: Are Women Really Taking Over the University?*(Stoke-on-Trent: Trentham Books, 2003).

3. Sharzad Mojab, 'War and diaspora as lifelong learning contexts for immigrant women, in Carole Leathwoood and Becky Francis eds, *Gender and Lifelong Learning* (London: Routledge, 2006).

4. Jocey Quinn, 'Belonging in a learning community: the re-imagined university and imagined social capital,' *Studies in the Education of Adults*, 37/1 (2005): 4-18; Jocey Quinn, 'Mothers, learners and countermemory,' *Gender and Education*, 16/3 (2004), 365-79.

5. Jocey Quinn, 'Welcome to the Pleasure dome: women taking pleasure in the university' in Pamela Cotterill, Gayle Letherby and Sue Jackson, eds, *Challenges and Negotiations for Women in Higher Education* (London: Kluwer, 2007).

6. Steve Pile and Nigel Thrift, *Mapping the Subject*, (London: Routledge,1995), 374.

7. Reay, Diane, David, Miriam and Ball Stephen, *Degrees of Choice* (Stoke-on-Trent: Tretham Books, 2005).

8. M. Jacqui Alexander, *Pedagogies of Crossing* (Durham and London: Duke University Press, 2005).

9. Miriam David, *Personal and Political* (Stoke on Trent: Tretham Books, 2003).

10. Valerie Hey, 'Perverse Pleasures: Identity work and the paradoxes of greedy institutions,' *Journal of International Women's Studies*, 3(3) (2004), 33-43.

11. Quinn, *Powerful Subjects,* 73.

12. Iris Marion Young, *Justice and the Politics of Difference* (Princeton: Princeton University Press, 1990), 318.

13. Quinn, *Powerful Subjects.*

14. Teresa de Lauretis, *Technologies of Gender* (Bloomington: Indiana University Press, 1987), 25.

Chapter Thirteen

Girl-Method: Placing Girl-Centred Research Methodologies on the Map of Girlhood Studies

Claudia Mitchell and Jacqueline Reid-Walsh

AS IS obvious in the range of methodological issues mapped out in various studies of girlhood, the notions embedded in ideologies of working *with* girls, *for* girls, and *about* girls are complex. These studies are ones that cross age, cultural contexts, and disciplinary boundaries and interrogate lines between the researcher and the re-searched. In particular, they contest feminist ideals of participation and "girls' voices" (our sisters/ourselves or our daughters/ourselves) and the accuracy of repre-sentations of girls' perspectives on issues that are key to their lives now and in the fu-ture. We are writing as daughters, as mothers of daughters, as former girls, and as feminist researchers who locate much of our research within studies of childhood, in-cluding the childhood of girls, who work within global frameworks, and who ap-proach girlhood studies within Age Studies more broadly. In this chapter, we present a framework for what we describe as "girl-method," a term we first used in *Seven Going on Seventeen: Tween Studies in the Culture of Girlhood* to talk about particular methodological approaches to understanding tween culture.[1]

To date, there remains a limited body of literature that attends to methodologies for work *with* girls or for facilitating research *by* girls themselves, even though the litera-ture on girlhood is replete with references to participation and the need for girl-centredness. Heather-jane Robertson's *A Cappella* studies of the early 1990s, the "lis-tening guide" research of Brown and Gilligan, or Holland et al's work on feminist tran-script analysis related to girls' sexuality are exceptions.[2] As has been evident in several regional, national and international conferences on girlhood, the methodological issues are ones that offer unique challenges to contemporary feminist scholars.[3]

What we propose in this chapter is a framework for deepening an understand-ing of what it means to do girlhood research. As a precedent for this work, we draw from the rich body of work on feminist methodology involving women, as well as the emerging body of literature within the new social studies of childhood looking at methodologies for working with children.[4] However, we also intersperse the chapter with retrospective accounts of some of our own work of more than a decade on girl-hood. This revisioning, as we see in the work of Brown and Gilligan among others, is arguably a component of girl-method.[5] In keeping with the overall theme of this book, some of the work we refer to is specifically Canadian, as we see in our studies of Canadian mail-order catalogues as girls' "texts of desire"; other studies, such as those on Barbie or Nancy Drew are simply Western in terms of content. Still other work applies to the broader context of girls' lives globally.

Girl-Centred Research and Girl-Method

We use the term "girl-method" as a short-hand way of referring to what Sandra Harding would describe as methodologies (theories and analyses of how research should pro-ceed) and methods (techniques for gathering and analyzing evidence) in girl centered re-search that assumes a political stance of defending and promoting the rights of girls.[6] It speaks to considerations such as who the researchers are, how girls participate, issues of girls' positionality, the cultural contexts of the girls, and the representations of girls his-torically, as well as in contemporary culture. More importantly though, the idea of girl-method indicates the need to make age and gender explicit both in relation to the re-searcher and to the researched. When working in girlhood studies, with very few excep-tions, power and age dynamics, as well as the intersectionality of race, class, ethnicity, and gender and sexuality need to be foregrounded in self-reflective ways. This fore-grounding is an extension of ideas of feminist scholars, such as those by Ann Oakley and Michelle Fine, who problematize the act of women researching other women.[7] It also un-derscores the inherent inequalities that arise when younger and older adults research girls of different ages, culture, and geographic locations. Like many other girlhood re-searchers, we are arguing against the tendency of lumping girls into one group or cate-gory. We believe that the key to avoiding this homogenizing is to develop methodologies that incorporate (and indeed, emphasize) the politics of girlhood within girlhood studies.

As editors of *Seven Going on Seventeen*, we drew on the category of "girl-method" as one of several ways to organize the chapters. Since we are interested in method work itself—in exploring different field sites for knowing in relation to the study of girlhood, childhood, popular culture, women's lives and so on—we were struck by the question of whether there are certain approaches that may be more suited than others to women researching preteen and young teen girls, age groups which are collapsed by marketers into the term "tween." Specifically, we were interested in whether there might be a framework that identifies kinds of method work that women could engage in *with* girls, *for* girls and *about* girlhood. Thus, the section in that book called "girl-method" includes a variety of methods, ranging from theoretical analysis, to participatory approaches, and to textual analysis that the authors use in a self-conscious, self-reflective way, with a focus on constructing a certain methodology and using it to study an aspect of tween girls and their culture.

In that volume, Elizabeth Seaton uses postmodern cultural theory to interrogate the biological phenomenon and critical reception of early puberty.[8] Both Marina Gonick and Kristina Hackman engage in participatory research with girls using aspects of video construction: Gonick involves girls aged twelve to fourteen of racially diverse backgrounds (Asian, Caribbean, European) in writing video scripts and then analyzes one of the stories as providing insight into how the politics of girls' school culture revolve around a "nerd-popular" axis inflected by race and ethnicity.[9] Hackman has a group of eleven and twelve year old German girls collectively produce a video centered on fan culture called "Girl Power" and then analyzes it in terms of their gendered identity in light of the dominance of heteronormativity.[10] In different ways, Kathleen O'Reilly-Scanlon, Sonya Dwyer and Meredith Cherland adapt feminist memory-work methods to self-study and to comparative age studies in order to work back to girlhood. The first two adapt Frigga Haug's work on studying parts of the body—here, hair—in relation to tweens' self image and sense of identity by analyzing photographs of themselves as white, middle-class pre-teens in the 1960's and 70's and comparing their own experiences with the experiences and expectations for tween girls today.[11] Cherland adapts Haug's method to auto-ethnographic study in order to situate girlhood historically. She compares memory accounts of her own childhood as part of a white working class family with that of her now adult daughter born of a professional couple. She focuses on the latter's tenth year and her reading of the *BabySitters Club* series in terms of how she constructed herself as part of a dominant and vulnerable group.[12] Miki Flockemann uses literary textual analysis to explore the representation of a tween voice in South African literature for adults in order to explore how the girl child, while often embodying the motif of social conflict as women characters do, is represented in such a way so as to revise and possibly subvert the existing hegemonic discourses.[13] In other chapters in *Seven Going Seventeen*, these research sites reappear. Particularly popular are participatory methods with tween girls used in visiting different field sites either physically, such as school yards, shopping malls or virtually, such as web sites.[14] Using various approaches, these essays seek ways to include the voices of girls between 8 and 12 in a respectful way, and to analyze their statements using different techniques of discourse analysis.

Sandra Harding states that while there is no *unique* feminist method, there is a distinctive methodological perspective or framework that challenges the implicit androcentric bias in research.[15] Although this statement has been modified in subsequent work by feminists occupying different marginalized positions due to race, ethnicity, class, sexuality, and geographical location, girls too often still seem to be subsumed under the category of women.[16] We argue that the statements of Harding and others need to be further adapted to include a feminist methodological perspective or framework that focuses on girls of different ages, as in the present volume. Whether there are unique methods that are better suited to a child population still needs to be discovered. Our point is simply that as researchers, we need to make a girl-centredness explicit in our work, and as a start, we need to think about the unique features of girlhood research within the larger map of girlhood studies. Indeed, even the term "mapping," as we outline in the next section, can have particularized uses when looking at girlhood studies.

Mapping

> Mapping, by forcing us to think in terms of discrete entities occupying specific spaces, makes us aware of the spaces we inhabit and the positions we take relative to others.[17]

A few years ago, we embarked upon a mapping project within girlhood studies that argued for the need to work across disciplinary borders, and to interrogate our own work for its potential to speak across generations, geographic spaces and so on. Our purpose in mapping was to ascertain possible points of convergence in terms of who was doing work on girlhood, and to discover what we could learn (and what we might lose) when we cross disciplinary borders. In so doing, we argued for the need for a discourse community that does not "cut up" girls' lives, but rather one that seeks to establish a framework for common understandings. Our aim ultimately was to begin to establish an "imagined community" among scholars, practitioners and activists.[18] In seeking to persuade the feminist community to contemplate such an aim, we used maps and mapping as metaphors in order to tap into the rhetorical persuasiveness often attributed to maps.[19] While we use "mapping" in a figurative sense, since it is important to remain cognizant of the patriarchal and colonial implications of the term, we also interrogate the limitations of our conceptual tools: "What can we learn when we cross the borders"? How can the work in one area inform the work in the other areas? How can we avoid unnecessary duplication? Is there any practical value to working with these comparative literatures?" This is a particularly key point when we think about the urgency for change in the lives of women in developing countries. Many countries do not have the luxury of twenty years or more to try to develop an action plan. In the developed world, where there may be only limited funds for researching girls' lives, we cannot afford to be scrapping over the small amounts of money that exists. We need to look critically at what the various areas say, not only in terms of how each can inform the others, but also in terms of the problems inherent in each area.

The strength of that exercise was in working out how feminist mapping, a term we borrowed from Nellie Stromquist, might help us to overcome what might at first appearance seem to be "just a review of the literature" or "just a carving up of the territory" into a who (or what agency) is doing what (or working in a specific area) of girlhood studies. In so doing, we did not claim to possess an objective world view. On the contrary, we approached the idea of mapping the scope of research on girls from the position of partial advocates. Nor did we presume a totalizing approach; our mappings left great areas of research uncharted. Instead, we thought our maps were to be done in the spirit of social cartography, which encourages the creation of smaller and contextualized narratives[20] – essentially what Donna Haraway would describe as a "boundary project" with fluid boundaries that may be able to resist established power relations and promote non-totalizing epistemological values.[21] Starting with the super-ordinate question, "Who cares about girls, anyway?" (a re-phrasing in some cases of "Who funds research about girls?"), we came up with the series of questions noted below that we have regarded as useful starting points for working across disciplines, across geographies, and acknowledging the significance of gender and generations.[22] Our goal has not been to re-position girlhood studies as some sort of monolithic enterprise, but rather to see the term "girlhood" as one that can (and should) invoke strategic alliances within research communities so that our overarching questions point to the strength of interdisciplinarity. Indeed, one might argue that interdisciplinarity is one key feature of redefining those limits.

The questions that we identify in Figure 1 provide for a meta-analysis on research on girlhood, with several of them specific to our discussion here on girl-method.

Figure 1: Questions For Meta-Analysis On Research On Girlhood

---

1. How is girlhood defined and why? Who is a girl?

2. What are the geo-political spaces in which the research takes place?

3. Who is engaging in this kind of research?

4. What is the critical reception of this research? Who funds girlhood?

5. Who are beneficiaries of the research on girlhood?

6. What are the kinds of questions that are being taken up?

7. What is the history of this field? How has the focus of the work changed over time?

8. How does the research link the lives of girls and women?

9. To what extent does the research draw on gender relations?

10. What is the main agenda of the work? To what extent is it regulatory and protective? Advocacy and action-oriented? Policy-oriented?

11. What methodologies are being employed? How do girls and women participate? To what extent is the work girl-centred?

Adapted from Mitchell et al., "Who Cares about Girls?" with emphasis added.

A Framework For Girl-Method

In this section, we look at four sub-themes of research methodology—age disaggregation, participatory process, situating the researcher, and historical context—that we regard as key to the development of a conceptual and practical map for both planning and evaluating girlhood research.

Age Disaggregation

How do we acknowledge and build in the significance of age? How and when do we disaggregate girlhood according to age and what do we lose when we do not? Can we talk across ages (and experiences) of girlhood? Does it matter if the girl is of pre-school age, between the ages of ten and fourteen (a very young adolescent, as defined by the Population Council), eighteen and at the age of consent in many countries, or twenty-four and at the far edge of North American adolescence, yet still within the category of "young" as defined by the UN? The category "girl" can re-

fer to the baby girl who is sexually abused by a man who believes the myth that having sex with a baby can cure AIDS; to the little girl knowers who are seen to be
controversial in Sally Mann's photography of her own daughters; or to the little
girls in Walkerdine's *Daddy's Girl* or to the tween age "whistle blower" girls of Lyn
Mikel Brown and Carol Gilligan's work.[23] "Girl" can also be a category within Youth
Studies – defined by UN agencies as being between the ages of fifteen and
twenty-nine. According to Fuchs, there are, at least five generations of women who
might classify themselves or be classified as girls, ranging from fifty-five year old
women as Gap shoppers shopping with their baby Gap grand-daughters; to girl rock
bands from Generation X; to Monica Lewinsky as "just a girl"; to the commodification of girlhood nostalgia girlhood through American Girl branding; to tween girls;
and to 'it's a girl' baby girls.[24] In some cases, who is a girl is defined by consumerism
(according to Gap, all females might be girls), but it can also be defined by the media or policy makers. If, for example, the young female is married, or if she is a
mother herself, or if she is orphaned and heading up the household of younger
brothers and sisters, as so many girls are in rural South Africa, is she still a girl?
What services can she access because she is a girl, or because she is a mother, or because she could be a property-owner?[25] Is the ten year girl-child in Rwanda still a
girl-child when she moves to Montreal as a refugee? When the life expectancy for
females is thirty-nine, as it now is in some countries in sub-Saharan Africa as a result
of HIV and AIDS, what does it mean to know that more than half of your life is over
by age twenty?

We would argue that as researchers, we need to be systematic and rigorous in
our analyses and in our work with other researchers, the media, and policy makers
when it comes to talking about age. The use of the term *balkishori* in India to refer
to the pre-adolescent girl suggests to us the value of more precise language to talk
about different times in the lives of young females in the context of policy and access to specific health and education services.[26] In an appendix in her book *Future
Girl: Young Women in the Twenty-first Century* (2004), Anita Harris includes a discussion of this very point "who is a girl?" and the issue of whether we ought to abandon the study of young women simply because of the challenges of definition.[27] We
concur with her position that researchers need to be very specific about the girls
they are describing. While we are not arguing for some universal definition of girlhood, nor are we making a claim that one set of studies is more "the girl" than others, we are suggesting that as feminist researchers of girlhood, we go one step
further and see that age dissagregation provides a useful audit tool for taking stock

of the research area, for identifying gaps, and for engaging in our own self-monitoring within a feminist community. To what extent, for example, does the whole area of Girlhood Studies privilege one set of girl-experiences over others and why? In an audit of studies that claim to be girlhood studies or girl-centred, how is girlhood defined and what are the dominant issues? How many of the studies are about adolescent girls, or girls and young women in their early twenties, or about girls between the ages of 5 and 8, and so on? As Harris observes, "when young women and girls did appear, this usually took the form of texts displaying an anxiety and fascination over sexuality, especially young women's involvement in prostitution."[28] If we were to engage in an audit of girlhood studies, to what extent does an age-bias privilege some issues over others (e.g. dating over play)? Finally, how might work on girlhood inform age studies more broadly where, as Kathleen Woodward observes, "old age and middle age are part of the larger continuum on a discourse on age itself, a system of age that includes infancy, childhood, adolescence and young adulthood."[29] To date, there are relatively few studies that provide for a cross-over from one stage (how ever defined) to another. A notable exception is the work of Jenny Hockey and Allison James *Growing Up and Growing Old* (1993), which includes a deconstruction of the notions of old age and second childhood.[30] We propose that age disaggregation could be an important component of any research which contests purely biological and essentialist meanings of age.

Participatory Process and Self-Representation

The notion of "girls' voices" is a critical one in Girlhood Studies. Many of us want to claim that the voices of the girls with whom we work (of whatever age) are heard. The study of the participation of those who are usually marginalized is an area of research that is burgeoning, both in terms of appropriate methodologies, but also in terms of fraughtness in relation to ethical issues, levels of participation, tokenism, privileging/romancing the voices of participants, putting our own interpretations on the words of our participants, and so on. When it comes to the participation of minors, the area becomes even more contested. Hart's discussion of a "ladder" of child participation is a useful one for monitoring levels of participation on a scale of one to eight.[31] A "one" might be children placed on a stage in front of a group of adults to sing "We Are the World." In an "eight" category, there might be no adults present at all; children have defined the issues (violence in schools, their right to hold an event) and have taken their own actions to consult with adults to bring about change. Most research studies, particularly those that are funded (and hence requiring adult participation), will be somewhere in the middle.

When acknowledging the power differentials between adult researchers and children participants, how do we minimize the presence of the former and maximize the presence of the latter? And equally important, are there specific issues that pertain to work with girls that we need to take account? We see the interrelatedness of these two questions. A good example is the devaluing of women's culture carried over into the devaluating of girl's culture.

Women in a Western context are often in the position of apologizing for romance reading, magazine reading, or for reading novels more generally, and as Gannett and many others point out, certain writing genres such as journal and diary writing, when they are associated with women, are often seen to have little value.[32] Even the status of girls' blogging and other computer use is under scrutiny.[33] Using the authentic voices of girls to understand girls' play, and particularly the links between girls' play and aspects of their identity, may be problematic. As David Buckingham, Julian Sefton-Green and others have pointed out in their work with children on their own television viewing, children usually figure out what they should say to adults.[34] As we argue elsewhere in our discussion of the political spaces of research with children, this self-censoring might be reconfigured as "what they can't say to adults," or even worse, the children might interpret the intrusiveness of the adult questioner to indicate that play activities must be secretly engaged in.[35] For girls, this might mean not admitting to having had a Barbie, or to still playing with Barbie dolls or My Little Ponies after the age of 9, or to buying *Sweet Valley High* books, and so on. The point is not that these political spaces cannot be negotiated (through child-to-child research, for example or studying our own daughters or nieces), but only that we devalue the genuine participation of girls if we don't make the actual status of the texts explicit in our formulations and if we don't take the low status of texts into account when we try to invoke the voices of girls. Even a savvy four year old will know enough to conceal a Barbie or other contraband on the way to day-care. In one study, we asked girls and boys to engage in their own self-representation by photographing their bedrooms with the idea that they would themselves represent their play and uses of popular culture.[36]

In other studies, as we explore in the next section, we have used retrospective memory work accounts, so that at least the participant has some distance for interrogating some of the things that have happened to them as powerless children.

The issues noted above are not easily separated from those that seem of an even more life-and-death status, because they also refer to sex and secrecy. Here we are thinking of girls' sexuality; the fact that worldwide, girls are more likely to be sexually abused than boys, the "gendering" of HIV and AIDS, and so on. As researchers, how do we ensure the full participation of girls in talking about what has happened to them or about what potentially is going to happen them? Retrospective accounts are too late! In one study with twelve and thirteen year old girls in a peri-urban school in Swaziland, where the incidences of sexual abuse at school, in the community, and at home are high, we used photo-voice techniques, where we asked them to photograph places at the school where they regard as "safe" and "not so safe."[37] We were struck by the numerous photographs they took of toilets (toilets, they said, were dangerous because they were too far from the rest of the school and you could be raped there, or there were in such a bad state that you had no privacy and could be attached). But we were equally struck by some of the responses of their teachers, who were surprised that the girls had taken such pictures. They had no idea of how the girls felt. We were also moved by a series of photographs of two girls, who staged being attacked and raped in the bushes around their school.

While it is beyond the scope of this chapter to articulate a more extensive analysis of this photograph—the expressions on the faces of the two girls who play the attacked and the attacker, speculation about the role of the girl-photographer and the discussions that must have taken place in order to pose the picture or even to decide to take such a picture in the first place—we think that it is this kind of method and analysis that could reposition girls as full participants.[38] In this particular study, we were not able to work over a long period of time with the girls, in another study in South Africa, it was the girls themselves who created an entire photographic narrative, where they interpret their photographs of children who work in the market on Fridays rather than attend school.[39] One of their narratives is around a grade 6 girl who skips school to avoid the inappropriate sexual advances of a male teacher. The girls can begin to see themselves as agents of change when their analysis convinces their principal to do something about the teacher.

What we want to emphasize here is that participation—hearing the voices of girls—should not be separated from taking action. Ethically, it may not always be possible to involve girls directly in taking action and indeed, we have to make sure that we don't put girls in a more dangerous position as a result of our interventions. At the same time, we must also adhere to a code of conduct where we don't simply "hear" the voices of girls for the purposes of our own research without ensuring that we take appropriate steps with policy makers. And it is here where we run the risk of devaluing girls' voices and experiences, not to mention putting their safety and security at risk.

Finally, though, we want to raise a point about the ways in which our research must respect young girls as children and their right to play and to an open future. As the VACHA women of India have described in their work with the *balkishori*,[40] researchers and policy makers might burden girls with all of the negative aspects of growing up. Our agenda may be a protective one, but by focusing on pregnancy, sexual abuse, and so on, we may unwittingly pathologize "growing up girl" and we may even reinforce a particular destiny. In asking girls to imagine their futures, to photograph, draw or perform their hopes, we may turn some of this work into a more futuristic mode. We might also see that photography, collaborative film making, drama and so on are pleasurable, drawing as they do on the principles of edu-tainment.[41]

Intergenerationality in the Unraveling of Girlhood

In the same way that Ann Oakley's "Interviewing Women: A Contradiction in Terms?" formulation has a particular place in women's research with older women, we think that methods for addressing intergenerationality have a particular place in our work with girls of various ages. While there may be a number of ways of thinking about what intergenerationality might mean in the context of girl-method, here we highlight memory work. In much of our previous work, we have drawn on specific memory-work approaches, as well as the work of those in the area of feminist nostalgia.[42] Far from seeing memory as what bell hooks describes as "useless longing,"[43] we have been working with the idea of interrogating memory by raising such questions as the following: Why do we remember things a certain way? What (or who) is left out? How can the past inform the future? How can we look at memory as a series of drafts? Retrospective accounts do not have to be far into the past, and indeed, in one study, we asked ten and eleven year old girls to look back at their grade one school photographs as a way to talk about their own experiences of schooling.[44] In other memory work studies where we have used photographs, we have highlighted the significance of working one just one or two photographs and have adapted Annette Kuhn's work to engaging in analysis and interpretation.[45]

We have been particularly interested in retrospective accounts in the context of lost photographs. Inspired by the work of bell hooks, who writes of a lost photograph of herself as a small girl in a cowgirl outfit and the ways in which the loss of the photograph is associated now with a loss of "that girl,"[46] Jacqui and Claudia have each written of other lost cowgirl photographs. Jacqui's account, like hooks', starts with the cowgirl outfit itself and demonstrates the ways in which items of clothing carry with them particular "dress stories" about identity, something that is articulated more fully in Weber and Mitchell's *Not Just Any Dress: Narratives of Memory, Body and Identity*.[47] There, we look at a number of girlhood stories through the conduit of communion dresses, school uniforms, little girl Polly Flinders' dresses, and even being dressed up like a Barbie doll.[48] In Claudia's case, it is a missing photograph of herself reading an Annie Oakley cowgirl book and the ways in which the photograph and the memory of its taking now conjure up particular relationships with her brothers, the place of girls in a 1950s household, and so on. And in a further analysis of memory work, feminist nostalgia and cowgirls, we go so far as to analyze the place of Jessie the 1950s cowgirl in the popular film ToyStory 2.[49]

In other memory work, we have looked at women's memories of playing with Barbie.[50] While Barbie is mostly regarded as a feminist nightmare in terms of emphasis on body, beauty, fashion and consumerism, we have encountered narratives where women talk about how Barbie was the first doll that did not require them to engage in conventional domestic play: feeding the baby doll, changing the diaper of the baby doll, and so on. In memory work involving the former readers of Nancy Drew books, we have noted again the ways in which participants revision their girlhood experiences through an adult woman lens. In one case, a woman who is now a police officer credits Nancy's amazing feats at solving mysteries as central to her career.[51] And in our study of memory work with the Eaton's and Sears' mail-order catalogue, it is the memories of our mothers as young girls that provide insights on girls' desires and dreams.[52] The point is not that memories can be taken at face value, or even that in working with memories, we therefore have "the truth." In her study of retired women teachers, Kathleen Weiler observes that although her participants look back at their decision to go into teaching as a "free choice" or as "a calling" ("I always wanted to be a teacher"), at the time, women only had three viable professional choices: teacher, nurse, or secretary.[53] Rather, we regard the uses of memory work as central to interrogating the autobiographical, theorizing the past, and as a starting point to asking what insights it provides for girls now.

Clearly, we do not believe that all published studies of girlhood research must necessarily begin with an explicit autobiographical exposé of the researcher's girlhood. However, we argue that somewhere in the process of doing research with and for girls, we should consciously work with our own histories as useful starting points, and that we should take full advantage of various approaches to working with the past as part of girl-method in informing our studies of contemporary girlhood. Three recent studies linked to girlhood in development contexts as part of a girlhood studies strand at McGill University used different intergenerational approaches: Jackie Kirk, for example, in her study of women teachers in Pakistan, drew on photographs and other forms of material culture so that the women currently teaching girls might invoke their own autobiographies. In her study of sexual violence in the Ghanaian context, Gladys Teni-Atinga had preservice teachers engage in written memory work about their own girlhoods as a way to not only learn more about the situation in schools in Ghana, but also as a way to involve new teachers as agents of change. Stephanie Garrow drew on techniques of feminist mapping in her study of girls' education in Uganda in order to engage the various partner organizations in reflecting on and "mapping futures" for girls.[54]

Girl History

Similar to autobiographical retrospective approaches, but on a collective scale, is the need for feminist researchers to contextualize a study of girls and girlhood within a historical–cultural framework. We attest that any attempt at a feminist mapping of girls and girlhood should include a temporal dimension (created in the context of multiple accounts of history, versus a monolithic "grand historical narrative"), in addition to the spatial. There is often a tendency in work focusing on the present day to disregard the past, relegating that approach to historians and to literary historians, who indeed years ago coined the term "presentist" for this attitude.[55] Feminist literary critic bell hooks has long urged for the need for historical approaches in feminist work, particularly if the history is a negative one as she points out in regard to the relations between black and white women in the United States and in North America generally, in order to appreciate the challenges for collective feminist projects today to proceed across and through boundaries of race, and class and we believe this perspective equally applies to women working on and with girls.[56] Keeping Walter Benjamin's dictum in mind, "the past haunts the present, but the latter denies it with good reason," we believe this stance of facing the past and trying to pick out one thread of a continuous or discontinuous narrative is necessary in order to study girls and girlhood in a scrupulous manner, no matter whether the topic is of urgent importance, such as girls and AIDS, or whether on the surface it appears trivial, as with work on girls' popular culture.

To take an example from girls' popular culture, as we have discussed in our earlier studies of fashion dolls, a historical contextualization will enable critics and researchers to approach a topic, such as the Barbie doll, in a more balanced and thorough way, to prevent needless repetition of work, and to stop the cycles of moral and media panics that seem to thrive on historical amnesia.[57] If we take the Bratz doll as an example of a recent artifact, we see that some critics regard it as yet another example of a long line of oppressive fashion dolls such as Barbie, while others see it as a parodic representation of a fashion doll.[58] Both historical views bring different insights to bear, one which stems from some 45 years ago, while another stems from some 200 year ago—the latter might argue that the parodic representation of a female form occurred in early commercial fashion dolls of the 18th century and link this parodic response to existing in different states of media and cultural transition, as argued by historical and comparative media critics David Thorburn and Henry Jenkins.[59]

Girlhood studies is a relatively new field of research and because of this, it is important methodologically to draw on the insights and to learn from the problems of other interdisciplinary studies, particularly in those that inform the perspective and background of the area. These would include Women's Studies, Feminist Studies, Sexuality Studies, Childhood Studies to name some of those most related. Similarly, more recent academic approaches, which cross the divide between the arts, humanities, and social sciences, such a New Media Studies, may prove to be helpful. For instance, here Thorburn and Jenkins call for new approaches to thinking about New Media:

> In our current moment of conceptual uncertainty and technological transition, there is an urgent need for a pragmatic, historically informed perspective that maps a sensible middle ground between the euphoria and the panic surrounding new media, a perspective that aims to understand the place of economic, political, legal, social and cultural institutions in mediating and partly shaping technological change.[60]

These proponents are arguing for a tone and a nuanced perspective that could fruitfully be adapted to Girlhood Studies, particularly since they too are responding to a sense of urgency, to the need to somehow be accountable, and to the desire to "get it right."

Girl-Method: Extending the Limits of Girlhood Studies

Some might argue that what we have mapped out is simply a version of "good method" within Women's Studies, an argument that we would reject on the grounds that attention to girls, particularly pre-adolescent girls and younger, has remained on the margins of the agenda of Women's Studies for the last 30 years. Somehow, when we factor in child development, the protectionist guidelines of the Convention on the Rights of the Child, and the politics of childhood more generally, the positions of child and adult, while blurred, remain nonetheless distinct within different cultural social and cultural contexts. An analogy could be made with Literary Studies and Children's Literature Studies, for the latter has similarly remained on the margins of the academy for a comparable length of time, and is recently emerging with a distinct child-centred identity. And when it comes to the girl-child, as we describe in our meta-analysis above, there are specific methodological issues that need to be factored in.

Others might argue that Girlhood Studies (and girl-method) simply complement Boyhood Studies, and that there is nothing that is unique to working with girls, other than seeing them (and possibly working with them) as a distinct grouping based on age and gender. Is there not also a need to disaggregate age in Boyhood Studies? Is there not a particular ethic of Boyhood Studies? Do adult male researchers also need to invoke some sense of their own boyhoods? While we think that there are important overlaps between Boyhood Studies and Girlhood Studies, we also see that they each have their respective "parent" groups and that Feminist Studies and Masculinity Studies inform the emerging areas and also inform one another theoretically. In all likelihood, there also needs to be a distinct discussion of boy-method.

We propose that the articulation of the idea of girl-method offers a platform for action, which includes particular tools and approaches; particular orientations that acknowledge, in a rights-based way, the unique historical and contemporary contexts for girls and young women; the position of women studying girlhood; and ways of taking action. Clearly what we have mapped out in this chapter leaves a great many gaps to be filled. However, through the emergence of strong academic, NGO, and activist alliances working with and for girls, new scholarship that provides a global and intergenerational context for understanding the lives of girls and young women, and the growth of Girlhood Studies more generally, girl-method itself will become the basis of studies. Indeed, it has only been in the last five years or so that it has been possible to go into some feminist bookstores and discover a section called Girlhood Studies! This discussion of girl-method has, we hope, extended the boundaries of what needs to be included in approaching and evaluating research with, for, and about girls into a methodological dimension as well.

Notes

1. On the term "girl-method": Although we first used this term in a publication in 2005, we would like to acknowledge discussions with Helen Berman in November, 2003 about the need for such a term and indeed for inspiring further explorations of the idea.

2. Heather-jane Robinson, *A Cappella: A Report on the Realities, Concerns, Expectations, and Barriers Experienced by Adolescent Women in Canada* (Ottawa, ON: Canadian Teacher's Federation, 1990); Lyn M. Brown and Carol Gilligan, *Meeting at the Crossroads: Women's Psychology and Girls' Development* (Cambridge, MA: Harvard University Press, 1992); Janet Holland, Caroline Ramazonuglu, Sue Sharpe, and Rachel Thomson, "Feminist Methodology and Young People's Sexuality," in *Culture, Society, and Sexuality*, ed. Richard Parker and Peter Aggleton, 457-472 (London: UCL Press/Taylor and Francis, 1999).

3. See for example, "A New Girl Order: Young Women and the Future of Feminism" conference at King's College, London, November 14-16, 2001; "Over There, Over Here" a conference on refugee and immigrant women in Montreal in November, 2002; and the "Transforming Spaces: Girls, Agency and Power" conference at Concordia University, Montreal, November 21-23, 2003.

4. For work on feminist methodology involving women, see Frigga Haug et al., *Female Sexualization: A Collective Work of Memory*, trans. Erica Carter (London: Verso, 1987); June Crawford et al., *Emotion and Gender: Constructing Meaning from Memory* (Thousand Oaks, CA: Sage, 1992); Lykes; and Ann Oakley, "Interviewing Women: A Contradiction in Terms?" in *Doing Feminist Research*, ed. Hele Roberts, 30-61 (London: Routledge and Kegan Paul, 1981). For work on methodologies involving children, see Allison Jenks, Chris James and Alan Prout, *Theorizing Childhood* (Cambridge, UK: Polity Press, 1998); Claudia Mitchell and Jacqueline Reid-Walsh, *Researching Children's Popular Culture: The Cultural Spaces of Childhood* (New York: Routledge, 2002).

5. Brown and Gilligan, *Meeting at the Crossroads*.

6. Sandra Harding, ed., *Feminism and Methodology* (Bloomington: Indiana University Press, 1987).

7. See for example Ann Oakley, "Interviewing Women"; and Michelle Fine, "Distance and Other Stances: Negotiation of Power Inside Feminist Research," in *Power and Method: Political Activism and Educational Research*, ed. Andrew Gitlin, 13-35 (New York: Routledge, 1994).

8. Elizabeth Seaton, "Tween Social and Biological Reproduction: Early Puberty in Girls," in *Seven Going on Seventeen*, ed. Claudia Mitchell and Jacqueline Reid-Walsh, 25-45 (New York: Peter Lang, 2005).

9. Marnina Gonick, "From Nerd to Popular? Re-figuring School Identities and Transformation Stories," in *Seven Going on Seventeen*, 46-62.

10. Kristina Hackmann, "Video Girls: Between Changing Exploratory Behavior and Self-authorization," in *Seven Going on Seventeen*, 63-78.

11. Kathleen O'Reilly-Scanlon and Sonya Corbin Dwyer, "Memory-work as a (be)Tween Research Method: The Beauty, the Splendor, the Wonder of My Hair," in *Seven Going on Seventeen*, 79-94.

12. Meredith Cherland, "Reading Elisabeth's Girlhood: History and Popular Culture in the Subjectivity of a Tween," in *Seven Going on Seventeen*, 95-116.

13. Marika Flockemann, "Mirrors and Windows: Re-reading South African Girlhoods as Strategies of Selfhood," in *Seven Going on Seventeen*, 117-132.

14. Deevia Bhana, "Show Me the Panties: Girls Play Games in the School Ground," in *Seven Going on Seventeen*, 163-172; Farah Malik, "Mediated Consumption and Fashionable Selves: Tween Girls, Fashion Magazines, and Shopping," in *Seven Going on Seventeen*, 257-277; and Willet, Rebekah, "Constructing the Digital Tween: Market Discourse and Girls' Interests," in *Seven Going on Seventeen*, 278-293;

15. Harding, *Feminism and Methodology*.

16. Feminist Epistemologies Collective, "Marginal Research Reflections on Location and Representation" (London: LSE, 2002) http://www.lse.ac.uk/collections/genderInstitute/pdf/marginalResearch.pdf.

17. See page 242 of Nellie P. Stromquist, "Mapping Gendered Spaces in Third World Educational Interventions," in *Social Cartography: Mapping Ways of Seeing Social and Educational Change*, ed. Rolland G. Paulston, 223-247 (New York: Garland, 1996).

18. Benedict Anderson, *Imagined Communities* (London: Verso, 1983).

19. Geoff King, *Mapping Reality: An Exploration of Cultural Cartographies* (New York: St. Martins' Press, 1996).

20. Stromquist, "Mapping Gendered Spaces."

21. See page 201 of Nikolas K. Huffman, "Charting the Other Map: Cartography and Visual Method in Feminist Research," in *Thresholds in Feminist Geography: Difference, Methodology, Representation*, eds. John Paul Jones, Heidi J. Nast, and Susan M. Roberts, 225-283 (Lanham, MA: Rowman & Littlefield, 1997).

22. Claudia Mitchell, "Mapping a Southern African Girlhood in the Age of AIDS," in *Gender Equity in Education in South African Education, 1994-2004: Conference Proceedings*, ed. Linda Chisholm and Jean September, 92-112 (Cape Town: HSRC Press, 2005); Claudia Mitchell and Jacqueline Reid-Walsh, "Nine Going on Seventeen: Boundary Crises in the Cultural Map of Childhood / Adolescence" (paper, American Educational Research Association annual meeting, Montreal, Quebec, April 19-24, 1999); Claudia Mitchell, Jacqueline Reid-Walsh, Marilyn Blaeser and Ann Smith, "Who Cares about Girls? Mapping Girlhood as a Cultural Space," in *Centering On ...the Margins: The Evaded Curriculum*, 169-176 (Ottawa, ON: Canadian Association for the Study of Women and Education, 1998).

23. Shannon Walsh, "Losers, Lolitas, and Lesbos: Visualizing Girlhood," in *Seven Going on Seventeen*, 191-205; Valerie Walkerdine, *Daddy's Girl: Young Girls and Popular Culture* (Cambridge, MA: Harvard University Press, 1997); Brown and Gilligan, *Meeting at the Crossroads*.

24. Cynthia J. Fuchs, "Girling Popular Culture: Proving What I've Got to Prove: Pop Culture, Sex, and the New Girl Power" (paper presentation, Modern Language Association Conference, Chicago, IL, December, 1999).

25. When it comes to HIV and AIDS prevention, defining the term "girl" is critical. It can mean the difference between seeing gender violence (and its links to HIV infections) as within the jurisdictions of schools, or it can "let schools off the hook" by seeing it primarily as an issue for health workers in the community who meet up with young women at antenatal clinics. Schools, for policy making purposes in South Africa often distinguish between learners who are affected by AIDS (orphans and especially children heading up families, extreme poverty) and learners infected by AIDS (typically, in the school context those who have been infected at birth). We are interested in the fact that so many school-related policy documents, in making a distinction between learners who are *affected* by AIDS and those who are *infected* with AIDS may not be addressing fully the vulnerability of girls who are in school. For example, the most recent statistics on the 'gendered face' of rates of infection show that the median peak age for infections for young women is at least five years earlier than it is for young men. These statistics also show that 29.2 per cent of young mothers in the province of Gauteng are test HIV positive. If these infection rates are accurate, then, it is likely that these young mothers were only very recently learners in school. In essence, then it is girls and young women who are in school *now* who are at a very high risk of infection.

26. Balkishori Team of VACHA Women's Resource Center and Jackie Kirk, "Reclaiming Girlhood: Understanding the Lives of Balkishori in Mumbai," in *Seven Going on Seventeen*, 135-147.

27. Anita Harris, "Appendix X: Who is a girl?" in *Future Girl: Young Women in the Twenty-First Century* (New York: Routledge, 2003).

28. Harris, *Future Girl*, 30.

29. See page x of Kathleen M. Woodward, "Introduction," in *Figuring Age: Women, Bodies, Generations,* ed. Kathleen M. Woodward (Bloomington, IN: Indiana University Press, 1999).

30. Jenny Hockey and Alison James, *Growing Up and Growing Old: Aging and Dependency in the Life Course* (Thousand Oaks, CA: Sage Publications, 1993).

31. Roger Hart, *Children's Participation: The Theory and Practice of Involving Young Citizens in Community Development and Environmental Care* (London: Earthscan Publications, 1997).

32. Janice A. Radway, *Reading the Romance: Women, Patriarchy, and Popular Literature* (Chapel Hill, NC: University of North Carolina Press, 1991); Claudia Mitchell, "I Only Read Novels and That Sort of Thing: Exploring the Aesthetic Response," *English Quarterly* (Summer, 1982): 67-77; Cinthia Gannett, *Gender and the Journal: Diaries and Academic Discourse* (New York: State University of New York Press, 1992).

33. Brandi L. Bell, "Girls and Blogging: Private Writing in Public Spaces?" (paper presentation, Childhoods 2005 Conference, Oslo, Norway, June 29-July 3, 2005).

34. See David Buckingham and Julian Sefton-Green, *Cultural Studies Goes to School: Reading and Teaching Popular Media* (London: Taylor & Francis, 1995).

35. Mitchell and Reid-Walsh, *Researching Children's Popular Culture*.

36. Ibid

37. Claudia Marshall and I. Mothobe-Tapela. *No turning back: Youth and sexual violence in and around schools in Swaziland and Zimbabbwe*. EASARO UNICEF: 2004.

38. Claudia Mitchell and June Larkin, "Disrupting the Silences: Visual Methodologies in Addressing Gender-based Violence" (paper presentation, Pleasures and Dangers Conference, Cardiff, Wales, June 29-July 1, 2004).

39. Claudia Mitchell, Relebohile Moletsane, Jean Stuart, Thabisile Buthelezi, and Naydene de Lange, "Taking Pictures / Taking Action! Using Photo-voice Techniques with Children," *ChildrenFIRST* 9, no. 60 (2005): 27-31.

40. Balkishori Team and Jackie Kirk, "Reclaiming Girlhood."

41. See also Jean Stuart, "Media Matters—Producing a Culture of Compassion in the Age of AIDS," *English Quarterly* 36, no.1 (2004): 3-5.

42. See, for example, Haug et al. *Female Sexualization*; Crawford et al., *Emotion and Gender*." See also Hampl's first draft and second draft work in Patricia Hampl, "Memory and Imagination," in *The Anatomy of Memory: An Anthology*, ed. James McConkey, 201-211 (New York: Oxford University Press, 1996). See also the photography and memory studies of Jo Spence and Annette Kuhn: Jo Spence *Cultural Sniping: The Art of Transgression* (London: Routledge, 1995); Jo Spence and Joan Solomon, eds., *What Can a Woman Do With a Camera?* (London: Scarlet Press, 1995); and Annette Kuhn, *Family Secrets: Acts of Memory and Imagination* (London: Verso, 1995). For an extended discussion of their work, see "Memory Spaces: Exploring the Afterlife of Popular Culture" in Mitchell and Reid-Walsh's *Researching Children's Popular Culture* and "Working Back Through Memory" in Claudia Mitchell and Sandra Weber, *Reinventing Ourselves as Teachers: Beyond Nostalgia* (London: Falmer Press, 1999). For a further discussion of feminist nostalgia, particularly the work of Adrienne Rich, Janet Flax, and Mary Jacobus, see "Theorizing Nostalgia in Self-study" in Mitchell and Weber's *Reinventing Ourselves as Teachers*.

43. See bell hooks, "In Our Glory: Photography and Black Life," in *Picturing Us: African American Identity in Photography*, ed. Deborah Willis, 43-54 (New York: New Press, 1994).

44. Mitchell and Weber, *Reinventing Ourselves as Teachers*

45. Mitchell and Weber, *Reinventing Ourselves as Teachers*; Mitchell and Reid-Walsh, *Researching Children's Popular Culture*.

46. hooks, "In Our Glory."

47. Jacqui's full story and its analysis appears in Mitchell and Reid-Walsh, *Researching Children's Popular Culture*; Sandra Weber and Claudia Mitchell (Eds.), *Not Just Any Dress: Narratives of Memory, Body, and Identity* (New York: Peter Lang, 2004).

48. Kathleen O'Reilly-Scanlon, "Communion Dress Violations," in *Not Just Any Dress*, 39-44; Sandra Weber, "Boxed-in by My School Uniform," in *Not Just any Dress*, 61-66; Carol Mavor "Collecting Loss: Photographs, Dresses, 'Paperies,'" in *Not Just Any Dress*, 15-38; Ardra L. Cole, "The Christmas Doll," in *Not Just Any Dress*, 137-144.

49. Mitchell and Reid-Walsh, *Researching Children's Popular Culture*.

50. Claudia Mitchell and Jacqueline Reid-Walsh, "And I Want to Thank You, Barbie: Barbie as a Site for Cultural Interrogation," in *Education and Cultural Studies: Toward a Performative Practice*, ed. Henry A. Giroux and Patrick Shannon, 103-116 (London: Routledge, 1997).

51. Jacqueline Reid-Walsh and Claudia Mitchell, "Romancing Nancy, Feminist Interrogations of Successive Version of Nancy Drew," *Review of Education / Pedagogy / Cultural Studies* 17, no.4 (1995): 443-455.

52. Claudia Mitchell and Jacqueline Reid-Walsh, "Mail-order Memory Work: Towards a Methodology of Uncovering the Experiences of Covering Over," *Review of Education / Pedagogy / Cultural Studies* 20, no.1 (1998): 57-75.

53. Kathleen Weiler, "Remembering and Representing Life Choices: A Critical Perspective on Teachers' Oral History Narratives," *Qualitative Studies in Education* 3, no.1 (1992): 39-50.

54. Jackie Kirk, "Reflexivity as Methodology for Studying Women Teachers' Lives in Development" (PhD diss., McGill University, 2003); Gladys Teni-Atinga, "Beginning Teacher's Perceptions and Experiences of Sexual Harassment in Ghanian Teacher Training Institutions" (PhD diss., McGill University, 2005); Stephanie S. Garrow, "Mapping the Gendered Nature of Inter-organizational Relationships in Girls' Education: A Case Study of the Alliance—Uganda Partnership" (PhD thesis, McGill University, 2004).

55. Gillian Beer, *Arguing With the Past: Essays in Narrative from Woolf to Sidney* (London: Routledge, 1989).

56. bell hooks, *Teaching to Transgress: Education as the Practice of Freedom* (London: Routledge, 1994).

57. Kristin Drotner, "Maternity and Mediapanics," in *Media Cultures: Reappraising Transnational Media*, eds. Michael Skovmand and Kim Christian Schroder, 42-62 (London: Routledge, 1992).

58. Mitchell and Reid-Walsh, *Seven Going on Seventeen.*

59. David Thorburn and Henry Jenkins, eds. *Rethinking Media Change* (Cambridge, MA: MIT Press, 2003).

60. Thorburn and Jenkins, *Rethinking Media Change*, 2.

EMMA GOLDMAN
Sexuality and the Impurity of the State
Bonnie Haaland

Focuses on the ideas of Emma Goldman as they relate to the centrality of sexuality and reproduction, and as such, are relevant to the current feminist debates.

> A model for "integrative feminism" that focuses on individuality rather than on rights. —*Common Knowledge*

> Haaland's work stands out among other literature. What is most valuable about Goldman is not her ideas so much as what she did with her ideas. —*Kinesis*

BONNIE HAALAND holds a PhD from the University of Toronto in feminist theory.

201 pages, paper 1-895431-64-6 $19.99 ❖ cloth 1-895431-65-4 $48.99

LOUISE MICHEL
Edith Thomas, translated by Penelope Williams

From the barricades of the Paris Commune to the spectacular trials and demonstrations, Michel is one of the most extraordinary legends in the literature of freedom.

> A very complete and very attractive biography, richly written. —*Le Monde*

> The book's first part is well done...especially the account of Louise's adaptation to life in New Caledonia. —*American Historical Review*

EDITH THOMAS was a French writer and author of *The Women Incendiaries*.

444 pages, paper 0-919619-07-4 $19.99 ❖ cloth 0-919619-08-2 $48.99

THE RAGING GRANNIES
Wild Hats, Cheeky Songs, and Witty Actions for a Better World
Carole Roy

Bursting with adventures, this is the tale of the Raging Grannies: their beginning, the invention of their identity, and their impact on issues, stereotypes, media, and people. Includes photographs and protest songs.

> Roy's examination of strategies of satire and humour, in particular, is groundbreaking. —Deborah Barndt, co-editor of *Just Doing It*

CAROLE ROY is an Assistant Professor in the Department of Adult Education at St. Francis Xavier University, Nova Scotia and a contributor to this volume.

355 pages, paper 1-55164-240-9 $24.9 ❖ cloth 1-55164-241-7 $53.99

Selected by the American Library Association for the Amelia Bloomer Award

GIRLHOOD
Redefining the Limits

Yasmin Jiwani, Candis Steenbergen, and Claudia Mitchell, editors

Girlhood is a collection of essays on girls, girlhood and girl culture. Drawing from the works of national and international scholars, this book focuses on the multifaceted nature of girls' lived experiences. Examined is racism, sexism and classism; the power and politics of schoolgirl style; encounters with violence; cyberspace; sexuality; identity formation; and popular culture. This groundbreaking collection offers a complicated portrait of girls in the 21st century: good girls and bad girls, girls who are creating their own girl culture and giving a whole new meaning to "girl" power. These provocative essays cover all aspects of girlhood as they bring to life the ever-changing identities of today's young women.

An excellent job…provides a diverse and vividly complicated picture of contemporary girlhoods. —*Feminist Collections*, University of Wisconsin

YASMIN JIWANI is an Associate Professor in the Department of Communication Studies at Concordia University, Montreal. She is the author of *Discourses of Denial: Mediations of Race, Gender, and Violence in Canadian Society*. Her work has appeared in *Violence Against Women, The Journal of Popular Film and Television*, and in *Critique: Critical Middle Eastern Studies*.

CANDIS STEENBERGEN is a PhD candidate in the Humanities: Interdisciplinary Studies in Society and Culture at Concordia University, Montreal. A former editor of *good girl magazine*, she has contributed to numerous publications including *Turbo Chicks: Talking Young Feminisms* and *The Encyclopedia of American Social Movements*.

CLAUDIA MITCHELL, PhD, is a James McGill Professor in the Faculty of Education, McGill University, Montreal. She is the co-author and the co-editor of a number of books including *Seven Going on Seventeen: Tween Studies in the Culture of Girlhood*, with J. Reid-Walsh, both of whom are contributors to this volume.

272 pages
Paperback ISBN: 1-55164-276-X $26.99
Hardcover ISBN: 1-55164-277-8 $55.99

OBSESSION, WITH INTENT
Violence Against Women
Lee Lakeman

Obsession, With Intent is an investigative report into one hundred cases of violence against women; in *all* cases the women tried to get help from the system. It is a harrowing account of individual women's stories, their understanding of the danger they faced, their attempts to get help, the incompetence and/or indifference they met, and, in those cases where someone was willing to prosecute, their vulnerability under/within the law. It reviews 911 procedure, from how the emergency operator evaluates the call, to the police (how, or if, they collect evidence), to prosecuting attorney, to court, to sentencing. This work also examines whether or not women are adequately protected under Canada's Charter of Rights and Freedoms.

Among the many narratives are "domestic dispute" cases, sexual assault cases, and cases of murder. The landmark decision, in the case of Jane Doe who fought for and won the right to sue the Toronto police force for the way in which they routinely dealt with rape victims is examined, as are a number of sexual assault cases—some high profile, some occurring more than forty years ago. Accounts of the serial killers Bernardo and Pickton are chilling, as are the other numerous accounts of impending murder. (As early as 1997 Pickton had been charged with confining, and repeatedly stabbing, Wendy Lynn Eisteler, but charges were dropped and Pickton released; the prosecutor judged that there was no likelihood of a conviction—the victim was "a drug-addicted prostitute." Thirty more women would die.)

Recognizing that violence against women is one of the strongest indicators of prevailing societal attitudes towards women, *Obsession, With Intent* screams out for social change at the individual, the institutional, and the political level.

LEE LAKEMAN works at the Vancouver Rape Relief and Women's Shelter. She has organized Take Back the Night marches, neighborhood confrontations of abusive men, and anti-violence lobbies petitioning government representatives. She is a contributor to *Not For Sale: Preventing the Promotion of Prostitution*.

256 pages, references, bibilography, index
Paperback ISBN: 1-55164-262-X $24.99
Hardcover ISBN: 1-55164-263-8 $53.99

PARTICIPATORY DEMOCRACY
Prospects for Democratizing Democracy
Dimitrios Roussopoulos, with C.George Benello
A completely revised edition of the classic and widely consulted 1970 version

First published as a testament to the legacy of the concept made popular by the New Left of the 1960s, and with the perspective of the intervening decades, this book opens up the way for re-examining just what is involved in democratizing democracy. With its emphasis on citizen participation, here, presented in one volume are the best arguments for participatory democracy written by some of the most relevant contributors to the debate, both in an historic, and in a contemporary, sense.

This wide-ranging collection probes the historical roots of participatory democracy in our political culture, analyzes its application to the problems of modern society, and explores the possible forms it might take on every level of society from the work place, to the community, to the nation at large. In the section entitled, "The Politics of Participatory Democracy," Porto Alegre, Montreal, the new Urban ecology, and direct democracy are covered.

> The book is, by all odds, the most encompassing one so far in revealing the practical actual subversions that the New Left wishes to visit upon us.
> —*Washington Post*

Apart from the editors, contributors include: George Woodcock, Murray Bookchin, Don Calhoun, Stewart Perry, Rosabeth Moss Kanter, James Gillespie, Gerry Hunnius, John McEwan, Arthur Chickering, Christian Bay, Martin Oppenheimer, Colin Ward, Sergio Baierle, Anne Latendresse, Bartha Rodin, and C.L.R. James.

DIMITRIOS ROUSSOPOULOS was a prominent New Left activist in the 1960s, locally and internationally. He continues to write and edit on major issues while being a committed activist testing theory with practice. He is the author and/or editor of some eighteen books, the most recent being *Faith in Faithlessness: An Anthology of Atheism* (2008).

380 pages
Paperback ISBN: 1-55164-224-7 $24.99
Hardcover ISBN: 1-55164-225-5 $53.99

WOMEN AND RELIGION

Fatmagül Berktay

While taking women's subjectivities and their reasons for their taking to religion into account, this book focuses mainly on the *functions* of religion: the way it relates to women; its contribution to gender differences; and the status of women within it, particularly the relationship between gender on the one hand, and power and social control on the other, and within this context, the meanings attributed to the female body. Undertaken as well, is an exposition of contemporary Fundamentalism (in both its Protestant and Islamic variants, in America and Iran) in the hope that a comparative approach to religious Fundamentalism will offer clues for a deeper understanding of the revival of religious belief in our modern world.

FATMAGÜL BERKTAY is an associate professor with the Department of Philosophy, and teaches feminist theory at the Women's Research Center, both of the University of Istanbul, Turkey.

240 pages, paper 1-55164-102-X $24.99 ❖ cloth 1-55164-103-8 $53.99

send for a free catalogue of all our titles

 BLACK ROSE BOOKS

C.P. 1258, Succ. Place du Parc
Montréal, Québec
H2X 4A7 Canada

or visit our website at http://www.blackrosebooks.net

to order books

In Canada: (phone) 1-800-565-9523 (fax) 1-800-221-9985
email: utpbooks@utpress.utoronto.ca

In United States: (phone) 1-800-283-3572 (fax) 1-800-351-5073

In UK & Europe: (phone) London 44 (0)20 8986-4854 (fax) 44 (0)20 8533-5821
email: order@centralbooks.com

Printed by the workers of
for Black Rose Books

imprimerie **gauvin**